# BLACK & DECKER ®

# HOME 101 IMPROVEMENT

## *E*veryday Care & Repair Made Easy

by Jerri Farris
with Thomas Lemmer

**Creative Publishing international**

CHANHASSEN, MINNESOTA
www.creativepub.com

# Credits

**Creative Publishing international**

© Copyright 2005
Creative Publishing international, Inc.
18705 Lake Drive East
Chanhassen, Minnesota  55317
1-800-328-3895
www.creativepub.com
All rights reserved

Printed by R.R. Donnelley
10 9 8 7 6 5 4 3 2

*President/CEO:* Ken Fund
*Vice President/Publisher:* Linda Ball
*Vice President/Retail Sales & Marketing:* Kevin Haas

*Executive Editor:* Bryan Trandem
*Creative Director:* Tim Himsel
*Managing Editor:* Michelle Skudlarek
*Editorial Director:* Jerri Farris

*Authors:* Jerri Farris and Thomas Lemmer
*Editor:* Andrew Karre
*Proofreader:* Charles Pederson
*Art Director:* Teresa Marrone
*Assisting Art Directors:* Dave Schelitzche, Jon Simpson
*Project Manager:* Tracy Stanley
*Technical Photo Editor:* Randy Austin
*Illustrators:* Earl Slack and Tim Himsel
*Photo Researcher:* Julie Caruso
*Photographer:* Tate Carlson
*Scene Shop Carpenter:* Randy Austin
*Production Manager:* Laura Hokkanen

Library of Congress Cataloging-in-Publication Data

Home improvement 101 : everyday care & repair made easy.
        p.  cm.
    Includes index.
    ISBN 1-58923-180-5 (soft cover)
  1.  Dwellings--Maintenance and repair--Amateurs' manuals.
2. Do-it-yourself work.
    TH4817.3.H649 2005
    643'.7--dc22                          2004029333

## NOTICE TO READERS

# table of contents

# introduction

*A good home must be made,
not bought.*

**JOYCE MAYNARD**

A wonderful thought, that. A good home must be made. While most homeowners are pretty sure this is true, many are not quite sure how one goes about doing it.

And no wonder. Turning a house into a home is a kind of alchemy. But the basis for the process, the base metal from which the gold arises, is caretaking. Somehow, when you care for a house, enhancing strengths and tending to weaknesses, it becomes yours in a way that reaches beyond mortgages, deeds, and surveys. You become part of it as you leave your mark on each task, and it becomes part of you through the lessons it teaches you.

The big question, if you're a typical cash-strapped, time-starved new homeowner, is: "What must be done and how?" And that's where this book comes in. In it, you'll find an introduction to the art of caring for your home. Like any intro class, *Home Improvement 101* is filled with basic information you can build on over time.

As you read these pages, you'll discover that caring for a home isn't rocket science. We're not claiming that it's always easy, and it can be frustrating. But it is so worth the effort, and in this as in all other endeavors, knowledge is power. When you recognize the components and systems of a house and understand how they're related, you are prepared to care for this marvelous structure that is becoming not just your house, but your home.

# How to Use This Book

*Home Improvement 101* begins with the premise that you own a house. You may be a first-time homeowner, but whether this is your first house or your fourth, you want information and guidance, or you wouldn't be reading this.

Whatever your reasons, you are reading it, and we aim to make it worth the investment. To that end, we ask you to start by reading through the Virtual Tour on pages 10 to 21. (If you've got the time, it will help to actually walk through your own house, identifying the elements and systems being described.) The tour explains how each part or system works and describes what it contributes to the overall picture. This understanding will serve as the foundation for the expertise that's sure to develop as you learn about and care for your home.

Following the tour, you'll find chapters, one for each of the main parts or systems of a house. In each chapter, you'll find information on:

▶ **Cleaning:** We highly recommend reading these pages, even if you don't think you need much help with cleaning—they offer a wealth of time- and money-saving hints and tricks.

▶ **Maintenance:** Routine maintenance—cleaning or replacing filters, filling holes, testing valves—helps you identify and resolve potential problems while they're small and can be fixed both easily and inexpensively.

▶ **Repair:** Sometimes, despite your best efforts, things break or wear out. No problem. We'll lead you through the most common home repairs. Best of all, we'll let you know when it's time for an average homeowner—and probably you—to call in professionals.

Along the way, we'll point out helpful bits of information, caution you about common hazards, and describe what has to be done, when, and why.

The information contained in the following pages is the result of decades of education and experience, and thousands of (sometimes painful) learning experiences. The writers and editors who worked together to bring it to you have come by their knowledge in many ways, including the hard way. We invite you to learn the easy way—by reading *Home Improvement 101*. And be sure to look at the pictures—every one really is worth a thousand words.

 Except for what's flowing to and draining from plumbing fixtures, water is your house's number-one enemy. When you see the water-drop icon, pay attention. If it involves water, procrastination can be ugly. And expensive.

 Some home maintenance projects—espcially those that involve electricity—call for specific safety measures and extra caution. When you see the caution sign, please be careful.

 There are a few things we've learned as we've worked on our own houses—shortcuts to take and shortcuts to skip, helpful hints, and so on. We've marked them with a check.

 And, of course, there are some times when you just need to call a professional. When you see the cell phone, it's probably time to call in the experts.

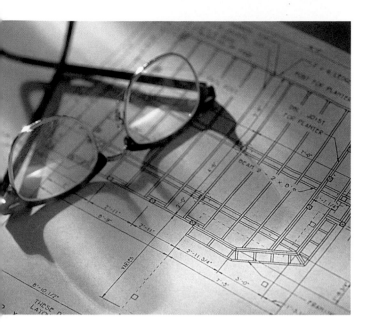

## Assess the Situation

If you're a new homeowner or if the responsibility of caring for a house is new to you, the very first thing you should do is assess the situation. Go through the entire house and familiarize yourself with its structure and systems. You might even want to walk yourself through a Virtual Tour (pages 10 to 21), identifying the various elements of the house as you read about how they work.

However you go about it, check out the house and survey its current condition. If you find situations you don't understand or uncover potential problems, seek expert opinions and help where necessary. Preventive maintenance is relatively inexpensive; emergency repairs can be extremely costly. For example, if you find insulation missing from an outside wall near a plumbing run, it doesn't take much time or money to replace it. But, if you leave the area unprotected through a cold winter, you could wind up with frozen pipes, an unpleasant and expensive situation.

So, check out the house. Make sure you understand how things should work so you'll recognize problems when they come up. List any issues you find and prioritize necessary repairs.

## Plan Ahead

It's time for a reconnaissance mission. Look at the door of your **electrical service panel**. If you find a map that lists each breaker and indicates what it controls, you're in luck. If not, you can make one. After all, almost every electrical repair starts with shutting off the circuit. If you know which breaker controls which circuit, this is a simple task. If not, the process can be frustrating and time consuming. Mapping the circuits eliminates all guesswork. If you don't plan to do electrical repairs yourself, it will take a professional less time—and cost you less money—to make repairs if they have an accurate circuit map. You can find instructions in a book on wiring (Black and Decker's *Basic Wiring & Electrical Repairs* is a good one) or on many DIY Web sites. (Accuracy is critical when you're working with electricity. Rely only on sources of information you know to be reputable.)

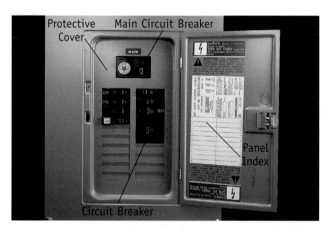

Next, identify the **main shutoff valve for the water supply** and the **main breaker or fuse on the service panel**. Teach other family members how to turn off the water and power in an emergency.

# Keep Records

There are few things you could do as a homeowner that will save you more time and aggravation than keeping good records. Set up a simple system and follow it. There are many good ways to keep records, but the easiest way we know of is to use a three-ring binder. Start with the blueprints or floor plans, if you have them. Add dividers for subjects such as *Improvement Receipts, Repair Receipts, Owner's Manuals,* and *Decor.*

**Improvement receipts:** When you buy a new fixture or appliance, put the receipt into the binder. If you need to save the original for tax purposes, put a photocopy into the binder. When you need to order a part or check to see whether the appliance is still under warranty, you've got all the information you need—date and place of purchase, model number, and so forth.

**Repair receipts:** When you buy parts for repairs or pay professionals to make repairs, save the receipts. The documentation comes in handy for warranties, but it also creates a record of what has been done to the house, when, and by whom. Records like this are invaluable to you as a homeowner and priceless to the next owner if you ever sell the house.

**Owner's manuals:** These manuals have a way of going missing unless you have a system for storing them. Send in the warranty cards and put the manual in your binder every time you purchase a fixture, appliance, or tool.

**Decor:** Set up a separate section of the binder with a page for each room. List everything you know about the surface treatments in the room—paint color, carpet type and color, wallpaper manufacturer and pattern number. Any time you make changes to the decor, make a note of the change and the date. Ten years from now, the local paint store may not offer Seabreeze Sunrise, but if you know the color number or have the color chip and the date you purchased it, they very well may be able to mix you up a batch.

Add any other categories that would help you keep track of what has been done to the house and what might be required in the future.

Keeping a notebook like this might sound tedious, but the time required is nothing compared to the aggravation you avoid by having such a resource.

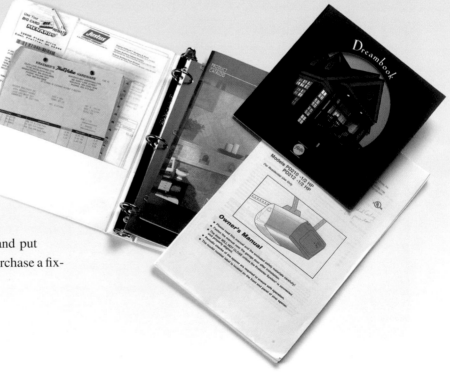

# virtual tour

## A LOOK INSIDE YOUR HOUSE

Before you can maintain or fix things, you need to know what they are, how they work, and what part they play in the general scheme of things. Before we do anything else, let's take a tour of a house and figure out what's what.

Starting from the ground up, the **foundation** is our first

stop. It might not be the most exciting part of a house, but it's among the most important. A good foundation is designed to be the link between a house and the earth. It supports hundreds of thousands of pounds—the weight of the building itself, all its mechanical systems, all your belongings, and even you and your family.

Soil Grading

Foundation Wall

Footing

Drain Tile

In a typical wall foundation (one that encloses a basement or crawlspace), the footings under load-bearing walls and posts are wider than the components they support. Footings do the same job for a foundation that snowshoes do for winter hikers: By distributing the load over a wider area, they keep the foundation from sinking.

Unless the house is very small, the foundation walls alone can't carry its entire weight. Large beams—supported on each end by the foundation walls and by vertical posts in between—carry some of the load, too. The location and size of each beam and the distances between support posts are regulated by local building codes, so problems are pretty rare.

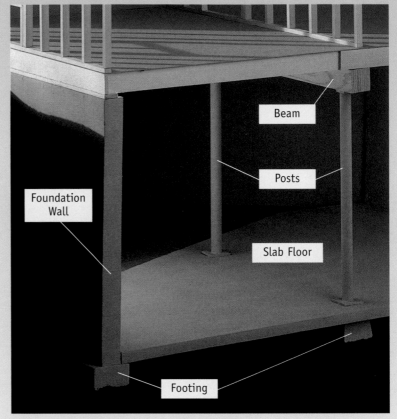

*Typical Wall Foundation*

A house is joined to its foundation by a 2 × 4 or 2 × 6 sill plate anchored to the top of the foundation walls. To prevent rot, the sill is made of treated lumber and the top of the foundation wall is covered with a fiberglass sealer. In regions where termites are a problem, metal or plastic termite guards cover the foundation to keep insects from migrating up into the framing lumber.

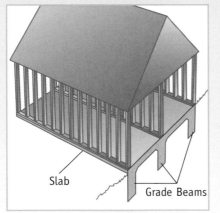

*Typical Slab Foundation*

Another common type of foundation is called a "slab" foundation, which consists of a layer of reinforced concrete laid over a bed of gravel. The areas directly under load-bearing walls or posts are supported by thickened areas of concrete, called grade beams. In areas with winter frost, the grade beams extend several feet down to a point below the frost line, forming frost footings. Without these frost footings, the slab would shift or heave considerably from season to season.

**Slab foundations** are most common in warm climates where deep frost footings aren't necessary. They're also used in areas with loose or sandy soil to distribute the weight of a house over a broad area in order to keep it from sinking.

Slab foundations don't need much maintenance—very little can go wrong. Water is the main enemy since slab houses are raised only a few inches off the ground. The most effective protection is to make sure the landscape slopes away from the house, directing runoff water away from the foundation. (See page 247 for more information on establishing grade.)

**Pier or grade-beam foundations:** With a pier foundation, the house rests on beams that are supported by columns called piers. The piers may be made of natural stone, brick, concrete, or even wood. These foundations are common in floodplains and other high-water areas, since such foundations can raise the house up off the ground and don't require much excavation. Grade-beam foundations, a newer version of pier foundations, are often used on hillside homes in the West. In this design, poured concrete columns are connected to an underground beam.

With a pier foundation, the space under the house is often hidden by an apron. That apron typically has an opening so you can get under the house to check on things from time to time. It's important to remove leaves, trash, and other debris that could trap moisture or shelter pests. You also need to make sure the insulation between the floor joists is in place and dry.

**Pole foundations:** Like pier foundations, pole foundations raise the house off the ground, but with this design the support columns—made of poured concrete and steel or wood—are directly connected to each story of the house. Pole foundations are earthquake resistant, well suited to steep slopes, and appropriate in areas where flash flooding is a possibility.

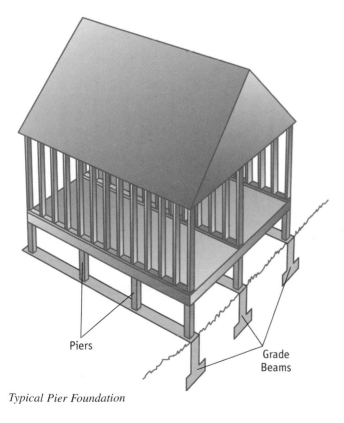

*Typical Pier Foundation*

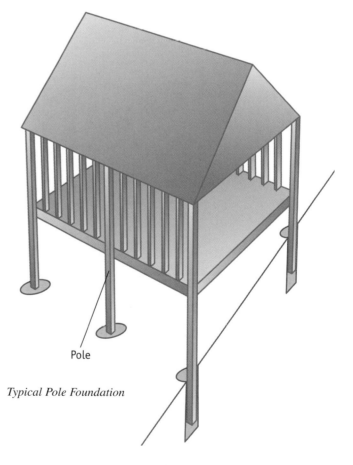

*Typical Pole Foundation*

Next stop on our tour: the **framing**. The framing is the wood (or steel) that shapes the walls, floors, ceilings, and roof of a house. It's a skeleton that includes these parts:

➤ **Posts** support the **beams**, which add strength to the foundation.

➤ The **sill plate** anchors the framing to the foundation.

➤ **Joists** form the floors and ceilings.

➤ **Studs** form the walls.

➤ **Headers** bridge the openings for doors and windows.

➤ **Load-bearing walls** transfer the weight of the house to the beam and foundation.

➤ The **ridge board and rafters** support the roof.

Now that we've got the basics down, let's take a closer look at wall framing. First, the studs: In exterior walls, typically they are 2 × 6s or 2 × 4s; in interior walls, they're almost always 2 × 4s. Studs are 16 inches apart, measured from the center of one to the center of the next. Any opening wider than 16 inches—a door or window for example—requires a header to transfer the weight to nearby framing.

Exterior walls are load bearing, and so are all interior walls aligned with the beams. Any interior wall that runs parallel to the floor and ceiling joists is a non-load-bearing, or partition, wall. Fixing cracks in partition walls is just a matter of surface repair, but substantial cracks in load-bearing walls need to be watched carefully for signs of underlying problems with the support structure.

Before we leave the framing, let's take a look at the roof, a system composed of three parts: the framework, decking, and covering.

**Framework:** Rafters and joists form triangles that support and balance the weight of the roof.

**Decking:** A base layer covering the rafters or trusses creates a sturdy foundation for shingles or other roofing material. In older homes, the decking usually is $3/4$-inch planks nailed to the rafters. In newer construction, the decking typically is $1/2$-inch exterior-grade plywood (with asphalt shingles, roll roofing, slate, and some tile roofs) or spaced slats (with wood shakes or shingles, some tile, and metal panels).

**Covering:** The first layer is the underlayment. Its job is to keep rain, snow, or ice from finding its way through the decking to the framing. Next comes flashing. At every interruption in the roofline—valleys, dormers, vents,

chimneys, and skylights—flashing directs surface water away from the decking and framework. Finally, comes the roofing material—shingles, shakes, tile, metal, or rolled roofing.

If you could look inside an exterior wall, you might be surprised at how little actually stands between you and the outside world. In new construction (below, left), walls usually have an exterior sheathing of rigid-board insulation; the framing cavities are insulated with fiberglass batts; a plastic vapor barrier covers the insulation, which in turn is covered by finished drywall.

In older construction (below, right), the exterior sheathing is made of wood planks; insulation—if there is any—probably is loose-fill cellulose; interior surfaces are made of lath and plaster.

Walls in heated basements are often insulated with rigid-board insulation installed between *furring strips* (a fancy

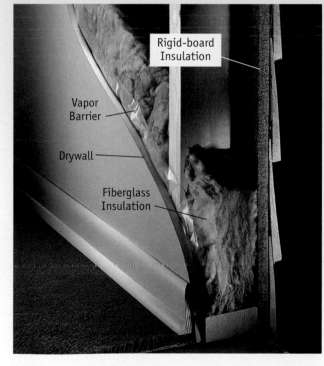

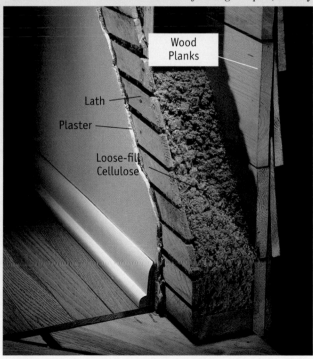

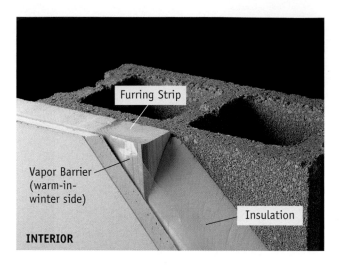

Furring Strip

Vapor Barrier
(warm-in-
winter side)

Insulation

**INTERIOR**

In warm climates (areas where the average January temperature is higher than 35°F), vapor barriers may or may not be required. Check with local building officials or a reputable contractor in your area.

Vapor barriers keep moisture from getting into the walls and condensing on interior surfaces. Trapped moisture reduces the R-value (efficiency) of the insulation and can cause framing and sheathing to rot. Plus, mold can form in damp walls, a very unhealthy situation for everyone living in the house—especially people who have mold allergies or respiratory problems.

name for 2 × 2 boards) attached to the masonry walls. The insulation and furring strips are covered with a vapor barrier and then wallboard or paneling.

A vapor barrier is any material that resists the flow of moisture, such as polyethylene film or aluminum foil. Also, some fiberglass insulation comes with a kraft-paper or foil facing that's intended as a vapor barrier.

If you live in a cold climate, listen up. This is important: Every exterior wall—wood framed or masonry—should have a vapor barrier.

In unfinished walls, you'll see a layer of polyethylene (looks like clear plastic) over the insulation or a paper or foil facing on the insulation itself. In finished walls, remove a switchplate or receptacle cover and look around; you may be able to see the edge of the barrier.

If you have damp or moldy walls, moldy insulation, or continually peeling paint on exterior walls, get serious about checking out your vapor barrier. Get a contractor's help if you need it.

Most of the major problems a house can develop can be traced back to misdirected, condensing, or intruding water—that is, water leaking from your pipes, water condensing from too-humid indoor air, or water getting in from outside. In severe climates, freeze/thaw can cycles exaggerate water damage (and repair costs) exponentially—especially to framing and coverings.

Not surprisingly, many repairs involve redirecting moisture and a whole lot of preventive maintenance is aimed at keeping water where it belongs in the first place.

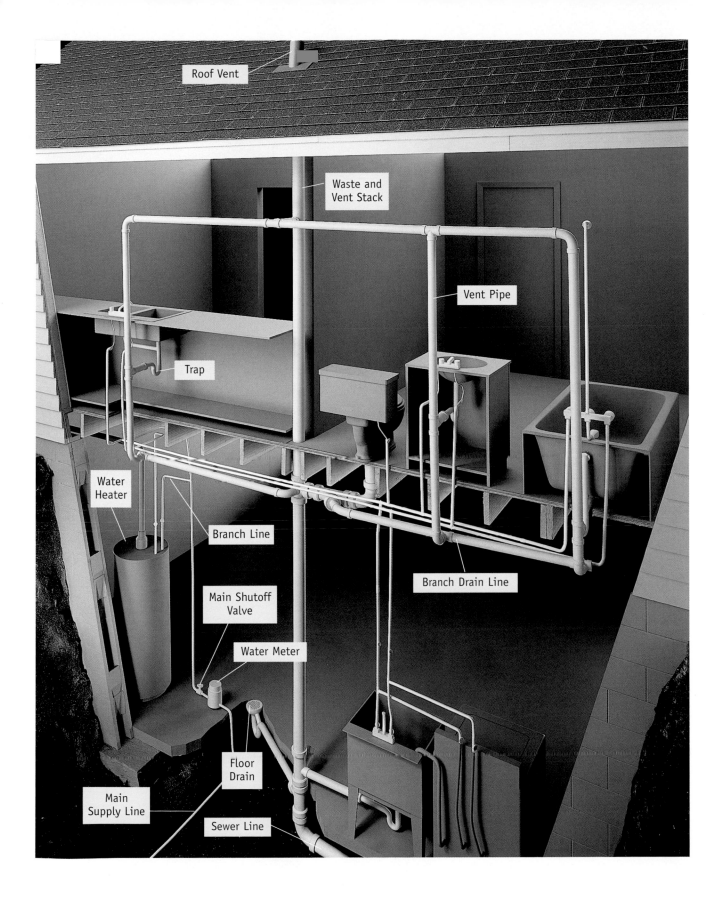

Roof Vent

Waste and Vent Stack

Vent Pipe

Trap

Water Heater

Branch Line

Main Shutoff Valve

Water Meter

Branch Drain Line

Floor Drain

Main Supply Line

Sewer Line

# Mechanical Systems

Now that we've covered the structure, let's look at the systems inside the house, starting with plumbing.

A **plumbing system** is responsible for both water delivery and removal. Water arrives under pressure and leaves by gravity, taking with it soap, dirt, human waste, and anything else put down the drains.

Of course, there are stops in between, such as water heaters and water softeners, but the basic system is incredibly simple: Water enters through a pressurized water line, gets split into hot and cold water lines, then delivered to faucets, toilets, and appliances. Once it's been used, the water is transferred to the sewer or septic system by the drain-waste-vent (DWV) system.

If you don't learn anything else about your plumbing system, learn where the shutoff valves are located, starting with the main water-supply shutoff valve. If a pipe bursts or a plumbing emergency arises, you may need to close this valve in a hurry.

Main Shutoff Valve

If you have municipal service, the shutoff is near the water meter, usually on a basement wall facing the street side of the house. In houses without basements, meters and shutoff valves are typically found in crawl spaces or along the ground-floor wall next to the street. If you have a well, the shutoff valve is probably located on the outlet side of the storage tank.

Sinks, tubs, and toilets typically have shutoff valves, too. You'll find these valves under the fixture, near where the water's being delivered. For example, the kitchen and bathroom sinks typically have shutoff valves under the sink, at the back of the cabinet.

Find these valves. Test them. Show family members how to use them. In an emergency, knowing how to turn the water off could mean the difference between a minor inconvenience and major damage.

*If you have municipal water service, your main shutoff is probably located near the water meter.*

Next stop: the **electrical system**. At this point, many of you are muttering that you have no intention of messing with electricity. If so, you're not alone. Plenty of homeowners are a little uneasy about working on their electrical system. But don't skip this part—really, there's nothing magical about electricity, no voodoo in your home wiring. Electricity abides by the laws of physics, and if you understand how it works, you'll be prepared to deal with minor problems and know how to describe and discuss the situation if you ever need to call in a professional electrician.

We'll go over this in detail in Electricity (page 166), but for now, we'll begin at the beginning: Service wires bring power into your home. Those wires may be strung overhead or buried, but either way, they run to the electric meter and service panel.

(Overhead wires run first to a service mast attached to the roof or siding. Buried wires enter straight into the basement or come up the foundation to the service panel.)

Current comes into the house through the electric meter, it goes to the service panel, which distributes it to individual circuits throughout the house. Each circuit is a continuous loop, and here's why: Electricity operates in a circle. It flows through the service panel to light fixtures, appliances, receptacles, and switches on hot wires and then goes back to the service panel along neutral wires. Electricity that escapes this defined loop is directed into the ground by a grounding wire. Anything that interrupts the circuit creates problems. In Electricity, we'll talk about those potential problems and what you should and shouldn't do about them. For now, just know that they're there and that they aren't nearly as intimidating as you may believe.

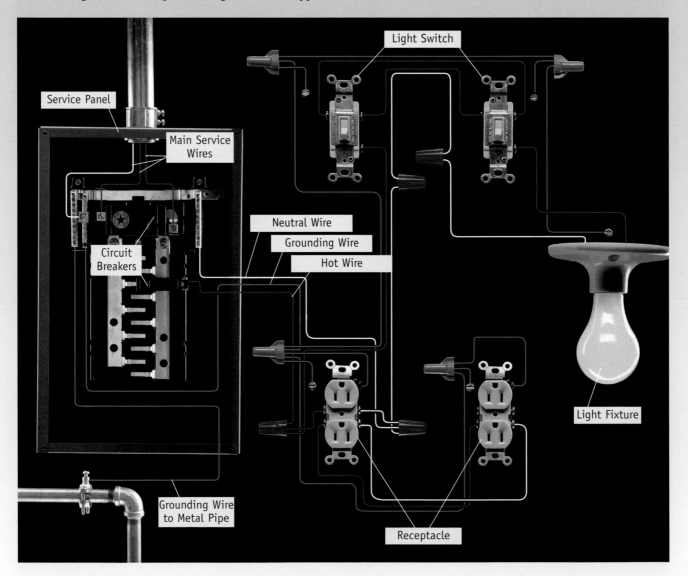

Light Switch

Service Panel

Main Service Wires

Circuit Breakers

Neutral Wire

Grounding Wire

Hot Wire

Light Fixture

Grounding Wire to Metal Pipe

Receptacle

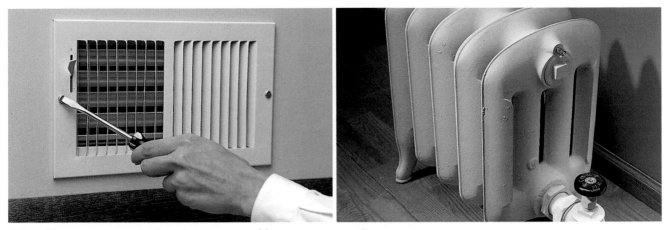

*Adjustable return air vent for forced air system and hot water system radiator.*

And finally, the system that's most responsible for your home's overall comfort and safety: the **HVAC system**. This system contains the heating, ventilation, and air conditioning units that help maintain consistent temperatures and humidity levels indoors, regardless of the weather changes outdoors. When the HVAC system functions properly, you're not aware of it because you feel comfortable. But when the system is failing, you'll quickly notice that it's too hot, too cold, too humid, too dry—or even that the air seems stale.

As you've probably guessed, "HVAC" is an acronym for—that's right—heating, ventilation, and air conditioning. We'll discuss how each particular subsystem works in HVAC (page 202), so for the sake of simplicity, here are the basics:

**Heating:** In your house, you most likely have a furnace or a boiler, where heat is released from burning fuel and transferred to air or water. The heated air or water is circulated through a series of ducts or pipes to registers, radiators, or convectors to warm individual rooms. Other common heating systems include electric baseboard heaters, fireplaces, and gas- or woodburning stoves.

**Ventilation:** Whether they're as simple as open windows and ceiling fans or as complex as air-to-air exchangers and elaborate filtering units, ventilation systems have a sole purpose: to supply fresh air to your house. Fresh air helps regulate both temperature and humidity, eliminate smoke and odors, and provide combustion air for fuel-burning appliances. Oh, yeah—fresh air keeps you and your family healthy, too.

The upside of the 1970s energy crisis was the advent of superefficient furnaces and elaborate house-wrapping techniques that helped homeowners conserve energy and save money. Unfortunately, the downside of this efficiency was the drastic reduction of fresh air cycling through our homes.

Just as we need fresh air to remain healthy, so do our homes. Good ventilation keeps indoor air from becoming stale, dusty, and too dry or too humid. A constant supply of fresh air reduces susceptibility—especially in children—to viruses, chronic respiratory ailments, and the effects of carbon monoxide. Ironically, older, drafty houses are often better ventilated than newer, superinsulated homes. Poor ventilation can actually reduce the efficiency of your HVAC system.

So, how do you know if your home is properly ventilated? Look for these telltale signs of excessive humidity and insufficient air exchange:
➤ Frequent condensation on the room side of windows
➤ Stale air
➤ Persistent, lingering odors
➤ Mold and mildew in carpets or on walls, especially in kitchens, bathrooms, and basements

Make sure vent fans work and furnace filters and humidifiers are clean. You can always add more ventilation, such as exhaust fans or an air exchanger.

Poor ventilation also could be the cause of chronic allergies or asthma. If you feel your family or home is at risk, don't hesitate to call an HVAC expert.

**Air conditioning:** Both central air-conditioning systems and window units work the same way: by capturing heat in a refrigerant and transferring it outside the house while cooled air is circulated through the furnace ducts or blown directly into a single room or area.

**Heat pumps:** If you live in an area with relatively moderate winter temperatures, you may have a heat pump that acts as both a cooling unit and a heating unit for your home. This single unit extracts heat from cool outdoor air during cold weather and removes heat from indoor air during hot weather.

**Humidity** refers to the moisture in the air. In winter, higher humidity makes air seem warmer; in summer, lower humidity makes air seem cooler. However, humidity is volatile—finding that delicate balance is key to keeping your home comfortable and safe.

Too much humidity can cause a lot of problems indoors, especially if your house is not properly ventilated.

Moisture condensing on old windows and wall surfaces can cause paint to peel, and if the moisture is trapped in wall and ceiling spaces, it can cause mold and wood rot. Newer, superefficient homes are particularly susceptible.

To help reduce indoor humidity levels, use portable dehumidifiers, fresh-air vents, and bathroom and kitchen vent fans. Additionally, clean furnace-mounted humidifiers as recommended by the manufacturer, typically once a month. This will help prevent mold and mildew from growing in the moist environment of the humidifier, where it can be dispersed throughout the house via the ductwork.

Heating and cooling is the biggest continuing expense related to your house. Regular maintenance will help ensure your HVAC equipment runs efficiently, keeping you and your family comfortable and healthy, as well as saving you money.

That's your home. Sure, each house has its own particular elements and idiosyncrasies, but at the very basic level, that's it. So, how do you maintain and take care of this structure and its interrelated parts? Well, turn the page and we'll get started . . . .

# tools & materials

*Tools have their own integrity.*

**VITA SACKVILLE-WEST**

Integrity: Kind of an old-fashioned word. Our tool-buying advice is kind of old-fashioned, too: Buy the best-quality tools you can afford and take good care of them.

Tools aren't disposable. They won't become obsolete. A well-balanced hammer will last for decades—so will good wrenches and pliers. There's a certain pleasure in using and caring for good tools, too. Each becomes something like a dependable friend, something you can count on.

Start small, with only the necessities. Buy more as you learn what you truly need and what qualities are important to you.

---

## With this chapter you'll . . .

- Find out what tools to buy to maintain your home—without taking out a second mortgage to pay for them.

- Know what hardware and fasteners to keep on hand for common household repairs.

- Learn how to mix your own cleaning supplies to save money and the planet.

# General Repair

*Tool lust. Almost every homeowner develops at least a mild case just about the time they discover how much easier it is to do a job with the right tool. It's easy to give in to the urge to splurge, but it's not necessary. For general repairs, you need good, durable versions of the basics and a few specialty tools for plumbing, electrical, and HVAC repairs. How much your tool kit expands after that is limited only by how much money and storage space you have to spare.*

Quick Clamps

## *Basic tools*

**Claw hammer:** drives nails. Also removes nails and pries things apart.

**Screwdriver:** drives and removes screws. Buy an assortment of sizes, including both slotted, which have flat tips, and Phillips, which are cross shaped.

**Utility knife:** cuts everything from cardboard to carpet. Choose one with a comfortable, easy-to-hold handle and a sturdy mechanism to extend and retract the replaceable blades.

**Tape measure:** measures anything. The metal tape and the mechanism should be sturdy enough to stand up to being used hundreds of times, and the hook at the end of the tape should be straight and true—a crooked hook can skew the result enough to ruin a measurement.

**Aviation snips:** cuts lightweight metal, such as flashing, and wire.

Claw Hammer

**Quick clamps:** hold pieces together when you need an extra hand; compress joints while gluing.

**Stud finder:** senses framing studs within walls. Some models also indicate the presence of wiring and other obstructions beneath the surface.

**Adjustable wrench:** tightens and loosens nuts and bolts; adjusts to a wide range of sizes.

**Flashlight:** illuminates dark corners and helps you find the service panel if the power goes out.

**Pliers:** grip objects tightly and give you extra torque as you turn, pull, or squeeze. Pliers with locking grips are especially helpful when you need an extra hand.

*Left to right: Needlenose pliers, channel-type pliers, blunt-nose pliers, locking pliers*

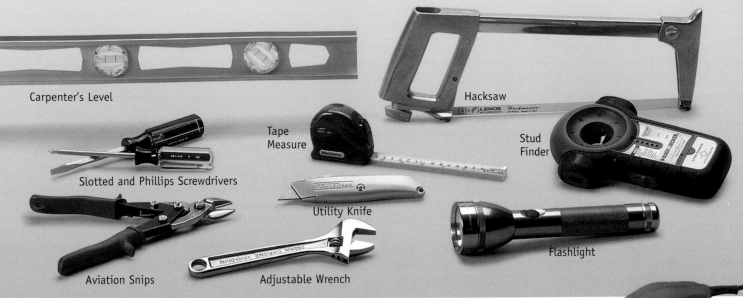

Carpenter's Level

Tape Measure

Hacksaw

Stud Finder

Slotted and Phillips Screwdrivers

Utility Knife

Aviation Snips

Adjustable Wrench

Flashlight

**Carpenter's level:** indicates true horizontal (level) and vertical (plumb) planes. A level helps you get it straight when you hang pictures, shelves, window treatments, and much more. Traditional levels use bubbles that float in small tubes; laser levels shoot out beams of light as reference points.

**Hacksaw:** cuts wood; cuts metal and plastic pipe. Choose a sturdy hacksaw with a comfortable handle and a replaceable blade.

**Caulk gun:** compresses caulk tubes to deliver beads of caulk.

**Palm sander:** quickly sands flat surfaces.

**Cordless drill and bit set:** drills holes in walls, wood, metal, and plastic; drives and removes screws; with attachments can be used to buff and polish. Choose a variable-speed, reversing drill with a keyless chuck. Get an extra battery so you always have a spare charged and ready to go, or invest in a quick charger that will put you back in business in minutes.

**Jig saw:** cuts plywood and other wood. Especially useful for making cutouts.

Palm Sander

Cordless Drill

Jig Saw

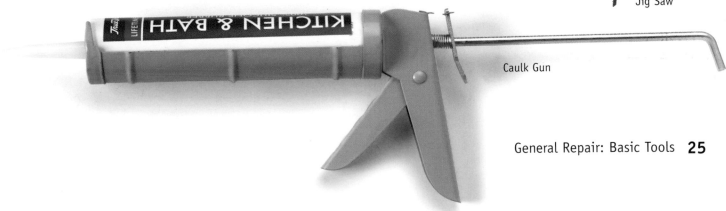

Caulk Gun

# Basic materials

*Every household needs a selection of fasteners, fillers, and adhesives. Day-to-day, there's always something that needs to be fixed, filled, or hung, and it's much easier to tackle the job when you have the materials on hand.*

**Screws:** are the fastener of choice for most jobs around the house. The threads bite into the materials being fastened— a big advantage when it comes to holding power. Just as importantly, screws can be removed as easily as they can be driven. No muss. No fuss. No damage to surrounding materials. Just switch the drill or driver to reverse, and you're there.

Like nails, screws come in various head styles and sizes. One look at a display in a hardware store or home center will convince you there's a screw for every possible task around the house. Don't worry—you don't need to buy them all. The trick is to have a good selection of commonly used screws and to use the right one at the right time.

The first basic distinction is between wood screws and machine screws. Wood screws are pointed at the end, and the ends of machine screws are flat.

Next comes head style. Round-head screws are domed and sit above the surface of the material when driven. They're best used where they won't show or where the work is likely to be taken apart later. Choose oval screws when you're going to drive the screw head below the surface, called *countersinking* it. Bugle-head screws are the answer when the screw head needs to be flush with the surrounding material.

*Wood screw (flat head)*  *Wood screw (oval head)*  *Machine screw with nut*  *Machine screw*  *Sheet-metal screw*  *Drywall screw*  *Lag-head screw*

The most obvious thing about a screw is the hole in its head. Slotted screws have straight grooves across the center, Phillips screws have cross-shaped holes, Torx screws have star-shaped holes, and not surprisingly, square-head screws have square holes.

Slotted screws work fine in situations where you're driving the screws by hand, but Phillips and square-head screws work better when you're using a power driver because they stand up to more torque without stripping.

Screws are described with two numbers. One number indicates the gauge, or thickness. The lower that number, the smaller the diameter of the screw. Most common household tasks can be accomplished with #5 to #14 screws.

Each gauge is available in a number of lengths, indicated by the second number. For example, #8 screws are commonly available in ½-, ¾-, and 1-inch lengths. When selecting screws, remember that they should extend about two-thirds of the way through the material being fastened.

## Tips on Driving Screws

Drill pilot holes before driving screws into hard woods or any dense or brittle material. Make the hole slightly smaller than the screw so it still bites into the material as it goes in. If you're going to countersink the screw, use a countersink bit for the pilot hole.

If you've drilled pilot holes and you're using the right size driver bit, the screws should go in easily. If you find yourself stripping screws, adjust the torque on the drill or driver. If you're having trouble with the wood

splitting, rub the screws on a piece of beeswax or a bar of soap before driving them. The wax or soap will help the screws slide into the wood without splitting it.

# F.A.Q.

**Q** *What's the deal with the different head styles on screws? Does it matter which I choose?*

**A** If you're driving them by hand into soft material, it probably doesn't matter. If you're driving them with a drill into hard materials, it does. In ascending order, Phillips, square, and Torx-style screws tolerate more torque (you can turn them with more force) without stripping or slipping than slotted screws. Not surprisingly, price per screw ascends in the same order. For almost all general screw needs, Phillips is the way to go.

**Nails:** come in a surprising assortment of sizes and styles, each with its own job to do. You can buy specialty nails if and when the need arises, but for basic maintenance and repair jobs, you need a selection of finish nails and a variety of brads, which are simply thin nails with small heads or no heads. It's good to have a few box nails on hand, too.

## Tips for Using Nails

Angling nails provides better holding power than driving them straight.

Staggering nails so they don't all enter the same part of the grain reduces splitting.

*Toenailing* is a method of joining two pieces of wood when endnailing isn't possible.

## Selecting Nails

Believe it or not, there's an art to selecting nails. First, the style: With or without a head? A box nail has a broad head, which is easy to drive, but too ugly to use where it can be seen. Finishing nails are harder to see, but they're also harder to drive and have less holding power than broad-headed nails. So, what's a handy person to do? Generally speaking, use broad-headed nails for rough carpentry and finishing nails for surface or trim work.

Next, the size: How big? Too short and they may not hold. Too long and they may protrude. Rule of thumb: Choose nails long enough to reach about two-thirds of the way through the second layer of material. Let's say you're nailing two 2 × 4s together. Since 2 × 4s actually are $1\frac{1}{2}$ inches thick, the nails should be the full thickness of the first board plus two-thirds of the thickness of the second ($1\frac{1}{2}$" + 1"), or $2\frac{1}{2}$ inches long.

Nail lengths are identified by numbers from 4 to 60, followed by the letter *d*, which oh-so-logically stands for "penny." The higher the number, the larger the nail. This means a 16d nail (read: 16 penny) is quite a bit smaller than a 60d spike.

**Glue and other adhesives:** bond materials of all types. Keeping a couple of bottles of glue on hand will spare you a trip to the store the first time something needs repair. Storing the glue bottles tightly closed and upside down

will spare you a trip the second time. With glue filling the tip of the bottle, it's easier to use, plus the bottle isn't filled with glue-drying air, and you don't end up with those irritating dried globs stopping up the bottle.

Good-old yellow carpenter's glue is still a staple, but every household also needs a bottle of polyurethane glue, which bonds with wood, stone, metal, ceramics, solid-surface

materials, and Styrofoam. Unless you're planning to do a tremendous amount of gluing, get a small bottle—polyurethane glue has a shelf life of about a year after it's been opened.

Silicone caulk is another adhesive that comes in handy in a surprising number of ways. The clear kind can be used as glue in many places, especially places that frequently get wet.

**Support anchors:** provide holding power to support window treatments, shelves, mirrors, pictures, and other hanging items in hollow walls. It's best to drive nails and screws into solid support, such as a wall stud, but it's not always possible. Adding the right support anchor neatly solves the problem. Which anchor you use depends on the size and weight of the piece you're hanging, so investigate before you hit the hardware aisle. When you get there, you'll find hollow wall anchors, molly bolts, toggle bolts, and other assorted fixings. Read the packaging to find a style that works for your walls—drywall, plaster, masonry—and the piece you're hanging.

*Toggle bolt*

*Wall anchor*

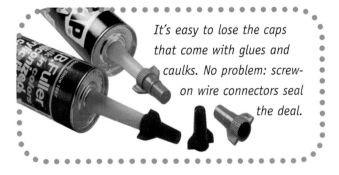

*It's easy to lose the caps that come with glues and caulks. No problem: screw-on wire connectors seal the deal.*

# Wall Repair & Painting

*Unless a house is brand new, the walls probably sport at least a few signs of wear and tear—dirt, scuffs, holes, cracks, maybe even paint combinations that were trendy before you were born. Wall repair—including painting—is pretty straightforward, and it's easy to tackle when you have the right tools and materials.*

**Putty and broad knives:** scrape walls and other surfaces in preparation for painting; smooths spackle and other fillers in walls and woodwork.

**Spackle and wood fillers:** patch holes in drywall, plaster, and wood. Ultralight spackle is fabulous for everyday wall repairs—easy to apply and dries in minutes. Plus, it can be painted over almost immediately.

Most brands of wood filler come tinted, neutral, and white. If you're trying to match a stain exactly, get the neutral and tint it yourself; the tinted versions are made to match several common stain colors. For painted woodwork, especially white, you may need to touch up the paint after you fill the holes—"white" comes in thousands of shades.

**Paint brushes and rollers:** apply paint and other finishes to small and large surfaces.

**Sandpaper and sanding sponges:** smooth rough surfaces. Available in different grades, from coarse to fine grit. One variety pack of sandpaper will probably serve you well for a long time when it comes to basic repairs. If you have a lot of painting ahead of you, try the sanding sponges. They're marked according to purpose—rough sanding, between coats, and so on—and they work wonders on rounded surfaces or in corners.

**Painter's tape:** masks off edges of a paint job. Painter's tape works better than standard masking tape because it's made to release easily without leaving any residue.

Finally, we can't say this often enough: Doing home repair safely means protecting your hands, eyes, and lungs from chemicals and flying debris. Buy safety glasses, dust masks, a respirator, and heavy gloves, and wear them when necessary.

**Safety glasses:** protect your eyes from flying debris and chemicals. Get the kind that protect your eyes from the side as well as from the front.

**Dust mask and respirator:** filter debris and chemical vapors. Dust masks are great when you're sawing, sanding, or using latex paint, but when you're dealing with harsh chemicals, it's best to use a respirator. It's so much better to be safe than sorry.

**Gloves:** protect your hands from harsh chemicals, contaminated water, splinters, and blisters. You need a pair of rubber gloves and and a pair of construction gloves, each durable enough to be used frequently.

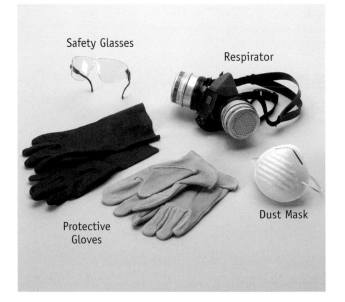

Safety Glasses

Respirator

Protective Gloves

Dust Mask

# Specialty Tools

*When it comes to the plumbing, all most people want is for water to arrive when and where they want it and to leave when they're finished with it. Sounds simple, but it doesn't always work quite that way. Most common problems involve leaks or clogs, which are fairly simple to fix as long as you have a few basic tools and a clear understanding of how the system is supposed to work (see page 128).*

## Plumbing

### Tools

**Plungers:** clear clogs in sinks, tubs, and toilet bowls. Good plungers are indispensible. A standard plunger has a flat face designed for clogs in sinks, tubs, and showers. Flanged plungers generate both pressure and suction to clear clogs in toilets. If you only want to buy one plunger (and you're willing to disinfect it scrupulously), you can fold up the flange and use a toilet plunger on sinks, tubs, and showers.

**Augers:** clear stubborn clogs. A closet auger is designed for toilet clogs; a hand auger (also called a snake) clears drain-line clogs.

**Wire brush:** cleans metal pipes and fittings. Choose one with bristles soft enough to clean pieces without damaging them.

**Wrenches:** Spud wrenches grab 2- to 4-inch nuts, allowing you to remove or tighten the nuts found on drain traps and tailpieces. Pipe wrenches have adjustable jaws for tightening a variety of pipes and fittings.

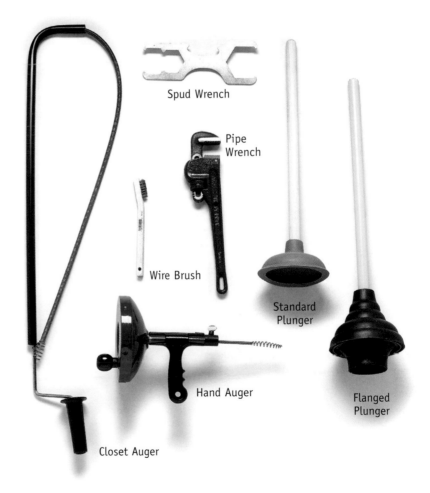

Spud Wrench

Pipe Wrench

Wire Brush

Hand Auger

Closet Auger

Standard Plunger

Flanged Plunger

## Materials

The materials required for a plumbing repair depend on the specific problem and its location. You'll need to buy pipe and fittings as the need arises, but it's a good idea to keep these basic supplies on hand.

**Plumber's putty:** fills gaps around faucets, drain bodies, and other parts of fixtures and drains to prevent leaks.

**Pipe joint compound and Teflon tape:** seal the connections between threaded components to prevent leaks.

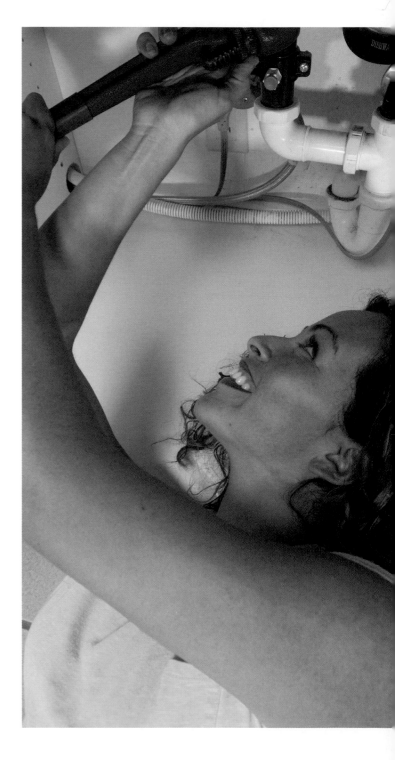

Putty

Teflon Tape

Pipe Joint
Compound

# Electrical

The tools you need for basic electrical repairs are simple and inexpensive. It's important to keep them clean and dry, and to keep the combination tool sharpened. Also, the batteries in the testing devices need to be changed from time to time, so keep spares on hand.

## Tools

**Combination tool:** cuts cables and wires, measures wire gauges, and strips insulation from wires. The insulated handles are extra protection against shock, although you should never work on circuits until you've confirmed that the power is off (see page 184).

**Continuity tester:** includes a battery that generates current and a wire loop that creates an electrical circuit so you can check switches, lighting fixtures, and other devices for faults.

**Neon circuit tester:** lets you check circuit wires for power. If you're going to do any electrical work at all, you have to have a neon circuit tester: confirming that the power is off is the first step in virtually every electrical repair.

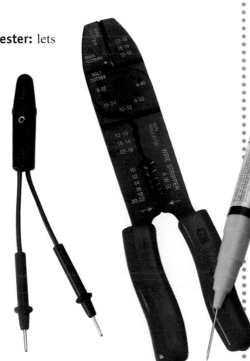

## Materials

**Switches:** control the flow of electricity to fixtures and some receptacles. They are extremely reliable but sometimes need to be replaced or updated.

**Receptacles:** provide access to electrical circuits, either standard (110, 115, 120, or 125 volts) or high (220, 240, or 250) voltage. Choose receptacles that match the amperage of the circuit.

**Wire connectors:** join wires safely. The color and size of a wire connector indicates the size and number of wires it's designed to accommodate. A small package of assorted sizes will meet most homeowners' needs for years.

**Cable:** carries electrical circuits throughout the house. Electrical cable consists of individual copper wires insulated with rubber or plastic (except for a bare copper grounding wire, which doesn't need to be insulated). The color of the insulation identifies the wire as hot (black or red), neutral (white or gray), or grounding (green or bare).

# HVAC

Most homeowners limit their work on HVAC systems to simple preventive maintenance, which doesn't require much beyond the basic tools and materials described already. There are, however, a few specialty tools you might want to keep on hand.

**Socket drivers, ratchet wrenches and extensions, and open-end wrenches:** tighten nuts and bolts on furnaces, flues, dampers, and small appliances.

**Fin comb:** straightens fins on heat pumps or air conditioners.

**Broad-billed pliers:** straighten convector fins.

**Pilot-jet tool:** clears a thermocouple tip.

Pilot-Jet Tool

Broad-Billed Pliers

Fin Comb

Socket Driver, Ratchet and Extension, and Open-end Wrenches

# Cleaning Tools & Supplies

*It's as simple as it is inevitable: When you own a home, you figure out that dirty things wear out faster than clean ones; you slowly realize that ground-in dirt breaks down fibers in carpet and upholstery and attacks the finishes on other surfaces. And since you want your belongings to outlast the payments, you begin to take cleaning seriously.*

There are thousands of cleaning tools and products on the market, but only a small handful are truly necessary. The basics include a broom, vacuum cleaner, mop, bucket, microfiber cloths, rags such as cotton diapers, rubber gloves, abrasive pads, scrub brushes, and a spray bottle.

**Microfiber cloths:** are super-absorbent nylon or nylon/poly weave cloths, great for dusting and other kinds of general cleaning. They're great for the environment since they can be reused repeatedly and even washed up to 500 times.

**Rubber gloves:** protect your hands from harsh cleaning products. Get a durable pair of rubber gloves and wear them whenever you're using cleaning chemicals.

**Vacuum cleaner:** sweeps and dusts. A good vacuum has plenty of suction power, is light enough to move easily, and has convenient attachments and a long power cord.

**Mop:** washes floors. Even if you prefer to wash the floors by hand, it's good to have a mop for quick pickups. Everyone has their own favorite type, and one isn't better than another as long it's durable, wrings out easily, and can be sterilized.

*You'll find recipes for cleaning solutions in individual chapters throughout this book. Most are simple combinations of very basic ingredients such as liquid dish soap, vinegar, isopropanol, and baking soda.*

**Brooms:** for quick pickups and daily sweeping. A good broom has plenty of bristles, the kind that are flexible but not wimpy.

**Abrasive pads and brushes:** make short work of ground-in dirt. Although you have to use common sense—avoid fragile finishes, for example—abrasive pads and scrub brushes easily earn a place in your cleaning caddy.

**Cotton diapers:** are soft, lintless cloths just right for many tasks. For some jobs—washing windows or mirrors—there's nothing like a cotton diaper. They're just the right size for many tasks.

**Disposable cleaning pads:** The brand we've used is Mr. Clean Magic Eraser. Put a little water on one and scrub away fingerprints, scuffs, black marks, even crayons from walls, floors, and woodwork. They aren't expensive and can be reused until they practically vanish.

**Squeegee:** You say you don't do windows? Well, someone has to, and if they know what they're doing, you can bet they use a squeegee. But forget about windows, and every household still needs a squeegee. If you wipe down the shower each day, soap scum, mold, and mildew never build up, and you never find yourself with an ugly job on your hands.

**Spray bottle:** You can buy a different product to clean every surface in your house. You can also keep the house sparkling with inexpensive, environmentally responsible cleaning solutions that you mix yourself, and that's where spray bottles come in handy. One caution: Label each bottle with its contents. Some chemicals create hazardous fumes when combined—you do not want to risk any misunderstandings about exactly what's in a bottle.

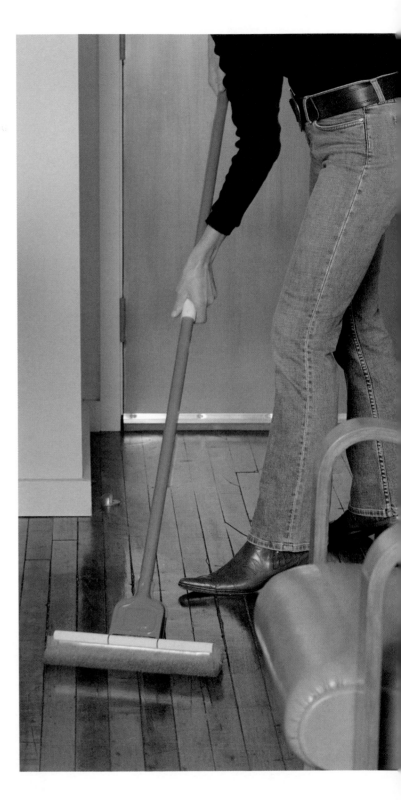

# walls & ceilings

*There was so much handwriting on the wall that even the wall fell down.*

CHRISTOPHER MORLEY

Your walls should stand strong, and straight, and true. And if there is handwriting on them, you should know how to get it off.

In this chapter, we'll show you how to keep walls and ceilings clean, in good repair, and freshly painted.

---

## With this chapter you'll . . .

- Learn how to remove old and damaged finishes quickly and easily.

- Find out everything you need to know about repairing drywall and plaster (but were afraid to ask).

- Paint walls and ceilings like a pro—with no drips, runs, or errors.

# walls & ceilings
## THE WAY THEY WORK

The walls and ceilings of your house are composed of layers of lumber, building materials, and decorative finishes. Sandwiched between the layers, you'll find plumbing, wiring, and HVAC ducts and vents. Walls also support doors and windows, and ceilings may frame skylights.

The basic structure of the walls and ceilings is formed by studs and joists. Wall studs, typically 2 × 4 or 2 × 6 lumber, are located every 16 inches. Ceiling joists, typically 2 × 10s, are also located at 16-inch intervals. (These intervals are *on*

*center*—meaning it's 16 inches from the center of one board to the center of the next.) In this chapter, we're concerned with the interior layers—the drywall or plaster and the finishes such as paneling, paint, wallpaper, and trim work.

Like veins and arteries beneath the surface of your skin, the basic systems of the house—plumbing, wiring, and HVAC—run beneath the walls and ceilings of your house. Find out what's back there before you probe, drill, or cut into a wall or ceiling.

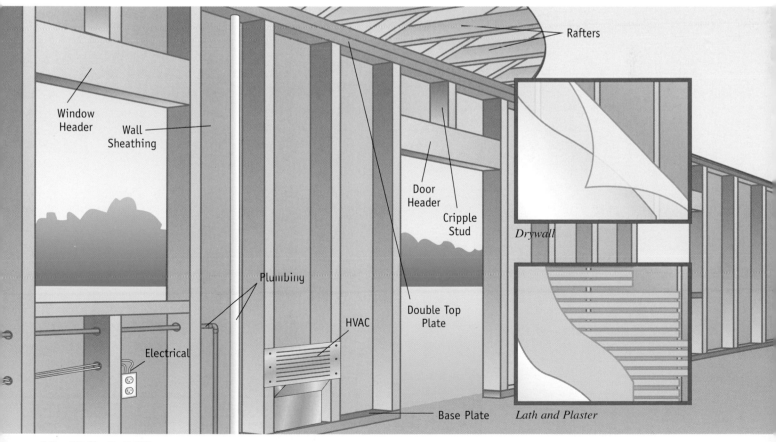

# F.A.Q.

**Q** *How do I find a stud?*

**A** If it's a framing stud you seek, there are several ways to search. The easiest method involves an inexpensive gadget called an *electronic stud finder*, available at home centers and hardware stores everywhere. The exact instructions vary from one brand to another, but the basic idea is that you push the gadget across the wall, and an indicator tells you when you're over a stud. No muss. No fuss.

If you've used a stud finder in the past and found it less than accurate, try one of the new models. The new electronic models work amazingly well over almost any wall surface, making them well worth the $15 to $25 they cost.

In a pinch, you can inspect baseboards or other trim molding for nail holes—molding is nailed to studs—and extrapolate from there. You can also remove the cover from an electrical switch or receptacle and check around. Electrical boxes typically are nailed to studs, and with the cover off, you can see which side the stud falls on, then measure in increments of 16 inches to estimate the location of the stud you're trying to find.

The old tapping-the-walls method is tried but not necessarily true. Some people say they can hear the difference between tapping on the hollow portion of the wall and the area in front of a stud. We find that's a good way to end up with a lot of holes to fill.

**Q** *What if there's no stud where I want to hang a picture, mirror, or heavy object?*

**A** You need hardware designed to support weight in hollow walls—wall anchors and toggle bolts, for example. Before you head to the hardware store or home center, you need to know the wall material (drywall or plaster) and the approximate weight of the object to be hung. Read the packages carefully and find the smallest anchor rated to support the object's weight. (Smaller holes are better if you have to fill them later.)

⚠️ If a repair makes it necessary to cut into walls or ceilings, **turn off the electricity** in the area before you start. First, identify the proper circuit, turn it off, and confirm that the power is off by testing a receptacle.

# Cleaning & Maintaining

*Today's furnaces may be the ultimate labor-saving devices. Their clean-burning fuels and efficient filters have virtually eliminated the need to clean layers of dust and soot from the walls and ceilings every spring. Our grandmothers probably scrubbed every surface they could reach as soon as it was warm enough to stop heating the house, but for the most part, we can keep things in great shape just by vacuuming the walls and ceilings and taking a damp cloth to switches, receptacles, and surrounding areas.*

## Painted Walls

**Dust the walls.** A vacuum with a long brush attachment is the tool for this job. Start at the top—work from the ceiling to the baseboards, and pay special attention to the corners.

**Wash fingerprints** from switches, receptacles, and surrounding areas. Use a slightly damp microfiber cloth or a disposable cleaning pad and a light touch. Remember, water and electricity don't mix: turn the switches to OFF and thoroughly wring out the cloth or pad before beginning.

**Wash walls that are dirty, greasy, or moldy.** Dirt and grease sometimes build up in kitchens, and mold does in bathrooms. You can limit problems by using the vent hood when cooking and the vent fan when showering.

First, vacuum the walls; then fill one bucket with cleaning solution and one with clean rinse water.

➤ For greasy or dirty walls, combine 1 cup of ammonia, 1 cup of white vinegar and ¼ cup of dishwashing liquid with 1 gallon of water.

➤ For moldy walls, add ¾ cup of chlorine bleach to 1 gallon of plain water. (*Never* mix chlorine with other cleaning chemicals, especially ammonia.)

Paint, especially the semigloss and glossy enamel types often used in kitchens and bathrooms, typically stands up well to washing, but you should test an inconspicuous area first.

Start at the top of the walls so dirty water doesn't drip onto clean areas as you work; wash a section with the cleaning solution, then rinse it thoroughly with plain water. Work in sections you can reach from one spot—about 4 feet square. Change the cleaning solution and rinse water frequently.

**Call a Pro!** *Are you regularly finding mold on walls or ceilings? It may be a symptom of a larger moisture problem. Call a mold abatement specialist.*

# Ceilings

**Acoustical tiles** can be carefully washed with a lightly dampened sponge or cloth. Use as little water as possible—too much moisture will ruin the tile. On some tile, you can cover small stains or marks with white shoe polish or with correction fluid, such as Liquid Paper. (Try it in an inconspicuous spot first to make sure it blends well.)

**Painted, textured ceilings** can be washed with a damp cloth and warm water. Don't use sponges—they leave crumbs in the texture's crevices.

**Sealed or varnished wood ceilings** can be washed with soap and water in the same way as other woodwork. For very dirty areas, try a solution of TSP and water.

**Flat, painted ceilings** can be washed in the same way as painted walls. (See page 42.)

**Popcorn ceilings** can't be washed with water. If you're having trouble getting spiderwebs and dust motes off the texture, slip a lint roller sleeve over the frame of a paint roller, attach a handle extension, and roll away. Roll lightly, and change the sleeve frequently. One lint roller covers a small roller frame, so you'll need two on a standard frame.

*Open a window, run a vent fan, and wear rubber gloves when using chlorine or other strong cleaning chemicals. These substances can burn skin and cause lung irritation.*

# Ceramic Tile

Ceramic tile walls are found mostly in bathrooms and kitchens. Warm water and a little bit of dishwashing liquid typically are enough to clean it; equal parts white vinegar and warm water will cut through heavy soap scum and water stains. Always rinse with clean water and dry the tile to prevent streaks.

To help **keep your ceramic tile clean:**

➤ Buff the walls with half a lemon. This will create a glossy finish that repels water. Liquid car wax does the same thing.

➤ After using the shower, wipe down the walls with a squeegee—removing the excess water before it has a chance to dry will reduce water stains and soap scum, as well as mold and mildew.

Scrub **tough stains** with a paste made of baking soda and bleach. Wear rubber gloves when making and using the paste.

☑ Save yourself some time and effort: Before cleaning shower or tub tile, **let the hot water run** for a couple minutes—the steam will loosen dirt and grime so it's easier to clean.

**To help grout resist water,** wear, and stains, apply sealer every year or two (above). Test the existing grout sealer by putting a few drops of water on a grout line. If the water beads up, the sealer is still effective. If it absorbs into the grout, it's time to reseal.

**Scrub grout joints** with a soft-bristle brush and a mild, nonsoap detergent to remove dirt and grime. To kill mold and mildew, mix one part chlorine bleach and ten parts water, put it on the moldy joints, and let it sit for ten minutes, then scour with a soft-bristle brush or toothbrush.

If the grout lines are not solid and full, **remove and replace it** (see page 55). Clean the wall, then spread the sealer on the grout lines, using a small sponge paintbrush. Follow the sealer manufacturer's instructions (three coats of sealer typically are recommended).

# Wallpapered Walls & Ceilings

Vacuum wallpapered walls in the same way as painted walls, but more gently. Remove the brush attachment from time to time and use the end of the hose to get the dust out of the brush itself, especially when cleaning flocked or textured wallpaper.

Wallpapers labeled *washable* can be gently cleaned with a damp sponge or cloth, papers labeled *scrubbable* can be washed in much the same way as painted walls. Disposable cleaning pads remove dirt or marks from most of these wallpapers without damaging them. Test gentle cleaners in an inconspicuous area, and never use abrasives or strong chemicals on wallpaper.

Get professional advice about cleaning wallpaper labeled *nonwashable*. You may be able to remove small spots with wallpaper-cleaning putty or an art-gum eraser, but test it in an inconspicuous spot first. If you can't find wallpaper-cleaning putty in your local home center or paint and wall-covering store, try the Internet.

# Protecting Walls & Ceilings

Walls and doorknobs don't mix. Or at least, they shouldn't. We won't name names, but all too often, someone in a hurry opens a door too energetically or the wind catches it at the wrong moment, and suddenly, there's a knob-shaped hole in the wall behind the door.

One of the most important things you can do to protect your walls is put sturdy stops on every door. Depending on a door's size and placement, the best choice may be a stop mounted on the door, the wall, the floor, or even slipped into the hinge pins. The idea is to stop the door just short of the point where the knob could make contact with the wall. It may take some experimentation to find the right stop for each door, but it's probably time well spent when you consider the alternative—patching and painting the walls over and over.

Once you have stops in place, make a point to check them now and then. In households with children or pets, the rubber bumpers disappear all too frequently, leaving the walls just as vulnerable as if the stops weren't there at all.

If you can't beat 'em, join 'em. In places where a stop alone won't do the trick, try a **protective guard**—they're available in styles ranging from paintable, paperable plastic shields that deflect the knob to molded-plastic cavities that accommodate it.

⚠ The rubber bumpers on some spring-type door stops come off easily, presenting a **choking hazard for young children**. If young children live in or frequently visit your home, avoid this danger by choosing another style of stop.

# Repairing Walls & Ceilings

*It happens all the time: slight miscalculations while moving furniture, undiscovered leaks from second floor bathrooms, swatting at spiders with a broom. . . . Whatever caused them, holes, cracks, and water damage to walls and ceilings are relatively easy to fix. Before making any repairs, check the overall condition of the walls and ceilings. If they feel spongy or have large bulges and cracks, consider hiring a professional to cover or replace the entire surface.*

## Drywall

If your home was built or remodeled after 1940, your walls are almost certainly made of drywall. Drywall panels are made up of a solid gypsum core wrapped in paper. The paper actually gives the panel most of its strength, so it's important that the paper remain intact.

Most drywall damage can be fixed using a few basic drywalling materials: screws, joint tape, drywall, and joint compound or spackle.

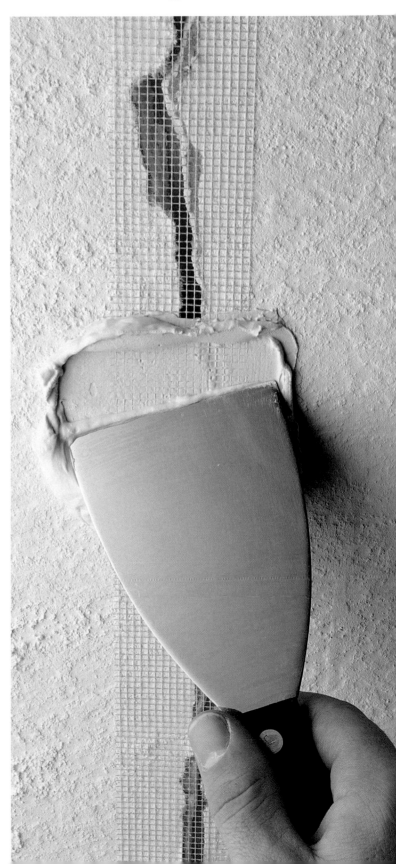

## Popped Drywall Nails

As a house settles, drywall nails pop to the surface. It's easy to drive the nails back down, but that's not a permanent solution. Drywall screws are the answer—they hold more firmly than nails.

**1.** Drive a drywall screw into a stud or joist, 2" above or below the popped nail. Be sure the screw pulls the drywall tight against the framing.

Scrape away loose paint or drywall compound. Drive the popped nail back into the framing so the head is about 1/16" below the surface. (Don't try to set the nail with a nail punch.)

**2.** Use a drywall knife to apply 3 coats of ultra-light spackle to the nail and screw holes, letting the spackle dry between coats. Sand, prime, and paint the patched area.

## Cracks

Settling also produces cracks in drywall, typically at seams where two drywall panels butt together or at the joints between ceilings and walls. When this happens, it's best to retape the joints to keep the crack from developing again.

**1.** Fill the crack with joint compound, using a taping knife. Center drywall tape over the crack, then smooth it with the taping knife, working from the center outward. Apply a thin layer of joint compound over the tape,  let it dry, then add a second coat, feathering the edges smooth. Once thoroughly dry, sand lightly and repaint.

**2.** For cracks at corners or ceilings, cut through the existing seam, then apply tape or inside-corner bead and two coats of joint compound.

# F.A.Q.

**Q** *Two nails popped out of the drywall of one of my living rooms walls. I've nailed them back in twice, but they keep reappearing. What's causing this?*

**A** As a house settles, nails often pop to the surface. After the nails have popped once, the nail holes are larger and the nail's grip is radically reduced. Replace the nails with screws (see above). The threads on drywall screws have much more bite than nails and will hold permanently.

## Dents and Shallow Holes

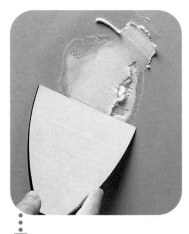

**1.** Scrape or sand away any loose drywall, face paper, or peeled paint. Fill the hole with ultralight spackle, using the smallest drywall knife that will span the entire hole.

**2.** Lightly sand the area, then prime and paint.

## Nail Holes

**1.** Apply ultralight spackle to the holes, using a putty knife or your fingertip.

**2.** Sand the area with 150-grit sandpaper. Wipe away dust with a damp sponge, then paint primer onto the spots. Paint the area, feathering the edges to camouflage the repair.

## Small Holes

**1.** Inspect the damaged area. If there aren't cracks around the edges of the hole, fill the hole with spackle, let it dry, and sand the area smooth.

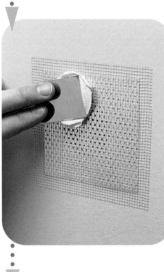

**2.** If the edges are cracked, cover the hole with a peel-and-stick repair patch. Use a putty knife to cover the patch with spackle or joint compound. When the spackle is thoroughly dry, add a second coat. Let the patch set until the spackle is nearly dry (consult the package for drying time).

**3.** Use a damp sponge or drywall wet sander to smooth the repair area.

### Again!?

If a doorknob repeatedly hits a wall, the problem isn't the doorknob (or the children), but the door stop. Either it's missing or not the right style for the situation. Experiment with different types until you find a stop that stops the knob short of the wall.

## Large Holes

**1.** Outline the damaged area. Use a drywall saw or jig saw to cut away the damaged section.

**2.** Cut two pieces of drywall to use as backer strips; use hot glue to attach the strips behind the opening. Let the glue cool and harden.

**3.** Cut a drywall patch to size. Run wavy beads of hot glue along the backer strips, and press the patch in place. When the glue is cool, cover the seams with self-stick drywall tape, apply joint compound, and sand the area.

**To patch a damaged drywall ceiling,** follow the same procedure as above; however, use wood for the backing. Cut the board so it is narrow enough to fit into the hole and long enough to span the hole by 2" on opposite sides. Fasten the backing in place with drywall screws.

# Plaster

Plaster walls are created by building up plaster in layers to form a hard, durable wall surface. Behind the plaster itself is a gridlike layer of wood, metal, or rock lath that holds the plaster in place. Keys, formed when the base plaster is squeezed through the lath, hold the dried plaster to the ceilings or walls.

Before you begin a repair, make sure the surrounding area is in good shape. If the lath is deteriorated or the plaster in the damaged area is soft, call a professional.

## Cracks in Plaster

**1.** Scrape away any texture or loose plaster around the crack. Reinforce the crack with self-sticking fiberglass drywall tape. Use a drywall knife to apply spackle or drywall joint compound, just enough to barely cover the tape. (If the compound is too thick, it will crack again.)

**2.** Apply a second thin coat if necessary to conceal the edges of the tape. Sand lightly and prime the area.

## Holes in Plaster

**1.** Scrape or sand any paint and all loose or soft plaster from around the edges of the damage. Probe the edges with the drywall knife to make sure the remaining plaster is solid and tight.

**2.** Apply latex bonding liquid liberally around the edges of the hole and over the exposed lath. Mix patching plaster as directed by the manufacturer and use a drywall knife or trowel to apply it to the hole.

**3.** For deeper holes, apply a shallow first coat, then scratch a crosshatch pattern in the wet patching plaster. Let it dry, then apply a second coat. Let the plaster dry, then sand it lightly. Use texture paint or drywall joint compound to recreate any surface texture. (See page 53.)

# Retexture Plaster Surfaces

**1.** First, take a look at the texture and consider how to reproduce it. You might want to practice on cardboard until you can re-create the pattern. Remember that the depth of the texture depends on the stiffness of the joint compound or plaster (which can be thinned with water), the amount you apply to the surface, and the type of tool you're using to create the texture. Here are some examples:

**2.** A long-nap roller produces a stipple-texture effect. For different patterns, vary the pressure on the roller and the amount of material on the surface.

**3.** Apply joint compound or plaster with a roller, then use a whisk broom to create a swirl pattern.

**4.** Trowel material onto the surface, then pile it in ridges to create an adobe pattern.

**5.** Dab, drag, or swirl a sponge through plaster or joint compound to create a variety of texture patterns. Or let the first course dry, then sponge another color on top for a two-tone stucco effect.

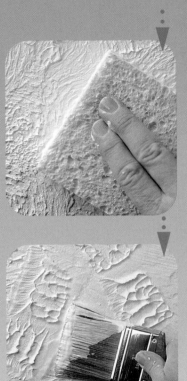

**6.** Apply material with a roller, rolling it out level. Randomly strike the surface with the side of a paint brush to produce a crowsfoot design.

**7.** Roll material onto the area, then press the flat side of a trowel onto the surface and pull it away to produce a stomp design.

**8.** Create a stomp design (above), then use a trowel to flatten the peaks and achieve a brocade design. Between strokes, clean the trowel with a wet brush or sponge.

# Acoustical Tiles

Acoustical ceiling tiles usually fit together with tongue-and-groove edges, so damaged tiles are easy to replace.

**1.** Cut the damaged tiles into pieces with a utility knife, then remove and discard the pieces. Use a straightedge to trim the upper (back side) lip of the grooved edges of the new tile. Also remove one of the tongues, if necessary.

**2.** Apply construction adhesive to the furring strips, then install the new tile, tongue first, and press it into the adhesive. Support large tiles with a flat board and a 2 × 4 post.

# Wallpaper

## Loose Seams

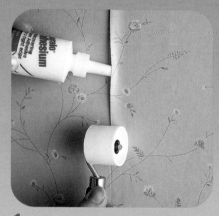

**1.** Squirt adhesive under the edge of the paper and firmly press the edge back into place. You can use a seam roller to create a better joint, though not with embossed or flocked papers. Wipe away excess adhesive with a clean, wet sponge.

## Bubbles

**1.** Cut a slit through the bubble using a utility knife. Apply adhesive to the wall under the bubble, then press the wallpaper into place. When the edges seem slightly set, wipe away excess adhesive.

## Patches

**1.** Using removable tape, position a scrap of wallpaper over the damaged area, lining up the pattern precisely. Cut through both layers, using a utility knife with a new blade.

**2.** Remove the patch, wet the wall, and peel away the damaged section. Put adhesive on the back of the patch and position it in the hole so the patterns match. Wipe away excess adhesive.

✔ If you don't have extra wallpaper, steal a section from a hidden spot, such as inside a closet or behind a door. Paint the hole a color that blends into the background of the wallpaper.

# Ceramic Tile

**Directing water:** You know that grout and caulk seal the edges of ceramic tile, but did you know they can protect ceilings? Imagine a second-floor bathroom with a tiled tub surround that has holes in the grout and gaps in the caulk at the edge of the tub. Every time someone showers, water finds its way into those holes and gaps and follows the path of least resistance, which in this case would be down the nearest wall stud and into the lowest spot in the ceiling below, probably near an opening for a vent fan or light fixture. Before you know it, the walls are wet, the ceiling's drooping, the fixture's shorted out, and you have a mess on your hands.

Inspect ceramic tile walls a couple of times a year. In a tub surround or shower stall, check the joints between walls as well as the edges where the tile walls meet the tub. If you find holes or gaps, regrout and recaulk them.

## Regrouting Ceramic Tile

**1.** Scrape out the old grout completely—a grout cutter (right) works really well for this. If you don't have one and don't want to buy one, try an awl or utility knife. Allow plenty of time for this step—removing grout isn't difficult, but doing it well takes more time than you might think. When all of the grout is out, cut out any caulk, and remove and replace any broken tiles.

**2.** Clean out the grout joints, then spread new grout over the entire tile surface, using a foam grout float or a sponge. Work the grout well into the joints. Let the grout set slightly, then tool it with a rounded object, such as a toothbrush. Wipe away excess with a damp cloth.

**3.** When the grout is dry, wipe away the residue and polish the tiles. Apply caulk (page 57). Don't use the tub or shower for 24 hours.

# Removing & Replacing Broken Tiles

**1.** Remove the grout from the surrounding joints. Break the damaged tile into small pieces using a hammer and chisel. Remove the broken pieces, then use a utility knife to scrape any debris or old adhesive from the open area.

If the tile to be replaced is a whole tile, you're ready to test-fit it in the open space (see Step 3 below). If it's a partial tile, cut a new one to match (see Step 2 below).

**2a.** Most tile stores will let you borrow a tile cutter or rent one for a very small fee. Ask store personnel to show you how to use the cutter, but basically you press down the wheel handle firmly to score a cutting line. Next, you snap the handle to quickly break the tile.

**2b.** You can also cut tile with a rod saw: Fit a tungsten carbide rod saw blade into a coping saw body. Firmly support the tile and use a sawing motion to cut the tile.

**2c.** If you need to cut a curved edge, mark the curve with a compass, then use the scoring wheel of a handheld tile cutter to score the cut line. Make several parallel scores, no more than 1/4" apart, in the waste portion of the tile. Use tile nippers to nibble away the scored portion of the tile.

**3.** Test-fit the new tile and make sure it fits and sits flush with the old tile. Spread adhesive on the back of the replacement tile, then place it in the hole, twisting slightly to make sure the tile makes good contact with the wall. Use masking tape to hold the tile in place for 24 hours so the adhesive can dry completely.

**4.** Remove the tape, then regrout the tile (see page 55).

## Recaulking a Bathtub or Shower Stall

**1.** Start with a completely dry surface. If possible, let the tub or shower dry for a few days before starting this project.

Scrape out the old caulk with an awl. Wipe soap scum from the joint with a clean, dry cloth dipped in rubbing alcohol.

**2.** If you're working on a bathtub, slowly fill it with water. (Don't let water splash onto the walls or into the joints.) Caulking the tub while it's weighted with water lets you fill the gap at its largest, reducing the possibility that the caulk will crack when you bathe.

If a joint tends to mildew, clean it with a product that kills mildew spores (available at hardware stores and home centers). Once the joint is completely dry, fill it with silicone or latex caulk.

**3.** Wet a fingertip with cold water (so the caulk won't stick to your skin). Use your finger to smooth the caulk into a cove shape. (A plastic straw works well, too.) After the caulk hardens, use a utility knife to trim away any excess.

The most important thing you can do to maintain your walls and ceilings is **protect them from water.** Most damage is caused by leaky plumbing fixtures or roofs. In cold climates, leaks related to ice dams often cause damage, too.

## Replacing Wall Accessories

**1.** To replace a built-in wall accessory, carefully remove the damaged piece as if it were a damaged tile (see page 56). Scrape away any remaining adhesive or grout. Apply dry-set tile adhesive to the back of the new accessory, then press it firmly in place. Use masking tape to hold the accessory while the adhesive dries. After 24 hours, remove the tape and regrout the tile.

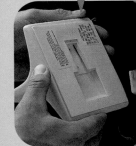

**2.** For a surface-mounted accessory, lift the damaged piece off the mounting plate. If the mounting plate screws are driven into studs or blocking, simply hang the new accessory. If not, install hollow-wall anchors appropriate to the weight of the accessory. Dab the pilot holes and the tips of the screws with silicone caulk, then attach the new mounting plate. Let the caulk dry before hanging the new accessory.

# Painting

*If you live in a house long enough, you will decide to paint. Maybe the ceiling looks dingy against the new window treatments, maybe the "baby" is now 11 and rebelling against pastel colors, maybe that aubergine wall has begun to look like last week's eggplant. Whatever the motivation, trust us—you will eventually paint. And it can be fun, with the right preparation.*

## Planning Ahead

Most municipalities allow you to put **empty latex paint cans** in the regular trash as long as the residue is completely dried out. If you have less than 1 inch of paint left in the can, let it dry out and throw it away. (Leave the lid off when you throw it out so your trash hauler can tell the paint is dried out and acceptable.)

**Never pour leftover paint thinner** down a drain. Let used thinner stand until the solid material settles (see photo at left). Pour off the clear thinner and reuse it.

*Waste not, want not. Reuse paint thinner after letting the solids settle out.*

**Leftover oil-based paint** must be disposed of as hazardous waste.

**Paint chemicals** don't store well. Buy only as much as is needed for the project and store them out of the reach of children. Don't use or store flammable materials, such as paint stripper, near an open flame or an appliance with a pilot light. (For example: Don't store paint cans near a gas furnace or water heater.)

Most communities now operate **latex paint recycling programs** in conjunction with their hazardous waste disposal facilities. If you have more than 1 inch of latex paint left in a can, recycle it. To protect its quality, put plastic wrap over the can before you replace the lid, don't let the paint freeze, and deliver it to the collection facility as soon as practical.

**Wear safety goggles** when you're working with chemical stripper or cleaning products, or painting overhead.

## Safety Issues

Always read the label information on paint and solvent containers. Chemicals that pose a fire hazard are listed as *combustible*, *flammable*, or *extremely flammable*. Be very careful when using these products, and remember that the fumes are also flammable. Follow the instructions on the label for safe handling.

The warning "use with adequate ventilation" means you should not let more vapor build up in a room than there would be if you were using the product outside. If the label carries the warning "harmful or fatal of swallowed," assume that the vapors are dangerous to breathe. Open doors and windows, and use a fan for ventilation. If you can't ventilate the area well enough, use a respirator mask.

**If your home was built before 1980,** the paint may contain lead, a hazardous substance. (Lead paint additives were banned in 1978, but supplies on hand were sold and used beyond that time.) Before sanding, scraping, or painting any surface in a home built before 1980, test for lead. You can find inexpensive test kits at hardware stores and home centers. If tests indicate lead, get expert advice. Most paint stores and the paint departments in larger home centers carry free brochures on what's known as "lead abatement procedures." You can also find information at www.epa.gov.

# Choosing Paint, Tools & Equipment

The right products will make the job a whole lot easier. Take a look:

**Primer:** If you're working with new drywall, plaster, or wood, you have to apply primer before painting. Yes, that's an extra step, but the results are worth the effort. Primer seals new surfaces and keeps finish coats from cracking or peeling.

You also need to use primer if you're trying to cover oil or water stains, rust spots, or other stains that might otherwise bleed through the paint. (The primer seals the stains, so the paint can cover them permanently.)

Primers are either water based or alkyd based. Choose a product designed for the application you have in mind—priming new surfaces, cov-

ering stains, or making the transition from a dark color to a lighter one. Follow label directions regarding coverage requirements and drying time.

**Paint:** Paint is either water based (latex) or alkyd based (oil). Latex paint is easy to apply and clean up, and it works in almost every situation. Some painters feel that alkyd-base paint has a smoother finish, but local regulations may restrict its use.

Paints come in various sheens. Paint finishes range from flat to high-gloss enamels. Gloss enamels dry to a shiny finish and are used for surfaces that need to be washed often, such as

## Just the Facts, Ma'am

*Paint departments are filled with products for faux finishing and other special painting techniques. Although we highly recommend that you try some of them, we stick to basic painting here. Once you have a handle on that, you'll be ready for any advanced technique that strikes your fancy.*

# F.A.Q.

**Q** *How do I know how much paint to buy?*

**A** Add the length in feet of each wall, multiply the total by their height, then divide the total by 400 to get a reliable estimate of how many gallons you'll need. For a 15 × 20-foot room with 9-foot ceilings, the calculations look like this:

$$15 + 15 + 20 + 20 = 70$$
$$70 \times 9 = 630$$
$$630 \div 400 = 1.575$$

Rounding up from 1.575, buy 2 gallons.

bathrooms, kitchens, and woodwork. Eggshell and flat paints have a nongloss finish and are used for most other wall and ceiling applications.

High-quality paint often costs more per gallon but typically covers more square footage and looks better longer than bargain brands. Good-quality paint covers about 400 square feet per gallon.

Consider buying recycled paint. It's sold for about 50 percent less than regular paint, so it's good for your budget as well as the environment. Recycled paint is made from unused paint combined with new materials that improve its consistency and produce standard colors. Check with your local recycling program to find authorized dealers in your area. (See page 58 for details about donating leftover paint to recycling programs.)

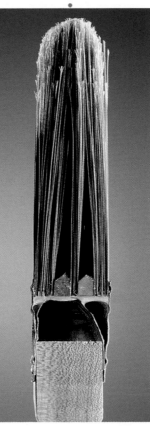

**Brushes:** Choose a straight-edged 3-inch wall brush for cutting paint lines (see page 69), a 2-inch straight-edged trim brush for woodwork, and a tapered sash brush for corners and window sashes. For latex paints, choose all-purpose brushes, which blend polyester, nylon, and sometimes animal bristles. Buy brushes made of hog or ox bristles to use with alkyd-base paints.

A good-quality paintbrush has a shaped hardwood handle and a sturdy reinforced ferrule made of noncorrosive metal. Multiple spacer plugs separate the bristles. It also has flagged (split) bristles and a chiseled end for precise edging.

**Paint trays:** A good paint tray is lightweight but stable and sturdy. You can clean the trays if you like, but it may be more environmentally responsible to let the paint dry and throw it away than to wash more paint down the drain.

**Rollers and covers:** The first roller you need is a basic 9-inch roller with a wire frame and nylon bearings. Choose one that feels well balanced and has a handle molded to fit your hand. Make sure the handle has a threaded end so you can attach an extension handle to paint ceilings and high walls. Next, check out specialty rollers, particularly smaller rollers and corner rollers, which make it easier to paint angles and contours.

Roller covers are available in a wide variety of nap lengths, including $1/4$-, $3/8$-, and 1-inch varieties. Most jobs can be done with $3/8$-inch nap, but rough surfaces call for $1/4$-inch nap. Always read the labels to make sure the covers you're choosing work well with the paints you've picked. Basically, for latex paint you need medium-priced synthetic roller covers that can be reused several times. Watch out for bargain roller covers—they tend to shed fibers onto the painted surfaces. When you're using alkyd-base paint, try lamb's wool or mohair covers.

**Tape and other masking products:** Careful masking creates crisp, sharp edges that divide the sheep from the goats when it comes to paint jobs. Good-quality painter's tape is sticky enough to stay where you want it but tack free, so it releases without leaving a tacky film. It's also flexible enough to follow curves and fit into corners. Wide paper tape catches spills and splatters, again without leaving a tacky film after it's removed. (Some masking tape has a time limit after which it may leave a residue or peel the paint. Be sure to follow the manufacturer's guidelines.)

Masking fluid simplifies the job of painting window trim and sashes. You paint the thick, white paste onto the trim, lapping it over onto the glass. When the fluid dries, it forms a thin sheet that protects the wood until you peel it away, leaving a clean, unpainted surface.

## Preparing to Paint

*New paint makes problems a little less obvious, but it doesn't make them go away. A finished paint job is going to look only as good as the surface being painted. If you want high-quality results, you've got to prepare the surfaces.*

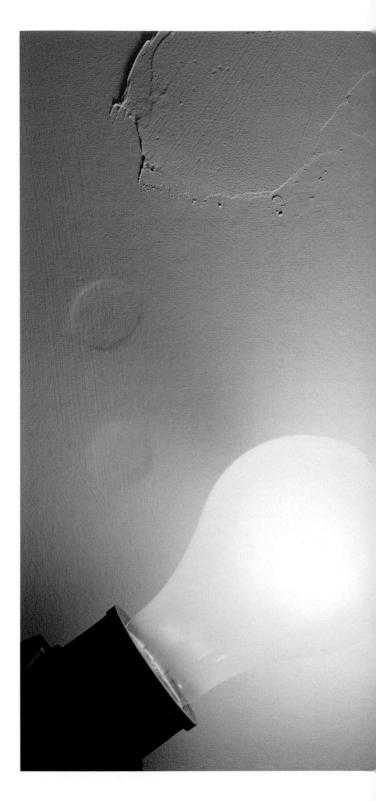

**1** Ceilings

**2** Woodwork

**3** Walls

If you're painting an entire room, do the ceiling first, followed by the trim, windows, and doors, and then the walls. Nothing magical about it, but tackling the jobs in order reduces the chances that you'll splatter freshly-painted surfaces.

You can go directly from painting the ceiling to the woodwork, but allow plenty of drying time between the woodwork and the walls. You don't want the tape to damage your freshly-painted trim. Check the paint label or ask your paint retailer about the curing time of the paint you purchase.

# Preparing Woodwork

Before painting or refinishing woodwork, take time to clean, repair, and sand it.

**Remove all hardware,** such as window handles and cabinet catches. If you're planning to install new hardware, buy it now and check to see whether the holes match. If not, fill the old ones and drill new ones as part of the preparation process.

If the wood's covered with thick layers or badly chipped paint, **strip it down to the bare wood.** We tell you how on page 65. Remember:

➤ If you use a heat gun, be careful not to let it scorch the wood or surrounding surfaces. Never use a heat gun after using chemical strippers: the chemical residue can be vaporized or ignited by the heat.

➤ If you use a chemical paint stripper, wear rubber gloves, heavy clothing, and safety gear, including safety glasses and a respirator. Follow the label directions for safe use, and keep the work area well ventilated.

➤ If your house was built before 1980, test for lead before disturbing the paint in any way (see page 59).

## Prepping Painted Woodwork

Scrape away any peeling or loose paint. If the woodwork is badly chipped, patch it (see page 65). Wash the wood with a solution of TSP and water, then rinse it clean with a sponge and water.

## Prepping Varnished Wood

Clean the wood with a soft cloth and odorless mineral spirits. Apply tinted wood putty to any holes and dents, using a putty knife. Allow the patch to dry, then lightly sand the area with 150-grit sandpaper. Wipe away any dust particles with tack cloth, then restain the patched areas to match the surrounding wood. When the stain is completely dry (check the label for recommendations), touch up the varnish.

## Stripping Old Paint

To strip wood with a heat gun, hold the heat gun near the wood until the paint softens and just begins to blister. Easy does it—too much heat can make the paint gummy or scorch the wood. Remove the softened paint with a scraper or putty knife.

To strip wood with a chemical stripper, apply a liberal coat of stripper to the surface, using a paintbrush. Let the stripper stand until the paint begins to blister. Scrape away the paint with a putty knife or steel wool. Rub the stripped wood with denatured alcohol and steel wool to help clean the grain. Next, wipe the wood with a  wet sponge or cloth dampened with solvent, as directed on the stripper label. (Be sure to wear safety glasses and rubber gloves, and make sure you have plenty of ventilation.)

## Repair Cracks, Dents & Holes

**1.** If necessary, use a putty knife to apply latex wood patch or spackle to any nail holes, dents, or other damaged areas. Allow the compound to dry. (This is also the time to fill old hardware holes and make new ones, if necessary.)

**2.** Sand the surfaces with 150-grit sandpaper until they're smooth to the touch. Wipe the surface with tack cloth before priming and painting.

# Preparing Ceilings & Walls

Repairing stains, water damage, holes, and cracks in drywall is simple. Small holes can be filled and large areas can be replaced. Plaster repairs are somewhat more involved, but easily accomplished.

If the walls aren't in good condition, hire a professional to re-cover or replace the entire surface.

**Removing stubborn stains:** Start with a cleaning pad, such as Mr. Clean Magic Eraser. If you can't completely remove the stain, seal the area with primer or white pigmented shellac to keep it from bleeding through the new paint.

**Removing mildew:** If a wall is mildewed, it's a waste of time to clean and paint it unless you first solve the fundamental problem. In bathrooms, the solution may be as simple as using the vent fan every time you shower or bathe. In other rooms, you may need to eliminate sources of moisture or provide additional ventilation. If necessary, bring in an expert.

Once the source is eliminated, wash the wall with soap and water, then with a bleach solution (¾ cup bleach in 1 gallon of water). Wear rubber gloves and safety glasses, and protect the floor and other surrounding surfaces.

Wash the wall with a TSP solution, following the manufacturer's directions. Rinse the wall with clear water.

**Remove all nails, screws, and pictures hangers** from the walls. To keep from damaging the walls, place a block of wood under the head of the hammer as you pull the nails.

**Peeling paint:** Painting over peeling paint guarantees that the new paint will peel, too. To permanently solve the problem, scrape away all the loose paint, then use a putty knife or drywall knife to fill in the chipped area with ultralight spackle. Feather the edges onto the surrounding wall.

Let the patch dry completely, then sand the area with 150-grit sandpaper. When the patch is smooth enough that you can't feel any ridges along the edges, put a coat of primer on the area.

**Repair holes and cracks** (see pages 48 to 53).

# Masking & Draping

Painting can be a messy business, so the less stuff in the room, the better. Remove everything you can, then put the rest in the center of the room and cover it with plastic. Cover the floor with drop cloths or masking paper.

 **Think taping's a hassle?** Try cleaning up mistakes and splatters. It's easy to imagine you can skip the masking and draping and be really careful, but think again. No one can be that careful. Mask it off. You'll be much happier with the results.

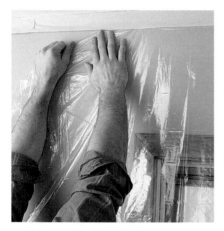

**Ceiling only:** Drape the walls and woodwork with sheet plastic. Press the top edge of 2-inch-wide painter's tape along the top edges of the wall, leaving the bottom half of the tape loose. Slide the plastic under the bottom half of the tape and press, draping the walls and baseboards.

**Woodwork:** Mask the walls by putting tape around all the edges, as close to the woodwork as possible.

**Walls:** Mask the baseboards, window casings, and door casings with painter's tape. Press one edge of the tape against the woodwork, right at the joint between the wood and the wall. Run the tip of a putty knife along the inside edge of the tape, pressing firmly enough to create a seal.

**Remove the covers** from outlets and switches as well as heating and air-conditioning duct covers. Remove thermostats or mask them with wide painter's tape.

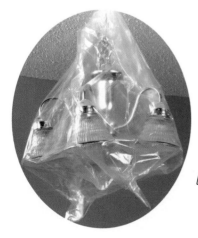

## Take Cover

*In rooms with hanging light fixtures, shut off the power to the circuit, lower the plate cover, and pull a trash bag up from the bottom of the fixture. Tie a knot at the top, neatly covering the entire piece. Trash bags come in handy in bathrooms, too: Drop a lawn-size bag over a toilet, and it's covered.*

# *Painting*

When you get right down to it, the mark of a professional paint job is the lack of marks. No runs or drips; no lap marks or patchy coverage; no splatters outside the work area. A good paint job is smooth, even, and seamless.

To get professional-looking results on ceilings and walls, work in small sections and start by "cutting in" all the edges, corners, and trim, using a brush. While the paint is still wet, roll the section. To avoid lap marks, always paint from a dry area back into wet paint.

Whenever possible, work in natural light—it's easier to spot missed areas.

**✔ Stir paint before using it.** A paint-mixer bit attached to a power drill stirs paint quickly and easily. Use a variable-speed drill at low speed to avoid introducing air bubbles.

# How to Paint Ceilings

**1.** Prepare the room as described on pages 63 to 67. Prime the area if necessary.

If you're using a new roller cover, blot the surface with masking tape to remove lint, then wet the cover (use water for latex paint or solvent for alkyd). Squeeze out as much liquid as you can and slide the cover onto the roller. Put the roller inside a plastic bag to keep it damp, and set it aside.

**2.** Load your brush—only about a third of the bristle length—then tap the bristles against the side of the can. (Don't drag the brush against the lip of the can—it wears out the bristles.)

**3.** Starting in the corner farthest from the entry door, use a paintbrush to cut in the edge on a 3-ft. section of the ceiling. Use the narrow edge of the brush to paint along the edge, pressing just hard enough to flex the bristles. Use long, slow strokes and paint from a dry area back into wet paint.

**4.** Attach a handle extension to a roller frame. Pour paint into a tray and push the roller down into the reservoir. Lift the roller and roll it back and forth on the textured ramp to distribute the paint evenly into the nap. The roller should be full—but not dripping—when you lift it from the pan.

**5.** Working in 3 × 3-ft. sections, roll on the paint with diagonal strokes. For the final smoothing strokes, roll each section toward the wall containing the entry door, lifting the roller at the end of each sweep.

⚠️ *Always wear eye protection while painting overhead.*

# How to Paint Trim

Prepare the wood as described on pages 64 to 66.

When painting woodwork, start by painting the inside portions, then work out toward the walls. On windows, for instance, first paint the edges close to the glass, then paint the surrounding face trim.

Trim work often requires two coats. Between coats, sand the wood lightly and wipe it with tack cloth so the second coat bonds properly.

## How to Paint Doors

**1.** Remove the door by driving out the lower hinge pin with a screwdriver and hammer. Have a helper hold the door in place. Then, drive out the middle and upper hinge pins.

**2.** Place the door flat on sawhorses. For paneled doors, use a brush to paint 1) recessed panels 2) horizontal rails, and 3) vertical stiles.

**3.** Let the paint dry. Sand the first coat lightly and wipe the door with tack cloth. Apply the second coat and let it dry. Finally, seal any unpainted edges of the door with a clear wood sealer. (Otherwise, moisture can enter those unsealed edges and make the wood warp and swell.)

## Casement Windows

**1.** Open the windows wide. Start by painting the hinge edge.

**2.** Paint the top rail, and then the vertical side rails. On the vertical rails, alternate sides, painting about a foot of each side before moving down the sash. Finish with the bottom rail.

**3.** Paint the window frame and then the sill.

☑ When **painting casement windows**, start early in the day on a warm, dry day. Casement sashes fit inside the frame, and the edges touch when the window is closed. Even with today's fast-drying latex paint, it's best to let the paint dry as long as possible before closing the window.

# F.A.Q.

Q *The baseboards in my living room really need to be painted, but I'm afraid I'll get paint on the carpet. What can I do?*

A Hold a wide drywall knife or plastic shielding tool under the baseboards to protect the carpet as you paint. Clean the tool thoroughly each time you move it.

Q *Painting the carved cove molding in my dining room is such a pain—the paint never gets all the way down into the crevices. Is there a better way?*

A Use a stenciling brush and work in small, circular strokes.

## Double-Hung Windows

**1.** If possible, remove the sashes from the frames. Drill holes and drive two 2" nails into the legs of a wooden stepladder. Set up the window easel-style for easy painting. Or lay the window flat on a bench or sawhorses. Do not paint the sides or bottom of the sashes.

If you have to paint the sashes in place, be careful not to get paint between the edges and the frame. As the paint dries, carefully move the sashes up and down several times to make sure they don't stick.

**2.** Using a tapered sash brush, begin by painting the wood next to the glass. Use the narrow edge of the brush, and overlap the paint onto the glass by about 1/16" to create a weatherseal.

**3.** Wipe away excess paint from the glass with a putty knife wrapped in a clean rag. Rewrap the knife often so you're always wiping with clean cloth.

**4.** Paint all flat portions of the sashes, then the case moldings, sill, and apron. Use slow brush strokes, and make sure you don't get paint between the sash and the frame.

## Painting Walls

Painting to a wet edge is the only way to avoid lap marks. It's best to have two painters, one to cut in with a brush while the other rolls the large areas. If you don't have a helper, work in small sections, quickly moving to the next section while the edges are still wet.

*Paint colors—even custom-mixed colors—may vary slightly from can to can. If the job requires more than one can, mix the paint together (called "boxing") in a large pail. Stir the paint thoroughly with a wooden stick or drill attachment.*

# How to Paint Walls

**1.** Prepare the walls as described on pages 66 to 67.

If you're using a new roller cover, blot the surface with masking tape to remove lint, then wet the cover (use water for latex paint or solvent for alkyd). Squeeze out as much liquid as you can and slide the cover onto the roller. Put the roller inside a plastic bag to keep it damp, and set it aside.

**2.** Starting in an upper corner, cut in the ceiling and wall corners with a brush. (See pages 68 to 69 for more information about cutting in.)

**3.** Switch to a roller, and slowly rolling upward, make a diagonal sweep about 4 ft. long (1).

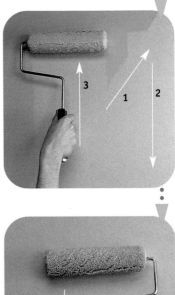

**4.** Draw the roller straight down (2) from the top of the sweep. Move the roller to the beginning of the diagonal and roll up (3).

**5.** Roll back and forth in light, horizontal strokes. Finally, roll vertically from top to bottom. Lift the roller and return it to the top of the area after each stroke. Continue with adjacent areas, cutting in and rolling the top sections before the bottom sections. Roll all finish strokes toward the floor.

☑ Brushed areas dry to a different finish than rolled paint. To make the brush-mark area as small as possible, slide the roller cover slightly off of the roller cage when rolling near corners or the ceiling slide. You can get closer to the edges that way.

# floors

*And each separate dying ember wrought its ghost upon the floor.*

EDGAR ALLAN POE

Creaking, squeaking floors bring to mind the kind of creepy things that go bump in the night. Don't let those squeaks give you the shivers—they're easy to fix.

In this chapter, we'll show you how to clean, maintain, and repair your floors so that they look better, last longer, and stay quiet enough to let you—and any household ghosts—sleep peacefully.

## With this chapter you'll . . .

- Make your kitchen floor sparkle without a trip to the chiropractor.

- Learn how to fix broken tiles and split boards to keep your floors on a solid footing.

- Clean and maintain carpet without toxic chemicals or expensive equipment.

# floors

## THE WAY THEY WORK

Floor covering—carpet, tile, wood, or resilient flooring—is the most obvious layer of a floor, but it's not the whole enchilada. Like walls, a typical wood-frame floor consists of several layers that work together to provide structural support.

At the bottom of the floor are the joists, the 2 × 10 (or larger) boards that support the weight of the floor. Joists typically are spaced 16 inches apart, measured from the center of one to the center of the next. For the floor to be structurally sound, the joists have to be solid and properly supported by posts and beams.

The subfloor is nailed to the joists. Most subfloors installed since the 1970s are made of ¾-inch tongue-and-groove plywood, but in older homes, the subfloor often consists of 1-inch-thick wood planks nailed diagonally across the joists. Properly supported subfloors last pretty much forever unless water gets to them, and then, like any other piece of unprotected wood, they will rot.

On top of the subfloor, most builders place a ½-inch plywood underlayment. For many types of floor coverings, such as resilient flooring, ceramic tile, or stone, adhesive or mortar is spread on the underlayment before the flooring is installed. Like subfloors, underlayment is extremely durable unless it's exposed to water. Some floor coverings, like carpet, may have an additional underlayment material, like cork or foam.

Finally, the floor covering, the only layer we see on a daily basis, presents a decorative, comfortable surface. Floor coverings wear out faster than other interior surfaces because they get more wear and tear. Keeping them clean and well maintained extends their useful life.

 If a floor seems to bounce when you walk across it, you probably have a joist problem called **deflection**.

Floors bounce when the joists span too great a distance for the weight they're carrying. When you step onto the middle of a poorly supported joist, it sags under your feet and comes up at the ends. When you step off, it settles back into place.

Although deflection typically is an annoyance rather than an emergency, sturdy floors make a house feel solid and secure. Correcting the problem involves adding extra support to the joists, usually a job for professionals. Solutions include adding an extra beam or adding an additional post.

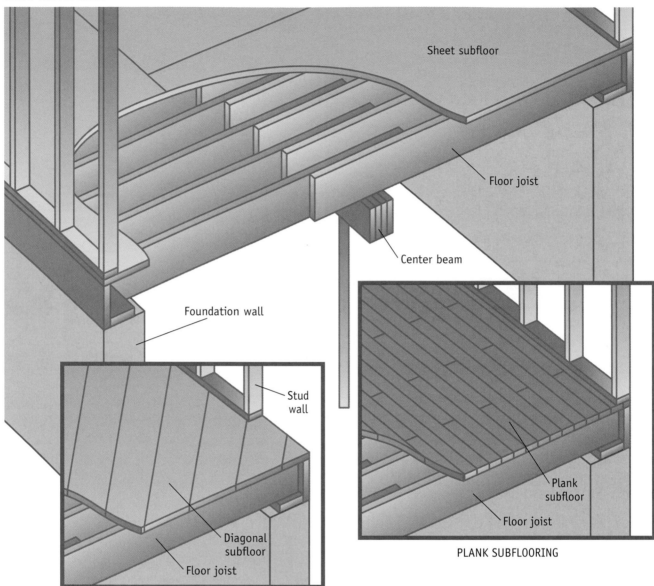

Sheet subfloor

Floor joist

Center beam

Foundation wall

Stud wall

Plank subfloor

Floor joist

PLANK SUBFLOORING

Diagonal subfloor

Floor joist

DIAGONAL SUBFLOORING

⚠ Resilient flooring manufactured before 1986 may contain **asbestos fibers**, which can cause severe lung damage if inhaled. The best way to deal with asbestos-laden flooring is to cover it with an underlayment. If the flooring has to be removed, hire a certified contractor. You'll find them listed on the Internet or in the yellow pages under "asbestos abatement."

# Cleaning & Maintaining

*Vacuuming and other regular cleaning keeps floors looking good and prolongs their useful lives. Dirt is made up of gritty, sharp particles that cut and tear at floor coverings, particularly the finish of hard flooring and the pile of carpet.*

*The Marble Institute of America estimates that it takes at least eight steps before the dirt on your shoes is removed after you walk in the door. To protect your floors, use mats and runners, and clean them regularly. To keep rugs from slipping on hard floors, use approved rug pads or underlays. Don't use rubber, foam-back, or plastic mats—they can discolor hardwood and other flooring materials.*

## Carpet

Many carpet companies recommend vacuuming every day. That's not realistic for most people, but it's important to vacuum as often as practical—several times a week if possible.

For most types of wall-to-wall carpet, its best to use a vacuum with a rotating brush or beater bar, but check the carpet manufacturer's recommendations—rotating brushes can damage some thick-loop pile or shag carpets. Use a bare-floor attachment for those carpets as well as antique or valuable Oriental rugs.

Manufacturers recommend having carpets professionally steam cleaned at least every 18 to 24 months. In fact, some warranties are void if you don't. So, have your carpets cleaned regularly, and keep the invoices.

**Call a Pro!** *If a burst pipe or other major water leak soaks your carpet, "letting it dry" isn't an option. Flooded carpet needs professional attention to prevent mold and rot.*

## Vacuum

Start opposite the door and slowly move the vacuum in long, overlapping strokes. Change the bags frequently, preferably outdoors.

✓ *When it comes to getting floors clean, more suction isn't always better. You need a slight gap between the tool and the floor in order to lift the dirt off the floor and into the vacuum.*

*The harder or denser the surface, the more suction you need. Use the highest setting for hard floors, a mid-level for carpets, and low for throw rugs, window treatments, and upholstery.*

## Spot Clean

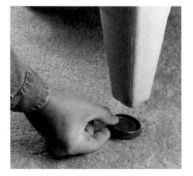

Treat stains and spots as quickly as possible. If you've spilled something fairly solid, use a spoon to scoop it up.

Using clean cloths, gently blot the area to remove as much moisture as possible. Don't rub or scrub—that just damages the fibers and grinds in the stain. Working from the outside edge toward the center, apply lukewarm water and blot until the stain is gone or until nothing more will transfer to the cloth.

If the stain is still visible, mix ¼ teaspoon of dishwashing liquid into a cup of lukewarm water. Pat the solution onto the area and let it sit for five minutes. Rinse the area with clear water, and blot with clean cloths to remove as much moisture as possible. Put several layers of white paper towels over the spill and weight them down with a fairly heavy, nonstaining object like a stainless-steel skillet or glass vase. When the carpet is thoroughly dry, vacuum the area.

To help your carpet maintain its color, protect it from direct sunlight by closing the blinds or drapes.

Use furniture coasters to distribute the weight of heavy furniture, especially pieces that have wheels.

Did you know you shouldn't walk on carpet with bare feet?

The natural oils in your skin and any lotion on your feet get into the carpet, where it attracts dirt and stains. Wear clean socks or slippers—your carpets will stay cleaner longer.

# Hardwood, Cork & Bamboo

There are many different types of wood floors, and it's important to know as much as you can about yours. It might be solid, tongue-and-groove planks. It also could be manufactured wood flooring, which consists of a plywood core topped by a layer of hardwood or cork.

With the right information, you can clean, maintain, and repair your floors properly. For example, solid hardwood floors can be sanded and refinished many times; manufactured floors can't. Also, urethane is a hard-wearing finish that can stand up to moisture. On the other hand, varnish, shellac, and lacquer finishes can't—not even water-based cleaning solutions.

Most of the time, hardwood, bamboo, and cork floors don't need much cleaning beyond regular sweeping. Experts, such as the National Wood Flooring Association, suggest sweeping every day for active or large families, using a soft-bristle broom or a vacuum and a bare-floor attachment.

Before you decide how to mop a wood floor, you need to know the type of floor you have. If it's solid hardwood finished with urethane, you can use a mild, neutral pH soap or detergent made to rinse clean. Use as little water as possible—your mop or cloth should be slightly damp, not wet. Never damp-mop bamboo—too much water can cause the flooring to swell or cup.

If you have manufactured flooring and know the manufacturer, follow their recommendations. Many manufacturers caution against using water or any cleaner that's mixed with water. The only way to maintain the warranty on these products is to know and follow the manufacturer's recommendations about cleaning products and methods.

No matter what type of finish it has, don't use ammonia on a wood floor.

## To help keep your hardwood, cork, or bamboo floors looking their best:

**Rearrange the rugs and furnishings periodically.**  Exposure to sunlight changes the color of hardwood over time. Anything that restricts light—furniture, area rugs, even draperies—discourages discoloration. Moving the furniture around evens out the floor's exposure to light and prevents sun damage.

**Avoid spike or stiletto heels.** Even on a small- to average-size person, high-heel shoes can produce dynamic loads of more than 1,000 pounds per square inch, more than enough to produce serious dents in resilient or hardwood flooring. Many manufacturers specifically exclude from their warranties damage caused by high heels.

**Maintain a humidity level of 35 to 55 percent.** Too much humidity can cause swelling; too little can cause shrinkage. Use a dehumidifier to reduce or a humidifier to improve humidity, depending on the season and the local climate.

**Replace small or narrow furniture wheels.** Barrel-type casters or wide, flat glides are best.

> ☑ *If you're not sure what type of wood floor you have, look at an edge under a floor register, a transition strip between floor coverings, or the shoe molding. You should be able to see either solid tongue-and-groove planks or a layer of veneer on top of a plywood or fiberboard core that tells you it's manufactured flooring.*
>
> *You may also be able to tell from the surface of the flooring. Planks or strips that were finished at the factory often have slight bevels or V-shaped grooves along the edges and ends where the boards meet. If you don't see these exposed and finished bevels, the floor probably is solid hardwood, custom finished after installation.*
>
> *If you know the flooring manufacturer, builder, or floor finisher, ask them about the finish. If not, the Wood Flooring Manufacturers Association recommends using your fingernail or a sharp instrument to scrape the finish in a hidden area. If a little clear finish material scrapes loose, you have a urethane or other surface finish; if not, you're probably dealing with a penetrating seal and should follow care recommendations for waxed floors.*

# Resilient & Laminate

The term "resilient" refers to sheet or tile vinyl and linoleum flooring. Vinyl flooring has a layer of vinyl bonded to a layer of felt or PVC backing. Linoleum is made of linseed oil mixed with cork dust or wood flour (or both), ground limestone, and resins on a jute backing. It's an environmentally responsible choice but does require a little extra maintenance. For instance, it has to be polished periodically (see page 83).

Laminate floors consist of a synthetic surface bonded to a fiberboard core. These floors are extremely easy to maintain. Consult the manufacturer for specific recommendations on cleaning products.

For all of these flooring materials, routine care is simple: vacuum the floor or use a dust mop to remove dirt, dust, and grit. Wipe up spills with a damp cloth or sponge.

On vinyl and laminate, you can remove tough spots like shoe polish, tar, or asphalt driveway sealer with nail polish remover containing acetone. When the spot is gone, wipe the area with a clean, damp cloth.

Vinyl and laminate flooring manufacturers suggest using special cleaning products rather than soap-based detergents or "mop and shine" products. These special products leave the floor shiny clean, which is good since you should never use wax or polish on vinyl or laminate floors.

## How to Polish Linoleum

Linoleum has to be polished periodically to look good and perform well. Eventually, it has to be stripped and repolished. Always read and follow the manufacturer's specific recommendations, but these general principles apply:

**1.** Start by sweeping, mopping, and rinsing the entire floor. Let the floor dry, then apply the polish with a clean, damp cloth. Don't pour polish directly onto the floor —that causes streaks. Instead, put it in a clean bucket, dip the cloth into it, and wring about half the polish out of the cloth. Working in a 3- to 4-foot square, wipe the cloth over the floor in straight lines.

**2.** Apply two to three coats; let the polish dry for at least 30 minutes between coats and as long as possible when you're done—an hour is the bare minimum; 24 hours is best.

When the floor no longer comes completely clean when you mop or when the surface is dull even when it's clean, the floor has to be stripped and repolished. Again, you should follow the manufacturer's recommendations, but this is the general routine: Start with a clean, dry floor. Dilute the stripper according to manufacturer's instructions, apply that solution to a 3- to 4-ft. square, and let it soak for a few minutes. Use a scrub brush or nylon pad to scrub the floor, then mop up the solution with a mop. Rinse the area with a second, clean mop. For best results, change the rinse water often. Let the floor dry completely, then follow the instructions at left to repolish.

## Ceramic Tile & Natural Stone

Tile flooring is virtually maintenance free. Whether your floor is glazed ceramic or natural stone, sweep regularly and damp-mop once a week to keep it looking new. Always wipe up spills and messes immediately so stains don't have time to set. Stay away from cleaners and detergents that contain soap; mild dishwashing detergent is okay.

For heavy stains and deposits on glazed ceramic tile, mix equal parts white vinegar and water. Test the solution in an inconspicuous area—some tile glazes can be damaged by vinegar. Wash the stained area with the solution, scrubbing it with a soft-bristle brush if necessary. Rinse with clear water, then dry with a towel to prevent streaks.

Use a soft-bristle brush and a pH-balanced stone tile cleaner to remove heavy stains from natural stone tile. Always get stone tile wet before applying cleaners and rinse them thoroughly when you're finished. If stone

cleaner doesn't do the trick, try poultice, a paste that lifts stains from porous stone materials. Cover the entire stain with the poultice, then tape plastic wrap over it. Let the poultice set, according to the manufacturer's instructions,

then remove it. Most poultice products draw the stain out of the stone, while others push it further down into the stone, away from the surface. Stone tile should be sealed after using a poultice product.

Grout joints are the most vulnerable part of tile floors. No matter what type of tile flooring you have, the grout needs to be cleaned. Scrub the joints with a soft-bristle brush and a mild, nonsoap detergent to remove dirt and grime. To kill mold and mildew, mix one part chlorine bleach and ten parts water. Put this solution on the mold and let it sit for ten minutes. Scour with a soft-bristle brush or toothbrush.

To help grout stay clean and fresh, seal it every year or two. First, test the existing sealer by putting a few drops of water on a grout line. If the water beads up, the sealer is still working. If the water absorbs into the grout, it needs to be resealed.

Before you seal grout, make sure it's in good shape. If it's not solid and full, remove and replace it first (see page 93). Clean the floor well, then spread the sealer on the grout lines, using a small sponge paintbrush. Follow the sealer manufacturer's instructions (most recommend three coats of sealer).

Unglazed tile is vulnerable to stains and water spots, but you can protect it by sealing the surface every year or two. Apply sealer to the tile as you would the grout. The same goes for natural stone, though stone tile products may require more than one coat of sealer. When sealing tile, always use the tile manufacturer's recommended sealer so you don't void the warranty.

# Repairing Floor Coverings

*Floor coverings wear out faster than other interior surfaces because they're subjected to more wear and tear. If scratches and cracks aren't repaired, moisture can get down to the wooden framing, which could eventually cause the subflooring to pull loose from joists, floors to become uneven and springy, and loose boards to squeak. Bathroom floors suffer the most from moisture problems. But you can fix many of these minor flooring problems yourself, with a few basic tools and materials.*

## Structural Squeaks

Houses settle; building materials expand and contract with changes in temperature and humidity. Before you know it, irritating floor squeaks develop. Most are harmless—just loose boards, such as the joists, subfloor, or finished floor, rubbing against one another. Once in a while, major squeaks are symptoms of structural problems. If you notice a squeak, check it out. Simple problems are easy to fix; even significant problems usually are manageable. If there's any question about the structural integrity of your floor or foundation, consult an expert.

Whenever possible, evaluate and repair squeaks from underneath the floor. First check for adequate support: joists longer than 8 feet should have X-bridging or solid blocking between pairs of joists. If necessary, install X-bridging every 6 feet to stiffen and help silence a noisy floor. Other ways to eliminate floor squeaks include:

➤ Drive wood screws up through the subfloor to draw hardwood flooring and the subfloor together—make certain the screws aren't long enough to break through the floorboards.

➤ Install shims coated with wood glue into any gaps between a joist and the subfloor (top photo at left).

If you can't reach the floor from underneath:

➤ Surface-nail hardwood boards to the subfloor with ring-shank flooring nails. Drill pilot holes and try to nail into joists, where possible. Sink the nails below the surface and cover the heads with matching wood putty.

➤ On carpeted floors, use a fastening device, such as Squeeeeek No More, to drive screws through the subfloor into the joists (bottom photo at left). The device guides the screws and controls the depth. Once the screw is set, break off the scored shank, just below the surface of the subfloor.

# Squeaks in Staircases

The risers and treads of a staircase rest on stringers that span the run of the stairs. The framing transfers most of the load of the staircase to the floor diagonally.

In the movies, creaky stairs have a part to play: they give away the bad guy's position or alert parents to teenagers sneaking in after curfew. In real life, they're just annoying. Creaks on individual treads typically are the result of an uneven plane across the tops of the stringers, a problem that can be caused by changes in moisture levels, poor construction, or just plain old wear and tear.

You can quiet squeaky treads without too much trouble. Try one of the following:

➤ Drive flooring nails at opposing angles into the treads to anchor them to the stringers. (If the treads are hardwood, drill pilot holes first.) Sink the nail heads and fill the holes with wood putty.
➤ Reinforce the treads by gluing small wood blocks to the underside of the risers and treads. Then secure the blocks to the risers and treads with wood screws.
➤ Shim the treads with hardwood wedges coated with glue.

Sometimes a stair tread can split or crack. If that happens, fix the problem right away. Also inspect the other treads—if one is weak, others may be, too. Problems often start with the stringers: Many stairways have only two stringers, one running down each edge. A third stringer added to the center of the stairway strengthens the whole structure. Of course, adding a stringer is much easier if the underside of the stairway is exposed.

Every stairway must have a secure railing. Make certain the rails are attached to studs.

Also check that any carpeting or rubber tread floor coverings are tightly attached.

Tread

Risers

Stringers

# *Carpet*

Small burns and stains are the most common carpeting problems. You can remove many stains (see page 79) and clip away superficial burns using small scissors, but deep burns and indelible stains require minor surgery and a patch.

Another common problem is carpet seams or edges that have come loose. You can rent the tools you need to fix these problems.

## Spot Damage

**1.** Remove the damaged areas with a "cookie-cutter" tool, available at carpet retailers. Press the cutter down over the area and twist it to cut away the carpet. (Leave the pad in place.)

**3.** Use the cookie-cutter tool to cut a replacement patch from scrap carpeting. Align the nap or pattern to match the surrounding carpet, and set the patch into place. Apply seam adhesive to the edges of the patch and press it in place.

**2.** Cut a piece of double-stick carpet tape large enough to extend beyond the edges of the cutout. Remove the backing, and position the tape under the cutout.

✔ When cutting a **large patch**, lay the new carpet over the damaged piece, then cut through both layers. When the cut strip of old carpet is removed, the new patch will fit tightly in its place. If the carpet is patterned, make sure the patterns are aligned before you cut.

## Reglue Loose Seams

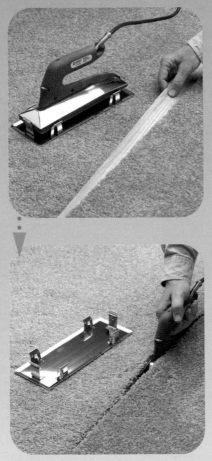

**1.** Remove the old tape from under the carpet seam. Cut a new strip of seam tape and place it under the edge of the carpet, centered along the seam with the adhesive facing up. Plug in the seam iron and let it heat up.

**2.** Pull up both edges of the carpet and set the hot iron squarely onto the tape. Wait about 30 seconds for the glue to melt. Move the iron about 12" along the seam. Quickly press the edges of the carpet together into the melted glue behind the iron. Separate the pile to make sure no fibers are stuck in the glue and the seam is tight. Place weighted boards over the seam to keep it flat while the glue sets. Remember, you have only 30 seconds to complete the process.

## Restretch Loose Carpeting

**1.** Adjust the knob on the head of a knee kicker so the prongs grab the carpet backing without penetrating it. Starting from a corner or near a point where the carpet is firmly attached, press the knee kicker head into the carpet, about 2" from the wall.

**2.** Thrust your knee into the cushion of the knee kicker, forcing the carpet toward the wall. Tuck the carpet edge down into the space between the tack strip and the baseboard, using a 4" wallboard knife. If the carpet is still loose, trim the edge with a utility knife and stretch it again.

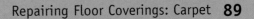

# Hardwood

Water and other liquids can penetrate deep into the grain of hardwood floorboards, leaving dark stains that are sometimes impossible to remove by sanding alone. Instead, try bleaching the wood with oxalic acid, available in crystal form at home centers and paint stores.

When small gouges, scratches, and dents aren't bad enough to warrant replacing a floorboard, repair the damaged area with a latex wood patch that matches the color of your flooring.

If a small area of a hardwood plank floor is badly damaged, it's even possible to splice in new planks. This requires carefully cutting out the damaged boards and replacing them with new planks of the same width and thickness. If you don't have much experience using power tools, this is a job for a flooring expert. Look in the yellow pages, under "floor repair."

## How to Bleach Hardwood

**1.** Start by sanding the stained area to remove the floor's finish. In a disposable cup, dissolve the recommended amount of oxalic acid crystals in water. (Always wear rubber gloves and eye protection when working with acid solutions.) Pour the solution over the stained area, taking care to cover only the darkened stain.

**2.** Let the solution stand for one hour. Repeat the application if necessary. Neutralize the acid by washing the area with 2 tablespoons of borax dissolved into 1 pint of water. Rinse with clear water and let the wood dry.

**3.** Sand the area smooth, then apply several coats of wood restorer until the bleached area matches the finish of the surrounding floor.

## Using Latex Wood Patch

**1.** Before filling nail holes, drive loose nails below the surface using a nail set and hammer. Apply wood patch to the damaged area, using a putty knife. Force the compound into the hole by pressing the knife blade downward until it lies flat on the floor.

**2.** Scrape excess compound from the edges and allow the patch to dry completely. Using a fine-grit sandpaper, sand the patch flush with the surrounding surface, following the wood grain. Apply wood restorer to the sanded area until it blends with the rest of the floor.

## Ceramic Tile

Ceramic tile repairs are manageable projects that should be tackled sooner rather than later. One of the keys to a long-lasting ceramic tile floor is a continuous field—broken tiles and cracked grout can let water get down to the underlayment, which eventually will destroy the floor.

Cracks in grout joints are a sign that the floor covering is moving. This causes, or is caused by, the deterioration of the adhesive layer. If more than 10 percent of the tiles are loose, you should remove all of them. Evaluate the condition of the underlayment—it must be smooth, solid, and level to ensure a long-lasting installation. If it is not, have it replaced.

Pay attention to the joints between the floor and a tub or shower; if water finds its way through the joint, the subfloor and joists are vulnerable to pests as well as rot. In fact, in areas where damp-wood termites live, 90 percent of termite reports relate to water damage around tubs and showers.

## Regrouting a Tile Floor

To begin, you need to remove the old grout without damaging any of the tile. The easiest way is to use a grout cutter rotary tool. You can also use a hammer, cold chisel, and a gentle touch. (Always wear eye protection when using a hammer and chisel.) Hold the chisel at a slight angle and break away small sections at a time. Clean out the joints with a stiff-bristle brush or a small vacuum. Evaluate the underlayment—repair or replace if necessary.

**1.** Prepare a small batch of grout, following the manufacturer's instructions. If you're working with porous tile, include an additive with a release agent that will keep the grout from bonding to the surface of the tile.

Starting in a corner, pour grout over the tile. Use a rubber grout float to spread the grout outward from the corner, tilting the float at a 60° angle to the floor and using a figure-eight motion. Press firmly on the float to fill the joints completely.

**2.** Remove excess grout from the surface of the tile by holding the float nearly vertically and wiping it across the joints diagonally. Continue to apply grout and remove the excess until you've grouted about a quarter of the floor surface.

**3.** Working in 2"-square sections, wipe a damp grout sponge diagonally over the tile to remove the excess. Rinse the sponge between each wipe, and wipe each area only once to avoid pulling grout from the joints. Continue this process until all the joints are filled.

**4.** Let the grout dry, then buff the surface with a soft, dry cloth. Apply grout sealer with a small sponge brush (see page 85).

## Broken Tile

**1.** Carefully remove the grout around the damaged tile (see page 93). After the joints are clean, use a hammer and cold chisel to break away the damaged tile (photo above), working from the center of the tile outward until the tile is removed.

**2.** Scrape away any remaining adhesive or mortar, leaving the underlayment smooth and flat. Fill any chips or dents in the under- layment using an epoxy-based, thin-set mortar for cement- board or a floor-leveling compound for plywood underlayment.

**3.** Apply thin-set mortar to the back of the replacement tile, using a notched trowel to furrow the mortar. If you're replacing several tiles, use plas- tic spacers to keep the spacing consistent. Set the tile in position and press down until it's level with the sur- rounding tiles.

**4.** Check the tile for level. If necessary, lay a piece of 2 × 4 padded with carpet across several tiles and pound it with a rubber mallet to level the new tile.

**5.** Take out any spacers, using a needlenose pliers. Remove wet mortar from the grout joints with a small screwdriver, and wipe off any that got on the surface. Let the mortar dry according to instructions, then fill the joints with matching grout. When the grout has cured, seal it (see page 85).

# Resilient & Vinyl Flooring

Small cuts and scratches in vinyl flooring can be fused permanently and nearly invisibly with liquid seam sealer, a clear compound that's available wherever vinyl flooring is sold. For tears or burns, the damaged area can be patched. If you can't find replacement vinyl in stores, you can remove vinyl from a hidden area—in a closet or under an appliance—to use as patch material. With vinyl tile, it's best to replace the whole damaged tile.

When vinyl flooring is badly worn or the damage is widespread, the only answer is to replace the flooring entirely.

## Patching Sheet Vinyl

**1.** Using a scrap of vinyl that matches the existing floor, place the patch over the damaged area so that the patterns match exactly. Tape the patch to the floor. Using a carpenter's square, outline the patch, drawing along pattern lines to help conceal the patch seams. Use a utility knife to cut through both layers. Remove the damaged vinyl with a putty knife.

**2.** Dissolve the old adhesive using mineral spirits, then scrape the subfloor clean with a putty knife or razor scraper. Apply new adhesive to the patch, fit it in place, and roll it with a J-roller. Let the patch dry for 24 hours, then apply a thin bead of liquid seam sealer to the edges.

## Replacing Broken Vinyl Floor Tiles

**1.** Use a heat gun to soften the underlying adhesive, moving the gun rapidly so as not to melt the tile. When the adhesive gives way, lift the tile out with a putty knife.

**2.** Brush on mineral spirits to dissolve any remaining adhesive, then scrape away all the residue, using a putty knife. If necessary, repair the underlayment. Apply new adhesive to the underlayment with a notched trowel. Set the new tile in place, then roll it using enough pressure to create a good bond. Wipe off any excess adhesive.

# windows & doors

*The closing of a door can bring blessed privacy and comfort.*

**ANDY ROONEY**

And opening one can lead to opportunities and adventures. Doors do, after all, swing both ways. No matter whether you're counting on them to keep things in or out, doors and windows are critical to the security, energy efficiency, and appearance of a home and keeping them clean and in good working order is essential.

---

## With this chapter you'll . . .

- Never again say "I don't do windows."

- Keep winter's worst at bay with airtight windows and doors.

- Learn a hassle-free way to replace drafty and worn-out windows.

# windows & doors
## THE WAY THEY WORK

Windows and doors have surprisingly complicated assignments. Doors, for example, are supposed to welcome family and invited guests but repel intruders. Windows are supposed to let in fresh air and sunshine, but only as much as we want. Pretty tricky, when you get right down to it.

The functionality of windows and doors starts with the framing that surrounds them. It may surprise you to learn that the security, maintenance requirements, and energy efficiency of your home depend to some degree on these frames of $2 \times 4$s.

Intruders can quickly remove or force poorly framed doors and windows, but that's much more difficult to do when doors and windows are framed and installed properly. Poorly supported doors and windows also tend to sag and shift, and you end up adjusting and repairing them in a variety of ways.

The rough openings for doors and windows are supposed to be slightly larger than the actual windows, but if those gaps are excessive, your energy bills will be as well. Good insulation reduces drafts somewhat, but it's hard to make up for poor framing.

Energy efficiency also depends on the type of windows and doors you have. Single-pane windows, for example, don't do much to keep heat or cold out or in. On the other hand, double- or triple-glazed, gas-filled windows are amazingly efficient. If you have old, inefficient windows, replacing them will make a world of difference in your energy bills.

Windows are available in several basic styles: casement windows, which crank open from one side; double-hung windows, which slide open from the top or bottom, horizontal sliders, which slide side to side, and fixed, which don't open at all.

Door styles include sliding doors, typically glass doors that slide open to one side; French doors, which are hinged doors that swing to meet at a center point; and pocket doors, which slide into recessed wall openings.

*Casement window*

*Double-hung window*

*Sliding window*

*Fixed window*

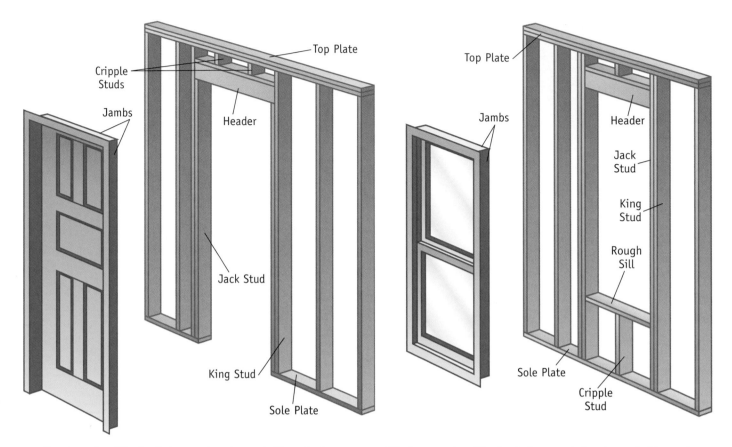

Top Plate

Cripple Studs

Jambs

Header

Jack Stud

King Stud

Sole Plate

Top Plate

Jambs

Header

Jack Stud

King Stud

Rough Sill

Sole Plate

Cripple Stud

*Door opening: The load above a door is carried by cripple studs that rest on a header. The header is supported by jack studs and king studs that transfer the load to the sole plate and eventually the foundation.*

*Window opening: The load above a window is carried by studs resting on a header. The header is supported by studs that transfer the load to the sole plate and foundation. The rough sill helps anchor the window unit but carries no weight.*

*Interior panel door*

*Bifold doors*

*Entry door*

*Storm door*

# Cleaning & Maintaining

*It's an old realtor's trick: If you want a house to sparkle, wash the windows and doors—everything else will look great, too. You can use commercial cleaning products if you like, but in many cases it's less expensive and just as effective to make your own.*

## Windows

**To wash windows,** you need a bucket, clean, lint-free rags, rubber gloves, and a good-quality squeegee. If you can be selective, wash your windows on days that are cloudy but dry. If you have to get it done whenever you can, at least try not to work in direct sunlight because the sun dries the cleaning solution before you get it wiped off, which causes streaks.

First, vacuum the screens, then remove them. If they're still dirty, wash them outside with a hose or in a bathtub. Next, vacuum or dust the frames and moldings and the sills (the woodwork around the windows), then wash them with detergent and water.

Add 2 or 3 tablespoons of white vinegar to a gallon of hot water. Or, combine a cup of water with a cup of rubbing alcohol and 2 tablespoons of ammonia. (Check the window manufacturer's recommendations about cleaning chemicals first.)

Dip a clean rag into the solution, wring it out, and wipe the glass. Rinse the rag and wipe the glass again. Dry a strip across the window and squeegee the window from that point. Start each stroke in a dry area; dry off the squeegee after every stroke. (If you're washing both inside and outside, work horizontally on one side and vertically on the other so you can easily tell which side any streaks are on.)

Change the water or cleaning solution as often as necessary to avoid streaks. If the squeegee blade gets nicked, replace it— nicks cause streaks.

# Improving Window Operation

If a window doesn't open or close easily, the problem typically is caused by some kind of obstruction. If wood windows aren't painted or finished properly, moisture makes the wood swell, which makes the window stick. Painted windows sometimes stick when paint has gotten into the channels. Newer vinyl or vinyl-clad windows typically need minor adjustments to their mechanisms; older models that won't stay open probably have broken sash cords or chains.

The best advice is try to open and close the window and watch what happens. It's usually easy to tell what's causing the problems.

## Casement Windows

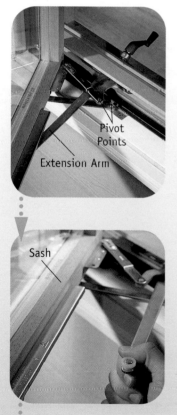

**1.** If a casement window is hard to crank, the problem may be as simple as a dirty crank assembly. To clean it, you have to take it apart enough to reach the mechanisms. Open the window until the roller at the end of the extension arm is aligned with the access slot in the window track.

**2.** Pull the extension arm down and out of the track. Clean the track with a stiff brush, and wipe the pivoting arms and hinges with a rag.

**3.** Lubricate the track and hinges with spray lubricant or household oil. Wipe off excess lubricant with a cloth, then reattach the extension arm.

**1.** If cleaning doesn't solve the problem, the crank assembly itself needs to be repaired or replaced. Remove the molding or cap concealing the mechanism. Unhinge the pivot arms.

**2.** Remove the screws that hold the crank assembly in place, then remove the assembly and clean it thoroughly. If the gears are worn, replace the mechanism. Note which way the window opens—to the left or right—and buy a replacement from a home center or the manufacturer.

**3.** Apply all-purpose grease to the gears and reinstall the assembly exactly as you removed it. Connect the pivot arms, and attach the extension arm to the window. Crank the window open and closed a couple of times to test it before you replace the cap and molding.

## Double-hung Windows

Newer double-hung windows with **spring-loaded sash tracks** don't need much maintenance. If you have one that sticks, use a toothbrush and damp rag to clean the vinyl tracks, then adjust the springs in or behind

the tracks. On each side, you'll find an adjustment screw on the track insert. Adjust both sides until the window opens and closes smoothly.

**Spring-lift windows** operate with the help of a spring-loaded lift rod inside a metal tube. To adjust one, unscrew the top end of the tube from the jamb, then twist the tube to change the spring tension. Turn the tube clockwise for more lifting power, counterclockwise for less. Maintain a tight grip on the tube to keep it from unwinding.

**Dirt buildup** is common on storm window tracks. Clean the tracks with a hand vacuum and a toothbrush.

Wooden double-hungs that stick may be **painted shut**. Slip a paint zipper or utility knife between the window stop and the sash, and slide it down to cut the paint film. Place a scrap of wood against the window sash and tap it lightly with a hammer. This should free the window. If necessary, sand the

channels lightly with very fine sandpaper, then rub them with pure bar soap or a white candle; open and close the window a few times. It should now slide easily. (Don't use liquid lubricants on wood windows.)

**Dirty or paint-spotted weatherstripping** can make double-hung windows stick, too. If that seems to be the problem, spray on some cleaner and wipe the weather-stripping with a cloth. Use a little paint solvent to remove any paint spatters. If the window still doesn't glide smoothly, put a little bit of lubricant on the weatherstripping and open and close the window a few times.

# Condensation

Energy-tight windows keep warm air from escaping and cold air from entering. Modern double- and triple-glazed windows often contain inert gases—which don't transfer heat as well as air does—between panes to help create sealed dead air space that blocks air movement. Older windows don't have that technology, but you can improve their efficiency by adding weatherstripping and good storm windows (see pages 107 to 108).

If your windows frost up or fog over, the cause and resolution depend on where the condensation is located.

Condensation on exterior glass isn't exactly a problem. If the surface of the outer glass drops below the dew point of the outside air, moisture gathers on the outer glass. The only way to prevent this is to warm the glass. Opening the drapes or blinds, or turning up the thermostat will help but probably won't entirely eliminate the condensation.

Condensation on the room side of a window is typically caused by too much indoor humidity (see the chart below). If you're using a humidifier, turn it down or off.

Windows with interior removable panels can get condensation between the panes of glass, typically because the breather holes in the sash are plugged with dust or dirt. Clean out the breather holes, using a pipe cleaner, nail, or wire.

Fog or moisture between panes of sealed insulating glass means the window's seal is compromised, and the window may need to be replaced. Check with the manufacturer for advice.

## Maximum Recommended Humidity Levels

(based on engineering studies at 70°F conducted at the University of Minnesota Laboratories)

| Outside Temperature F° | Inside Humidity |
|---|---|
| 20°F to 40°F | Not over 40% |
| 10°F to 20°F | Not over 35% |
| 0°F to 10°F | Not over 30% |
| -10°F to 0°F | Not over 25% |
| -20°F to -10°F | Not over 20% |
| -20°F or below | Not over 15% |

# F.A.Q.

**Q** *The double-hung windows in my bedroom won't stay open. The house was built in 1942, and the windows are original. Can they be fixed?*

**A** Yes, they can be fixed. In all probability, the sash cords are broken. Replacing them isn't difficult, but it may not be the best idea. After all, windows from 1942 probably aren't very energy efficient. Consider replacing the sashes, a surprisingly easy project. Check out the instructions on page 123.

**Q** *My bathroom door gets stuck on the floor when we open or close it. How can I fix it?*

**A** It depends on what's causing the problem. If you've changed the floor covering or done some other type of remodeling project that altered the dimensions of the doorway, you can remove the door and sand or plane the the bottom edge (see page 126). On the other hand, if the door suddenly started sticking for no apparent reason, check the hinges. If they're sagging or loose, the door is sticking because it isn't square within the opening. Tightening the hinges (see page 124) should solve the problem.

**Q** *The sliding glass door to my patio is very hard to open and close. Any suggestions?*

**A** Absolutely. First, clean and lubricate the track. If that doesn't solve the problem, you'll need to remove the door and tighten or loosen the roller adjustment screws (see page 113). Don't worry—this is much easier than it sounds.

# Weatherizing Windows

The goal of weatherization is to block air movement—keep interior air in and exterior air out. There are lots of simple steps you can take to improve the energy efficiency of your windows.

Apply **clear silicone caulk** around interior window casings (shown). For added protection in extreme weather, lock the window in the closed position and caulk the gaps around the interior edges of the sash with clear, peelable caulk. Remove the caulk when more moderate temperatures return.

On **casement windows**, improve seals by attaching self-adhesive foam or rubber compression strips on the outside edges of the window stops.

Add **plastic sheeting or shrink-wrap product** on the room side to block drafts and keep moisture away from window surfaces. Read and follow manufacturer's directions, which often include using a hair dryer to tighten the plastic and remove wrinkles.

Create a tight seal by attaching foam compression strips to the outside of the **storm window** stops. After installing the storm window, fill any gaps between the exterior window trim and the storm window with caulk backer rope. Check the inside surface of the storm window during cold weather for condensation or frost. If moisture is trapped between the storm window and the permanent window, drill one or two small holes through the bottom rail of the storm window to let moist air escape. Drill at a slight upward angle.

# Weatherstripping a Double-hung Window

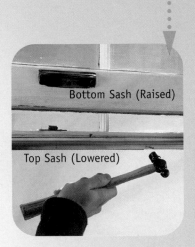

**1.** Cut metal V-channel to fit in the channels for the sliding sash, extending at least 2" past the closed position for each sash (do not cover the sash-closing mechanisms). Attach the V-channel by driving wire nails (usually provided by the manufacturer) with a tack hammer. Drive the nails flush with the surface so the sliding sash won't catch on them.

**3.** Lift the bottom sash and lower the top sash, and tack metal V-channel to the bottom rail of the top sash. Make sure the open end of the V is pointed downward so moisture can't collect in the channel. Flare out the V-channel to fit the gap between the sashes.

Bottom Sash (Raised)

Top Sash (Lowered)

**2.** Flare out the open ends of the V-channels with a putty knife so the channel is slightly wider than the gap between the sash and the track. Avoid flaring the channel too much at once—it's hard to press V-channel back together without buckling it.

Clean the bottom edge of the sash, then attach self-adhesive compressible foam.

Treat **side-by-side sliding windows** as if they were double-hung windows turned 90°. For even better durability, use metal tension strips rather than self-adhesive compressible foam in the sash track that fits against the edge of the sash when the window is closed.

# Storm Windows

Whether you have removable storm windows or combination windows, a few handy tips can make maintaining them much simpler:

**Build a storage rack** for removable screens and storm windows. Carefully stored storms and screen will last longer. Simply attach a pair of 2 × 4s to the rafters of your garage or the ceiling joists in your basement, then

attach eyescrews in matching rows. Finally, attach window-hanger hardware to the top rails of the screens and storm windows, if they do not already have them.

**Lubricate sliding assemblies** on metal-framed combination storm windows or doors once a year, using penetrating lubricant.

**Replace turnbuttons and window clips** that don't hold storm windows tightly in place. Fill old screw holes with wood putty or toothpicks and glue before driving screws.

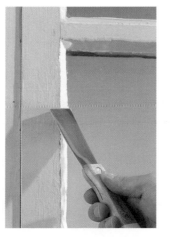

**Replace deteriorated glazing** around glass panes in wood-framed windows. Sound glazing makes windows more energy efficient not to mention more attractive.

# Securing Windows

**Pin together sashes** of single- and double-hung windows with $1/4 \times 3$-inch eyebolts. With the window closed, drill a $1/4$-inch-diameter hole, at a slight downward angle through the top rail of the bottom sash and into the bottom rail of the top sash. Avoid hitting the glass, and stop the hole three-quarters of the way through the top sash. To lock the window in open positions, drill holes along the sash stiles (vertical pieces) instead.

Intruders would rather not crawl through broken glass to get into your home. That's why they usually break casement or awning windows, crank them open, then enter through the open window. **Removing the handles** at least slows down intruders and may even encourage them to pick easier targets.

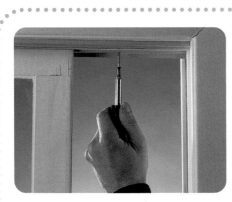

Standard sliding windows lift out easily if you know how—and criminals know how. To foil the bad guys, **drive screws to fasten the window** to the top channel. Use sturdy screws, spaced about 6" apart. Drive the screws far enough in that they don't get in the way when you open and close the window. You can also **add auxiliary locks** on sliding windows. Most types can easily be installed on the upper or lower tracks.

## Doors

Begin cleaning by vacuuming the door and frame, especially the molding above the door. Wash the door and frame with mild detergent and water. Sponge paintbrushes clean corners quite nicely on raised panels, and microfiber pads do wonders when it comes to removing fingerprints and smudges. If stained wood doors have gotten scratched, polish them with furniture polish designed to cover scratches (Old English Scratch Cover, for example)—they'll look practically new again.

When washing exterior doors, don't forget the thresholds. Entries brighten up considerably when the thresholds are clean. (Many exterior thresholds are aluminum: don't use ammonia or products containing ammonia on aluminum.)

If the door hardware looks grungy, wash it with a mild detergent, then polish it with paste wax.

Most brass door hardware is covered with a protective clear coat. If that clear coat gets scratched or worn off, the brass tarnishes. If your doorknobs or other hardware are covered with a brown-, black-, green- or copper-colored film, it's time to remove the damaged clear coat, clean the brass, and reapply clear coat (see page 111).

## Cleaning Door Hardware

**1.** Take all the hardware off the door. Fill a plastic container with a paint stripper that contains methylene chloride and soak the hardware (read and follow manufacturer's directions).

**2.** Rub the pieces lightly with #00 steel wool to remove any remaining clear coat. Rinse each piece thoroughly.

**3.** Use a copper or brass cleaner to clean the brass, following manufacturer's directions.

**4.** Spray each piece with a clear lacquer spray and let it dry. When the clear coat is dry, re-install the hardware.

✔ To spray a finish onto brass hardware or other small items, suspend each piece from a board or shelf, using nylon filament (fishing line, for instance). Tie one end of the filament to a tack or push pin, and the other to the hardware piece. To avoid smudges and drips, leave plenty of room between pieces and be careful not to overspray.

# Improving Operation

Almost all problems with door hardware are caused by a lack of lubrication. The best way to unstick a door is to spray the moving parts with spray lubricant and wipe them down. You can also keep door hardware in good condition by cleaning all hinges, tracks, and other hardware regularly.

 **Don't use graphite** in locksets. It can abrade some metals with repeated use.

## Locksets

Door locksets are very reliable, but they do need to be cleaned and lubricated occasionally. One simple way to keep an entry door lockset working smoothly is to spray a light lubricant into the keyhole, then run the key in and out a few times.

A sticking latch bolt is a sure sign the lockset needs to be cleaned and lubricated (see below).

## Cleaning a Lockset

**1.** Disassemble a lockset by unscrewing the connecting screws and remove the parts carefully.

**2.** Wipe clean each part, then spray moving parts with lubricant. Reinstall the lockset, tightening the connecting screws an equal amount. Don't overtighten the screws; overtightening can cause binding.

## Bifold Doors

Open or remove the doors and wipe the tracks with a clean rag. Spray the tracks and rollers or pins with silicone lubricant. Close the doors and check their alignment. If the gap between the closed doors is uneven, adjust the top pivot blocks with a screwdriver or wrench.

Pivot blocks are found at the bottom of some doors. Adjust the pivot blocks until the gap between the door and frame is even.

## Sliding Doors

Use a toothbrush and a damp cloth or a hand vacuum to clean the tracks above and below the doors. Spray a silicone lubricant on all the rollers but not on the tracks. Replace any worn or bent parts.

If the gap along the bottom edge of the door isn't even, rotate the mounting screw (left) to raise or lower the door's edge.

## Sliding Glass Patio Doors

**1.** Slide the door to the middle of the tracks. Adjust the roller adjustment screws to lower the rollers, then lift the door up out of the sill track. Glass patio doors are heavy; have someone help you.

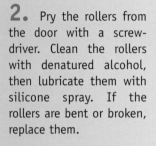

**2.** Pry the rollers from the door with a screwdriver. Clean the rollers with denatured alcohol, then lubricate them with silicone spray. If the rollers are bent or broken, replace them.

**3.** To reinstall the rollers, align the adjustment screw with its access hole on the door. Use a wood block and rubber mallet to protect the rollers and tap them in place.

**4.** Vacuum the tracks, then clean them with alcohol. Lubricate the header track with silicone spray and the sill track with paraffin wax. Reinstall the door, guiding the top of the door into the header track and lifting the bottom into the sill track. Move the door to within a 1/2" of the latch-side jamb, then adjust the roller adjustment screws until the door is parallel with the jamb and the latch catches properly.

# Weatherizing Doors

Most heat loss from doors occurs around the jambs and at the threshold. If the opening is just too large, it's possible to adjust the door frame, but most other weatherization is quite a bit simpler.

## Exterior Doors

They're typically small, but **cracks in wood doors** do leak air. Fill the cracks with wood filler, caulk, or (if the door has a stained finish) tinted wood putty. Fill the cracks from the inside, then sand the area and touch it up with paint or stain. (Make sure all the edges of the door are finished, including the top and bottom. If not, paint or varnish them. Uneven expansion of unfinished edges encourages cracking.)

Add a **door sweep** to the bottom of the door, on the interior side. Tack the sweep in place, then open and close the door to make sure you've left just enough clearance. When the sweep is positioned correctly, drive screws to hold it in place.

If the door frame doesn't have **weatherstripping** or it's damaged, add or replace it. Cut two pieces of metal tension strip or V-channel, one the full height of the door opening and the other to fit the full width. Use wire brads to tack the strips to the door jambs and door header, on the inside of the door tops. Start nailing at the top and work your way down the edges of the door. Flare out the tension strips—a little at a time—with a putty knife to fill the gaps between the jambs and the door when the door is closed.

Add **reinforced felt strips** to the edge of the door stop, on the exterior side. The felt edge should form a close seal with the door when it's closed. (Don't drive the fasteners too far or they'll buckle.)

Large gaps between the door and jamb can create significant drafts. The answer is to **adjust the door frame**, which isn't as complicated as it sounds. First, remove the interior case molding (the wood trim) around the door. (Be careful with the pry bar—you'll replace this molding later.)

Drive new shims between the jamb and the framing member on the hinge side to reduce the size of the door opening. Close the door to test the fit, and adjust as necessary. Replace the molding and caulk the gap between the molding and the wall.

## Sliding Glass Doors

Add rubber compression strips to seal the channels in patio door jambs. You can also cover the glass with plastic sheeting similar to the sheeting used for windows (see page 106).

# Storm Doors

You'll get the most out of your storm doors if you inspect them every year and keep up with basic maintenance:

**Add a wind chain** to keep the door from blowing open too far, which can damage the door hinges or the closer. Set the chain so the door can't open more than 90°.

**Adjust the door closer** so it has just the right amount of tension to close the door securely, without slamming. If a closer stops working effectively, replace it right away.

**Tighten storm door latches** by redriving loose screws on the strikeplate.

# Garage Doors

Most garage door problems are caused by moisture, dirt, and neglect. Common symptoms include rusted or rotted panels, loose hinges, squeaky or stuck rollers, and a door that binds or seems heavier than usual.

**Call a Pro!** If the door doesn't open smoothly, check the lift springs—a well-balanced door should stay open about 3 feet above the ground. Above or below that position, it should open or close by itself. If your door fails this test, call a professional to have the springs adjusted or replaced.

Except for adjusting or replacing the lift springs, you can make the most common garage door repairs yourself:

**Replace worn or damaged weatherstripping** along the bottom of your garage door to protect against moisture damage and rot.

**Tighten all hinge screws or bolts**, and replace any missing or broken hardware and loose or bent hinges.

If you have an **automatic garage door opener**, disengage the lifting mechanism by pulling the emergency release cord before making repairs on the door.

**Adjust the lock** so the lock bar meets the lock hole in the door track. Loosen the lock assembly's mounting screws or bolts to adjust the position of the bar.

**Clean and lubricate** the rollers, door tracks, locks, cable pulleys, hinges, and the chain and track of chain-driven automatic door openers. Use a silicone lubricant or a small amount of 3-in-1 oil.

**If the door rubs** against the stop molding, or if there is a large gap, loosen the bolts securing the tracks to the lower track bracket. Adjust the tracks so there's a slight gap between the door and the stop, then retighten the bolts.

Track Bracket

# Securing Doors

Adding security at entry doors is easy, and it won't make your house look like Fort Knox:

**Install plywood shims** in the gaps between the door frame and wall studs, to prevent pry-bar attacks. Be sure to shim directly above, below, and behind the strike plate.

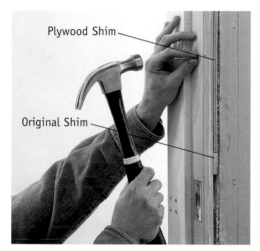

Plywood Shim

Original Shim

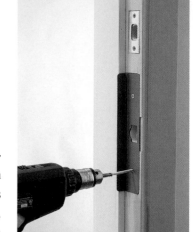

Add **metal door reinforcers** to strengthen the areas around locks to prevent kick-ins. Another option is to add a heavy-duty latch guard to reinforce the jamb around the strike plate. For added protection, choose a guard with a flange that resists pry-bar attacks.

**Replace hinge screws** with 3- or 4-inch screws that extend through the door jamb and into the wall stud. This helps resist kick-ins.

## Securing Sliding Glass Doors

**Make a custom lock** for your door track, using a thick board and a hinge. Cut the board to fit behind the closed door, then cut it again a few inches from one end. Install a hinge and handle so you can flip up the end and keep the door secure while it's ajar.

**Drive sturdy, pan-head screws** into the header track every 8 inches to keep the sliding panel from being pried up and out of the lower track. For metal frames, use self-tapping screws and a low drill speed.

 In case of a fire or another emergency, make sure everyone in your family knows where sliding-door locks are located and how to remove them. If you have children, don't install any security devices that they won't be able to unlock easily from the inside.

**Attach a sliding-door lock** to the frame of the sliding panel. Drill the hole for the deadbolt into the upper track.

# Repairing Windows & Doors

*Whether it's due to an accident, neglect, or just good ol' fashion wear and tear, a time will come when a window or door will fail. And though there are occasions when the faulty or broken unit needs to be replaced, more often than not a simple adjustment or repair will restore the window or door back to working order.*

## Replacing Screen in Storm Windows

If your window screens are damaged, replace the old screening with new fiberglass screen. It's inexpensive and easier to install than metal screening.

### Wood Frames

**1.** Pry up the screen molding with a small chisel or screwdriver. If the molding is sealed with paint, use a utility knife to cut the film. Cut the new screen 3" wider and longer than the frame.

Staple the screen along the top edge of the frame, then stretch it tight and staple it along the bottom edge. Stretch and staple the screen to the sides, one at a time.

**2.** Nail the screen molding back in place with wire brads or finish nails. Cut away excess screen using a utility knife.

### Aluminum Frames

**1.** Pry the vinyl spline from the retaining groove around the edge of the frame, using a screwdriver. You can reuse the old spline if it's still flexible, or simply replace it with a new one.

Stretch the new screen tightly over the frame so that it overlaps the edges of the frame. Keeping the screen taut, use the convex side of a spline roller to press the screen into the grooves.

**2.** Use the concave side of the spline roller to press the spline into the groove (this is much easier if someone helps you). Finally, cut away the excess screen, using a utility knife.

# Replacing Window Glass

Replacing glass in single-pane windows is an easy DIY project, but never try to replace double- or triple-glazed glass panels: that is a job for a professional glass installer.

Putty

**1.** To begin, remove the sash from its jambs, if possible. Break out the big pieces of glass, then wiggle the small pieces out of the glazing, along with the glazing points. Make sure to wear gloves and goggles. With traditional glazing, soften the old putty with a heat gun, but be careful not to scorch the wood. Scrape away the soft putty with a putty knife. On newer windows, pry out the vinyl glazing strips. On metal windows, pry out the "spring clip" molding that holds the glass in place, using a small screwdriver.

**2.** Sand the L-shaped groove to clean away old paint and putty. Coat any bare wood with sealer to prevent rot and absorption of oils from the glazing compound and let it dry.

**3.** Take the exact dimensions of the window frame opening to a hardware store or home center. Purchase glass that is an $1/8$" less than both the width and length of the opening to allow for expansion.

**4.** Apply a thin layer of glazing compound along the L-groove. Install the glass, pressing lightly to embed it in the compound. Press in new glazing points every 10" using the tip of a putty knife.

Glazing Points

**5.** Apply a bead of glazing compound around the edges of the glass. Smooth the glazing with a wet finger or cloth. When the glazing is dry, paint it to match the window frame. Overlap the paint onto the glass by $1/16$" to create a good weather seal.

# Replacement Window Inserts

Replacement window inserts make repairing old and damaged windows largely unnecessary—you're still welcome to do it for fun, but we don't recommend it. Because the units are self-contained with their own sash and jamb, the existing jamb doesn't need to be perfectly square. But it is important to measure the window dimensions carefully: many inserts are custom made and nonreturnable. For best results, measure the window frame in three spots for both the height and width and use the smallest dimensions for ordering. Make sure to measure from the jambs and not the blind or stops.

Installing a replacement insert is easy, but because procedures vary slightly, always follow the manufacturer's instructions for your specific product. To see just how easy installation is, check out the overview on page 123.

⚠ Houses built before 1978 may contain **lead paint**. Contact your public health department for information regarding lead paint analysis and handling procedures.

# Installing Replacement Inserts

**1.** Remove the existing interior stops using a putty knife or pry bar. Cut the sash cords and remove the lower sash, then remove the parting stops and the upper sash.

*Note: If your insert is banded around the center of the unit, do not remove the banding until the insert is installed.*

**2.** Install the sill angle to the bottom side of the insert; attach the head expander to the top side. Apply caulk to both the sill angle and the expander. Also apply caulk to the inside edge of the blind stop, then lift the insert into the window frame.

**3.** Once the insert is set in place, remove the sash stops on the unit. Drill pilot holes at the four screw mounting holes, then drive the installation screws. Turn the jamb adjustment screws to align the sash and jambs.

**4.** Fill any gaps or seams between the molding and the insert frame with caulk. On the exterior side, caulk any gaps between the insert frame and the sill or brick molding.

# Repairing Doors

The most common door problems involve loose hinges, which can cause a door to rub, stick, or just hang funny, as well as throw off the latch mechanism. Simple adjustments and repairs can fix these problems.

## Removing a Door

Have someone hold the door steady as you drive out the hinge pins from bottom to top, using a screwdriver and hammer. For stubborn pins, use a nail set or small punch to tap the pin up from underneath. Remove the door.

## Tighten Loose Hinges

**1.** Remove the door from the hinges (at left) and tighten any loose screws. If the wood won't hold the screws, remove the hinge, then coat golf tees or dowels with wood glue and drive them into the worn screw holes. Let the glue dry before cutting off the excess wood.

**2.** Drill pilot holes in the new wood, and reinstall the hinge.

## Aligning a Latch Bolt & Strike Plate

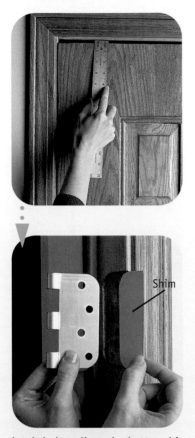

**1.** Fix minor side-to-side alignment problems by filing the strike plate until the latch bolt fits. If the latch falls above or below the strike plate, check the door to make sure it is square with the frame.

**2.** If the door is far out of square, remove it from its hinges. To change the angle of the door, drive 3" wood screws at the top or bottom hinge to pull the jamb into the framing stud, or install thin cardboard shims behind one of those hinges. To raise the latch bolt, adjust the bottom hinge; to lower it, adjust the top hinge.

Shim

## Fixing a Warped Door

**1.** Use a straight-edge to check the door for warpage. If the door is slightly warped, remove the door from its hinges and lay it across a pair of level sawhorses.

**2.** Place weights on the bowed center of the door, using cardboard to protect the finish. Leave the weights in place for several days, checking the door periodically with a straight-edge. Once the door is straight, seal the bottom edge to prevent moisture from warping it again.

**3.** Extremely warped doors can't be corrected, so you'll have to adjust the door stop to follow the door. Start by removing the stop using a small pry bar. If it's painted, cut the paint film with a utility knife.

Remove all nails, pulling them through the backside of the stop to prevent splintering the piece. Close the door and latch it. Starting at the top, nail the stop in place, keeping the inside edge flush against the door. Test the door operation, then set the nails with a nail set.

## Shortening an Interior Door

If an interior door binds on thick carpet or a large threshold, trim off a bit of the bottom edge to allow the door to swing freely.

**1.** With the door in place, measure 3/8" up from the top of the floor covering and mark the door. Remove the door from the hinges. Mark the cutting line and cut through the door veneer using a utility knife and straightedge to prevent chipping when it's sawed.

Lay the door on sawhorses and clamp a straightedge to the door as a cutting guide. Saw off the bottom of the door.

**2.** If the door has a hollow core that is now exposed, reinstall the cutoff frame piece to the bottom of the door. First, chisel off the veneer from both sides of the removed portion.

**3.** Next, apply wood glue to the piece and insert it into the opening at the bottom edge. Clamp it in place and wipe away any excess glue. Let the door dry overnight.

## Freeing a Sticking Door

**1.** Tighten all the screws on the hinges. If the door still sticks, mark the area where it sticks with light pencil. Then remove the door. It's important that the door not be swollen by moisture, so don't do this on or right after a rainy day.

**2.** Sand or plane the door at the marked locations until it fits smoothly into the frame.

**3.** Seal the ends and edges with a clear wood seal, then rehang the door.

## Replacing an Entry Threshold

**1.** Remove the old threshold. This may be as easy as pulling the screws and prying it out. If necessary, cut threshold in two carefully, so as not to damage the flooring, sill, or door frame.

**2.** When purchasing the new aluminum threshold, make sure it matches the old one as closely as possible, with the same width, thickness and beveled edge. If the clearance between the bottom of the door and the new threshold is less then $1/8$", trim the door to accommodate the new threshold (see page 126).

Measure the distance between the jambs and cut the new threshold to length using a hacksaw with a fine-tooth blade or a power saw with a metal cutting blade. Make sure to wear safety goggles. Test-fit the threshold and trim if necessary.

**3.** More than likely, you will have to notch the threshold to properly fit around the door stops. Make sure to carefully mark the threshold and trim slightly within the lines to prevent taking off too much material. Test-fit and trim as needed until the threshold fits snugly in place, centered under the door.

**4.** Thoroughly clean the sill. Caulk the underside and ends of the threshold, then center it in place under the door.

At each screw hole in the threshold, drill pilot holes into the sill, then fasten the threshold in place with 2" screws.

# plumbing

*There must be quite a few things a hot bath won't cure, but I don't know many of them.*

**SYLVIA PLATH**

Whether a hot bath actually cures anything may be open to debate, but there's no doubt it's worth a try. With the information in this chapter and a can-do attitude, you'll be prepared to make sure there's always plenty of hot water and a clean bathtub waiting—just in case.

You'll also know how to turn the water off, remove stubborn clogs, and stop a running toilet, among other things.

---

## With this chapter you'll . . .

- Fix leaks before they drain your wallet.

- Stop a running toilet in its tracks.

- Learn to fix and install faucets.

# plumbing

## THE WAY IT WORKS

It's not glamorous and most of us barely notice its existence, but a plumbing system does a very important job. According to the United States Geological Survey, the average American uses 80 to 100 gallons of water every day. That means a family of four goes through about 400 gallons a day. Every day. All that water is delivered to its various destinations throughout the house and then returned to the sewer or septic system by . . . none other than the plumbing system.

What's really amazing is that most plumbing is quite simple. If you have municipal water, the system doesn't even include motors or engines—just gravity and pressure. Water towers are usually quite tall or located on hills, or both. Gravity pulls the water down toward your home, drawing it along with enough pressure to push it out of the tap every time you open a valve (turn on a faucet). If you have a well, a motorized pump draws water into a pressurized system and an ingenious collection of pipes and valves takes it from there.

Fresh water provided by either a municipal water company or a well comes into the house through a main supply line. If a municipality is supplying the water, it passes through a meter that keeps track of how much you use.

Just after the supply line enters the house, a branch line splits off to supply the water heater. From there, supply pipes—one for hot and another for cold—run together inside wall cavities or underneath floor joists.

Hot and cold water supply pipes are connected to fixtures such as sinks and tubs, and appliances such as dishwashers and clothes washers. Toilets, hose bibs, and refrigerator icemakers use only cold water.

When you flush a toilet or open the drain in a sink or tub, gravity carries the water down the drainpipes, out of the house, and into a sewer system or septic tank. Drainpipes typically are plastic or cast iron. In some older homes, they may be made of copper or lead. Because water flows through them only as it leaves the house, lead drain pipes aren't hazardous to your health, but they're no longer manufactured for home plumbing. Drain pipes range from $1\frac{1}{4}$ to 4 inches in diameter.

Traps are another important part of the plumbing system. These curved sections of drainpipe, found near every drain opening, hold standing water. The water they hold seals the drain and keeps sewer gases from backing up into the house. Each time a drain is used, the standing water is flushed away and replaced by new water. When a drain is clogged, often the problem lies in the curve of the trap.

The drain system needs air to work properly, so drainpipes are connected to vent pipes. One or more vent stacks, located on the roof, provide the air needed for the drain-waste-vent (DWV) system to work smoothly.

Without vents, draining water from a sink would work like pouring soda from a can, and draining your bathtub would create a vacuum strong enough to suck the water out of every trap in the house.

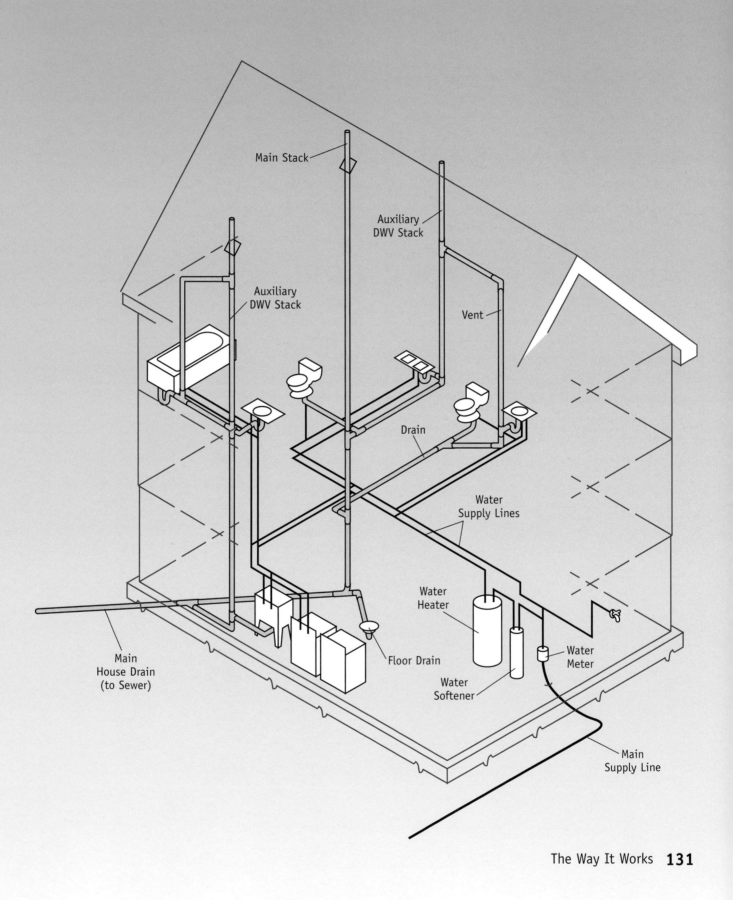

Main Stack

Auxiliary
DWV Stack

Auxiliary
DWV Stack

Vent

Drain

Water
Supply Lines

Water
Heater

Floor Drain

Water
Softener

Water
Meter

Main
House Drain
(to Sewer)

Main
Supply Line

# Cleaning & Maintaining

*When it comes to plumbing, cleaning generally involves the fixtures, mostly in kitchens and bathrooms. And although these rooms are quite different, many of the cleaning principles are the same: Clean frequently to avoid grease, soap, or mineral buildup. Use the gentlest cleaner that will do the job, and avoid abrasives. If you can identify a fixture's manufacturer, follow its recommendations for care.*

Germs are an issue in both kitchens and bathrooms. To avoid contamination, don't use sponges—they're difficult to disinfect. Use clean rags each time and wash them in hot water immediately after you're done. Start with the areas with the least germ potential and work your way toward the areas with the most. In bathrooms, this means you should start as far from the toilet as possible and work toward it. In kitchens, start with eating areas and work toward food preparation areas. And it has to be said: Use a clean rag for each room.

Maintaining the plumbing system largely means keeping the drains clean and flowing and taking care of the water heater. Neither is difficult.

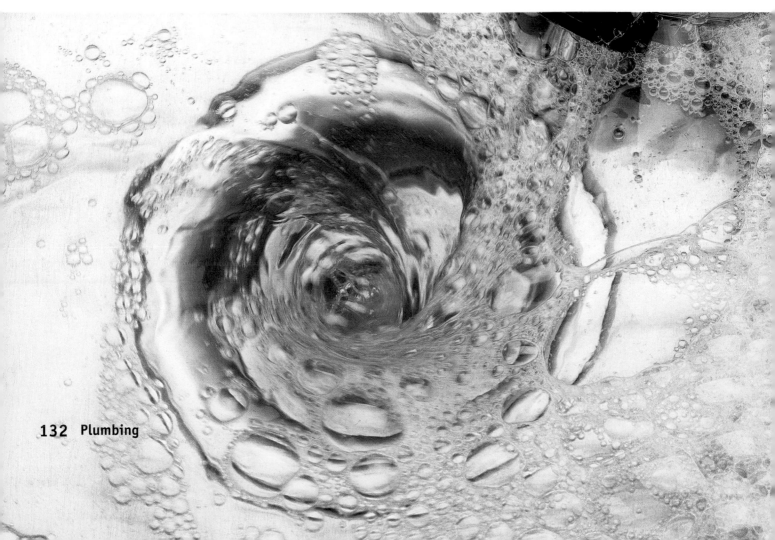

# Sinks and Tubs

Here are the general rules: In kitchen sinks, use accessories like basin racks and rinse baskets to help protect the surface. Don't leave dirty dishes, food, or other stain-producing substances in the sink. If you're not sure about a cleaner, test it in an inconspicuous area first. Don't use steel wool on any sink, including stainless steel. Don't let cleaners sit or soak for long periods. As soon as a sink or tub is clean, rinse it thoroughly and dry it with a soft cloth. A 50/50 solution of white vinegar and water will remove hard-water stains and mineral deposits from many sinks, but don't use vinegar or other acids on natural or artificial stone.

**Cast iron and vitreous china:** Wash with soap or detergent. Soft abrasives or abrasive cleaners are acceptable if you use them sparingly. A paste made from baking soda and water removes many stains gently and inexpensively.

**Stainless steel:** Wash with soap or detergent. Stainless steel polishes are effective; work with the grain as you clean or polish. Don't use bleach or cleaners that contain chloride on stainless steel.

**Solid-surface materials:** Wash with soap or detergent, or use a spray cleaner that includes ammonia. Rinse thoroughly and wipe dry.

If a sink is deeply stained, fill it with a 50/50 solution of chlorine bleach and water, and let it soak for 15 minutes. Drain the sink, then wash and dry it as usual. (Never combine chlorine with products containing ammonia.)

A countertop polish, such as Countertop Magic or Hope's Countertop Polish, helps hide scratches and restores the gloss on a semigloss or high-gloss surface. Read and follow label directions.

**Natural stone:** Use a soft cloth or medium-bristle scrub brush along with a mild detergent and water. Don't use ammonia, strong detergents, abrasives, or anything acidic, such as vinegar.

Small scratches, water rings, and some stains can be removed with stone or marble polish, a mildly abrasive powder you can find at home centers and hardware stores. Read and follow label directions carefully.

# Whirlpool Tubs

Soap residue, oils, and mineral deposits are hard on a whirlpool's pumps and jets if they constantly get recirculated with the water. Keeping the tub clean is actually part of maintaining a whirlpool, and it isn't much different from cleaning a standard tub.

Use water and a nonabrasive cleaner to clean the surface regularly. Remove tough stains by dabbing rubbing alcohol onto them. Rinse thoroughly. To remove minor scratches and protect the whirlpool's finish, apply a rubbing compound, buff out any scratches, then polish the surface with a car wax or other product recommended by the manufacturer.

Many whirlpool systems should be flushed out once a month to clean out the hydrojets and the water lines. Check your owner's manual for specific recommendations, but here are some general recommendations:

Fill the tub with warm water and add automatic dishwasher detergent—2 tablespoons of liquid detergent or 2 teaspoons of dry crystals. Run the system for 10 to 20 minutes, then drain the tub. Refill it with cool water and run the pump for ten more minutes to clear all the detergent from the lines.

Bleach can help remove bacteria from a whirlpool system. Some manufacturers recommend using $1/2$ cup of bleach instead of detergent on alternate monthly cleanings.

# Showers

The best thing you can do to keep a shower clean is dry it after each use. Yes, that sounds like a hassle, but it really doesn't take much time to wipe the walls and door with a shower squeegee. It saves untold amounts of time in the long run, because you never have to scrub away mold or mildew.

If the shower already has mold or mildew, you can use a detergent/bleach solution to remove it from most surfaces. (See page 44 for more information on cleaning ceramic tile.) Don't use bleach on natural stone.

## Faucets

Wash faucets with mild soap and water, rinse, then wipe the entire surface dry. Don't use cleaners that contain ammonia, bleach, acid, or chemicals that could damage a faucet's finish. Chrome shines up beautifully if you wipe it with rubbing alcohol and dry it thoroughly.

## Toilets

In-tank cleaners may seem like the easy way to keep a toilet clean. The problem is, most manufacturers don't recommend using in-tank cleaners because many of them can damage flush valves and other working parts. That means you need to clean the toilet frequently.

Most toilet bowl cleaners work well, as long as you use them only on the inside of the bowl and immediately wipe away any splashes from plastic or plated surfaces. You can use soft abrasive cleaners when necessary, but avoid scouring powders or other strong abrasives that can scratch or dull the surface. And after you clean the lid, dry the hinges so they don't rust.

Finally—did you ever wonder where the water comes from when you flush a toilet? Look under the toilet's rim. It's ringed with dozens of little holes. Over time, those holes can get clogged with debris or minerals from the water, and then the water flow is diminished and the toilet doesn't flush well. You can prevent this problem. Unbend a paper clip or wire hanger and carefully poke it up into each hole. Wiggle it around until you force the debris out. Follow up by scrubbing the rim with a stiff toilet brush and *voilà*—full water flow.

# Drains

The best way to keep your drains running smoothly is to keep them clean. The less gunk stuck inside the pipes, the less likely it is that problems will develop. Besides, clean drains smell fresh. You can keep drains clean by developing a few simple habits.

➤ **Daily:** Use cold water when you run the garbage disposal. Cold water washes any congealed grease down the drain and out of the plumbing system. Warm water softens grease, which then leaves a slight residue as it passes through your pipes. Over time, this residue builds up, narrowing the inside diameter of your pipes and making it more likely that clogs will develop.

➤ **Once a week:** Pour several quarts of boiling water down the kitchen sink. Also, whenever you're boiling water for cooking—coddling eggs, cooking pasta, or making tea, for example—pour some down the drain. Boiling water flushes out grease that might otherwise build up and become a problem.

➤ **Once a month:** Fill the sink with about a gallon of warm water. Add ¾ cup of chlorine bleach and about a tablespoon of powdered laundry detergent. Drain the sink, then rinse it with plain hot water. Detergent contains surfactants that loosen dirt and grease; bleach disinfects and deodorizes the drain and sink.

# Drain Hoses

Dishwashers and clothes washers drain into the DWV system through flexible hoses attached to internal drains.

These hoses deteriorate over time and should be replaced when necessary. It's pretty easy to tell if they're going bad—they develop hairline cracks or just feel brittle rather than soft and pliable. The owner's manual should have instructions for a simple replacement process.

Clothes washers use 40 to 65 gallons of water for a load; dishwashers use 12 to 18 gallons. Quite a mess if a drain hose bursts in the middle of a load. Just to be on the safe side, it's a good idea to run these appliances only when you can be home throughout the entire cycle.

⚠ Warning: Do NOT mix **chlorine** with other household chemicals or products except laundry detergent. It's vitally important not to combine ammonia and chlorine: Dangerous gases result.

## *Shutoff Valves*

Kitchen and bathroom sinks, toilets, washing machines, and refrigerator ice makers all have shutoff valves—that is, valves that you can use to shut off the water quickly in case of an emergency. These valves are durable, but they can deteriorate over time and sometimes get stuck so that you can't turn them either way. This is not a good situation because the last thing you need if a toilet's overflowing is to find out that the shutoff valves don't work.

To avoid a minor catastrophe like that, check all the shutoff valves every month or two. It's easy—just look to see if the valve is leaking. If not, turn the handle back and forth to open and close the valve a couple of times. If the handle is stuck, don't force it. Call a plumber and have it checked—sooner rather than later. This advice holds true

if a valve is leaking, too. Replacing a valve with a minor leak is much less expensive than replacing the valve and repairing the damage it would cause if it burst.

While we're talking about shutoff valves, let's take a moment to think about supply lines, too. These carry water from the copper supply pipes to your faucets and appliances. In many cases, these are thin, rigid lines that can corrode or rust over time. Many people prefer lines made of stainless steel braided over rubber with threaded couplings on the ends—they're quite reliable and easy to install. No matter what material the lines are made of, you should check all of them regularly and replace them every five to seven years.

# Water Heaters

Water heaters are the second largest energy user in a home. In fact, heating water is responsible for 4 percent of America's total energy consumption, according to the United States Geological Survey. It's easy to see that maintaining your water heater saves money, but did you know it also protects your family and your home itself?

Water heaters are simple devices and easy to maintain, but at the heart of it, they're very large containers filled with extremely hot water. Problems are rare but significant.

**The best setting** for a water heater is between 120° and 125°F, or L for Low. If the  thermostat's set too high, the water coming from your faucets can be hot enough to cause serious burns, especially on children or the elderly. To check the temperature, let the water run for a few minutes, then check it with a candy thermometer. Adjust the water heater's thermostat as necessary.

Dirt and dust are combustible, so **keep the area around the water heater clean**, and store any flammable materials well away from it.

**Don't add an insulation blanket** around a gas water heater. Insulation can block the air supply or keep the water heater from venting properly. Before adding an insulation blanket to an electric water heater, check the caution labels. Most newer water heaters have so much insulation that it isn't a good idea to add more. If you're worried about saving energy, insulate the hot water pipes with sleeve-type foam insulation.

Water heaters have **pressure relief valves** that guard  against ruptures caused by steam buildup in the tank. Once a year, you should test this valve: Lift up on the lever and let it snap back. The valve should allow a burst of water into the drain pipe. if it doesn't, it needs to be replaced.

The average family of four wastes over 15,000 gallons of water a year waiting for the water to get warm in the shower. If that's a problem at your house, add a hot water recirculating pump—a relatively inexpensive system that makes hot water available immediately.

## Flushing a Water Heater

Over time, sediment can build up in the bottom of a water heater. It makes the heater less efficient and can even reduce the amount of water the tank can hold. If the sediment hardens, it can clog the drain valve. All of this can be avoided by flushing the tank once a year.

**1.** First, turn off the heater. (If you have a gas unit, set the gas valve on "Pilot." If it's electric, turn the circuit breaker to the OFF position.) Keep all children and pets away from the area.

**3.** Open the drain valve at the bottom of the heater. Be careful: hot water will flow out. (If the tank doesn't drain, sediment probably is clogging the drain valve. Close the pressure relief valve and turn on the cold-water inlet valve. If it still doesn't drain, it's time to call a plumber.)

Keep an eye on the water coming out of the hose. When it runs clear, you've removed as much sediment as possible. Close the drain valve and disconnect the hose. Close the pressure relief valve and open up the cold-water inlet valve.

**2.** Connect a garden hose to the drain valve at the bottom of the tank. Close the shutoff valve on the cold-water inlet. Open the temperature/pressure relief valve, and leave it open. Run the hose to a nearby sink or floor drain.

**4.** Open a hot faucet (on the top floor if you have a multistory house) and let the water run until no air bubbles come out. Finally, turn the heater back on. (If you have a gas unit, set the gas valve to ON; if it's electric return the circuit breaker to the ON position.

# F.A.Q.

**Q** *I noticed a small puddle under my water heater. Should I worry about it?*

**A** No, you shouldn't worry—you should take action. Immediately. Have the water heater replaced as soon as possible. A leak, even a small one, can be dangerous. Leaks generally mean that the inner tank has rusted through. If the tank gives way, the flood of scalding water could cause serious injury and ruin the surrounding floors and walls.

# Repairing Plumbing

*When it comes to plumbing, the most important issue is keeping water contained and under control. Leaky pipes and fixtures, if left alone, can damage the structural framing of your house, leading to expensive repairs down the road. But this is easy to avoid—most common plumbing problems are a lot easier to fix than you may think.*

## Faucets

Fix leaky faucets as soon as possible. Although the trickle or drip from your faucet may not seem like much, it can quickly make an impact on your water bill, adding up to 25 gallons per day. And if left unrepaired, a leak can also cut a channel in the metal faucet seat, which may require that the entire faucet be replaced.

Most faucet problems are easy to fix, generally a matter of cleaning or replacing washers, O-rings, or seals. When purchasing new faucet parts, select replacements that match the original parts. Parts can be identified by faucet design, brand name, and model number.

 A leaking toilet or hot water faucet will cost you money. The following chart offers examples of just how much water and electricity you may be losing in kilowatt hours (KWH):

| Drops per Minute | Gallons per Month | KWH per Month |
|---|---|---|
| 60 | 192 | 48 |
| 90 | 310 | 78 |
| 120 | 429 | 107 |

To keep your channel-type pliers from **scratching the finish** when you take a faucet apart for repair, wrap masking tape around the jaws of the pliers.

# Repairing Ball Faucets

Ball faucets have a single handle with a hollow metal or plastic ball contained in the faucet body that controls the temperature and flow of water.

**1.** If a ball faucet leaks from the spout, first tighten the cap with channel-type pliers. If this doesn't work, take the faucet apart and inspect for worn-out valve seats or springs or a damaged ball.

Turn off the water at the shutoff valves or the main supply valve near the water meter. Loosen the handle setscrew with an Allen wrench, then remove the handle to expose the faucet cap.

**2.** Remove the faucet cap with channel-type pliers. Lift out the cam, cam washer, and ball. Using a small screwdriver, remove the old springs and neoprene valve seats. If any of these parts are worn or damaged, replace them.

**3.** Leaks around the base of the faucet are usually caused by worn O-rings. Remove the spout by twisting it upward, then cut off the old O-rings.

Coat new O-rings with heatproof grease and install them. Reattach the spout, pressing downward until the collar rests on the plastic slip ring, then reassemble the handle assembly, using new parts as necessary.

**4.** Turn the faucet to ON, then slowly open the shutoff valves to restore the water supply. Check for leaks and tighten connections as needed.

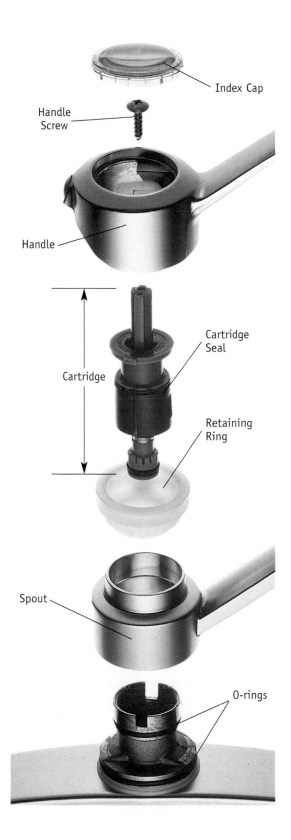

Index Cap

Handle Screw

Handle

Cartridge

Cartridge Seal

Retaining Ring

Spout

O-rings

## Repairing Cartridge Faucets

Inside the body of a cartridge faucet is a cylindrical metal or plastic cartridge that holds a movable stem. Lifting the faucet handle causes the stem to rise, where its holes align with the cartridge holes, allowing hot and cold water to mix. Rotating the handle adjusts the mix of hot and cold.

Spout drips are generally caused by worn cartridge seals. Other problems, such as decreased water flow, may be caused by clogs in the cartridge holes or a corroded cartridge. If a cartridge is worn or damaged, replace it.

**1.** Start by turning off the water at the faucet shutoff valves or the main supply valve. Pry off the index cap and remove the handle screw underneath the cap. Remove the faucet handle by lifting it up and tilting it backward.

Using a channel-type pliers, remove the retaining ring. Also remove any retaining clip holding the cartridge in place.

**2.** Grip the top of the cartridge with channel-type pliers, then pull straight up to remove the part. Because cartridges come in many styles, bring yours along for comparison when shopping for a new one.

When installing the new cartridge, align it in the same position as the old one. If the cartridge is not aligned correctly, the hot and cold water may be reversed. If that happens, just take the faucet apart and rotate the cartridge 180°.

Leaks around the base of a cartridge faucet are typically caused by worn O-rings.

**3.** To remove the spout, pull up and twist it. Use a utility knife to cut the old O-rings, then coat new O-rings with heatproof grease and install.

**4.** Reattach the spout and reassemble the faucet body. Turn the faucet to ON, then slowly open the shutoff valves to restore the water. Check for leaks and tighten connections as needed.

☑ Close the sink drain before disassembling the faucet. Then, if parts fall as you work, they'll stay in the sink rather than falling down the drain and into the trap.

# Repairing Disc Faucets

A disc faucet has a single handle with a wide cylinder inside the faucet body. The cylinder contains two ceramic plates that, when the handle is lifted, slide against each other and align inlet holes to allow hot and cold water to mix and move out through the spout.

Leaks at the spout or around the body of a disc faucet usually can be fixed by cleaning the seals and cylinder openings.

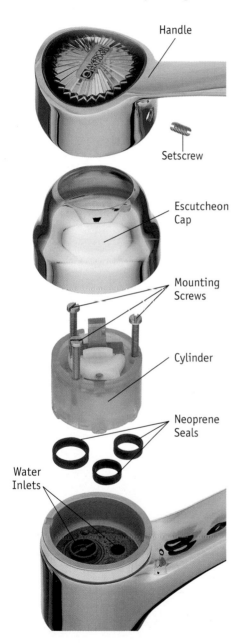

Handle

Setscrew

Escutcheon Cap

Mounting Screws

Cylinder

Neoprene Seals

Water Inlets

**1.** Turn off the water at the faucet shutoff valves or the main supply valve. Rotate the faucet spout to the side, then raise the handle. Remove the setscrew, then lift off the handle and escutcheon cap. Unscrew the mounting screws and lift out the cylinder.

**2.** Remove the neoprene seals from the cylinder openings. Do not use sharp or metal tools—you could scratch or chip the smooth ceramic discs. Clean the openings with an abrasive pad, then rinse clean the cylinder with clear water. If necessary, clean the inlet holes in the faucet body with the abrasive pad.

**3.** Reinstall the seals to the cylinder, then reassemble the faucet. Be sure to line up the holes of the cylinder with the correct inlet and outlet holes in the faucet body. Move the handle to the ON position, then open the shutoff valves very slowly until water runs steadily. If the faucet continues to leak, install a new cylinder.

☑ Be very careful when you turn the water back on: The ceramic discs can be cracked by air rushing through the faucet when the water is restored. After making repairs, place the handle in the ON position, and then very gradually open the shutoff valves. Don't turn the faucet off until the water runs steadily, without bursts of air.

# Repairing Compression Faucets

Compression faucets have separate handles for hot and cold water (some may even have separate spouts for hot and cold) and can be identified by a threaded stem assembly inside the faucet body. The stems come in many styles, but all stems use neoprene washers or seals to control the flow of water. Spout drips are usually caused by worn stem washers, and leaks around the handle typically are caused by worn O-rings.

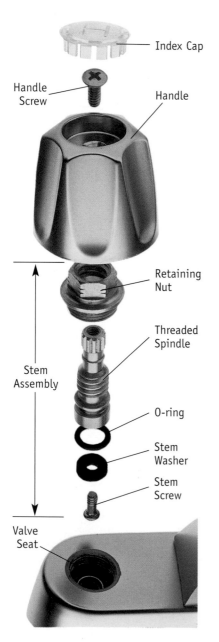

Index Cap

Handle Screw

Handle

Retaining Nut

Threaded Spindle

Stem Assembly

O-ring

Stem Washer

Stem Screw

Valve Seat

**1.** Turn off the water at the shutoff valves or the main supply valve. Remove the index cap, unfasten the handle screw, then pull off the handle. If a handle won't pull free, use a handle puller tool.

Unscrew the stem assembly from the body or the faucet with channel-type pliers. If the faucet body or stems are badly worn, replace the entire faucet.

Faucet Stem

**2.** Remove the brass stem screw from the stem. Remove the worn stem washer, then unscrew the threaded spindle from the retaining nut. Cut off and replace the O-ring with an exact duplicate.

If the faucet has packing string rather than an O-ring, wrap new packing string around the stem, just beneath the packing or retaining nut. Install a new washer and stem screw, then coat all parts with heatproof grease.

**3.** If the metal seats inside the faucet body are rough, replace them. Remove the valve seat, using a seat wrench. Select the end of the wrench that fits the seat, and turn counterclockwise to remove the seat. Install an exact duplicate. Reassemble the faucet, then turn both handles to ON. Open the shutoff valves very slowly until water runs steadily.

Old compression faucets need frequent repairs. If yours are troublesome, it may be better to replace them.

# *Faucet Pressure Problems*

Low water pressure is typically the result of a dirty or clogged aerator, a screw-on spout attachment with a small metal screen that mixes tiny air bubbles into the water flow. To fix the problem, unscrew the aerator from the spout and clean it with a small brush dipped in vinegar. The same trick works on a clogged sink sprayer.

# Fixing a Sink Sprayer

The diverter valve, located inside the faucet body, shifts the water flow from the spout to the sink sprayer when you press the sprayer handle. If you still have water pressure problems after cleaning the sprayer head, the cause may be a dirty or faulty diverter valve.

**1.** Turn off the water at the shutoff valves, then remove the faucet handle and spout to expose the diverter valve. Remove the diverter with needle-nose pliers.

**2.** Use a small brush dipped in vinegar to clean the valve. If possible, replace any worn O-rings or washers. Coat any new parts with heatproof grease, then reinstall the diverter valve and reassemble the faucet.

**1.** If the sprayer hose is damaged, turn off the water at the shutoff valves and unscrew the hose from the sprayer nipple on the faucet using channel-type pliers. Pull the hose through the sink opening.

Unscrew the sprayer head from the handle mount and remove the washer to expose the retaining clip.

**2.** Remove the retaining clip with a needlenose pliers and slide off the handle mount from the end of the sprayer hose.

**3.** Attach the handle mount, retaining clip, washer, and sprayer head to the new hose, then attach the new hose to the faucet sprayer nipple.

**4.** If you find the sprayer still isn't working properly, replace the sprayer head.

# Replacing a Faucet

If a faucet continues to leak after repairs have been made, it's time to replace the whole thing. Replacing a faucet is an easy project that takes about an hour to complete.

When shopping for a new faucet, choose one that matches the size and configuration of the existing sink openings so the tailpieces will fit in place. Also, choose a well-known brand—replacement parts will be easier to find when you need them.

Some faucets are sold with preattached copper supply tubing while others are sold without supply tubes, which means you need to purchase them separately. It really doesn't matter which style you purchase—both are easy to install.

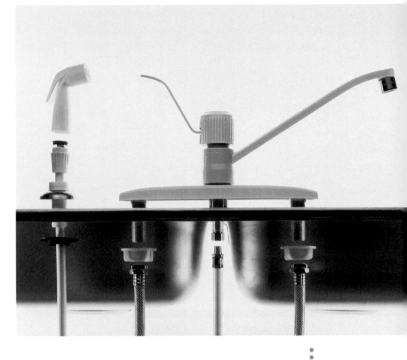

**1.** Turn off the water at the main shutoff, located near the water meter. To remove the old faucet, spray penetrating oil, such as WD-40, on the tailpiece mounting nuts and supply tube coupling nuts. After a few minutes, remove the nuts using a basin wrench or channel-type pliers.

Mounting Nut

**2.** Pull the old faucet out of the sink openings, and clean away the old putty from the surface of the sink, using a putty knife.

Tailpieces

**3.** Apply a ¹/₄" bead of silicone caulk or plumber's putty around the base of the new faucet. Insert the tailpieces into the sink openings. Position the base so it's parallel with the back of the sink, then press it down to make sure the caulk forms a good seal.

**4.** Screw the metal friction washers and the mounting nuts onto the tailpieces using a basin wrench or channel-type pliers. Wipe away excess caulk from the faucet base.

**If your fixture has flexible supply tubes:**

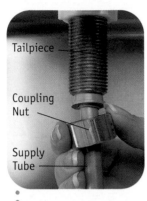

Tailpiece

Coupling
Nut

Supply
Tube

**5a.** If you need to add **flexible supply tubes**, cut the new tubes to fit between the tailpiece and the shutoff valve plus an extra 1/2" to fit inside the valve. Connect the tubes to the tailpieces and tighten the coupling nuts.

**6a.** Connect the supply tubes to the shutoff valves with compression fittings. Slide the compression nut over the tube (threads toward the valve), slide on the compression ring, then apply a continuous bead of pipe joint compound or Teflon tape over the compression ring.

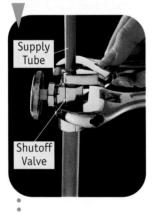

Supply
Tube

Shutoff
Valve

**7a.** Insert the supply tube into the shutoff valve, slide the compression ring and nut against the valve threads, then tighten the compression nut using two adjustable wrenches. Don't overtighten the compression nuts; turn them just enough so they're snug.

**If your fixture has preattached supply tubes:**

**5b.** If you bought a faucet with **preattached supply tubing**, apply caulk or plumber's putty around the base and position the new faucet as described on page 148. If the faucet has a decorative coverplate, attach its washers and locknuts to the coverplate bolts.

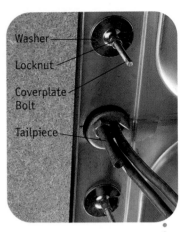

Washer

Locknut

Coverplate
Bolt

Tailpiece

**6b.** Attach the faucet to the sink by placing the rubber gasket, retainer ring, and locknut onto the threaded tailpiece. Tighten the locknut.

Rubber
Gasket

Retainer
Ring

Locknut

**7b.** Connect the supply tubing to the shutoff valves with compression fittings, as described in steps 6a and 7a. Each of the preattached tubes is color coded: The red-coded tube connects to the hot water supply and the blue-coded tube connects to the cold water supply.

**8.** After the new faucet is installed, restore the water supply and check for leaks.

# Tub & Shower Faucets

Tub and shower faucets have the same four basic designs as sink faucets, so the techniques for repairing leaks are the same (see pages 140 to 145). However, to determine the design, you may have to disassemble the faucet.

Many tubs and showers are combined, which means the showerhead and the tub spout share the same water supply lines and handles. And though these combination faucets are available in three-handle, two-handle, or single-handle designs, don't think that complicates matters—the number of handles provides clues as to the design of the faucets and the kinds of repairs that may be needed.

With combination faucets, a diverter valve or gate divert-

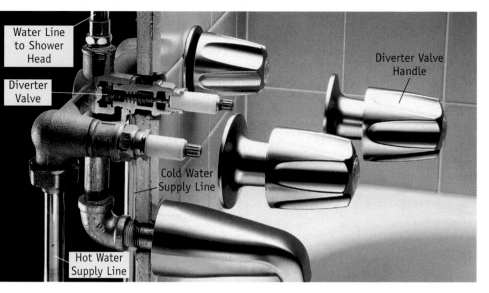

Water Line to Shower Head

Diverter Valve

Cold Water Supply Line

Hot Water Supply Line

Diverter Valve Handle

er is used to direct the water flow to the tub spout or the showerhead.

**Three-handle faucets** indicate either a cartridge or compression design, with the middle handle controlling a diverter. If water doesn't shift easily from tub to showerhead, or if water continues to run out of the spout when the shower is on, the diverter valve probably needs attention.

## Fixing the Diverter Valve of a Three-Handle Faucet

**1.** Turn off the water at the shutoff or main valves. Shutoff valves can typically be accessed by removing a panel in the "wet wall" (the wall that contains the shower supply pipes).

Remove the diverter valve handle and unscrew or pry off the escutcheon plate. Remove the bonnet nut. If necessary, carefully chip away any mortar surrounding the valve. Using a deep-set socket, unscrew the stem assembly (shown), and remove the diverter valve.

**2.** From the bottom of the diverter valve, remove the brass stem screw. Replace the stem washer with an exact duplicate. If the stem screw is worn, replace it.

**3.** To clean the diverter valve, unscrew the retaining nut from the threaded spindle, then scrub it using a wire brush dipped in vinegar. Coat all parts with heatproof grease and reassemble the valve.

Stem Washer

Stem Screw

Like three-handle faucets, **two-handle faucets** have either a cartridge or a compression design. The water supplies—one handle controls the hot water, the other controls the cold—flow into a mixing chamber and flow out of the spout.

**Single-handle faucets** have one valve that controls both the water flow and temperature. These faucets may feature a ball, cartridge, or disc design.

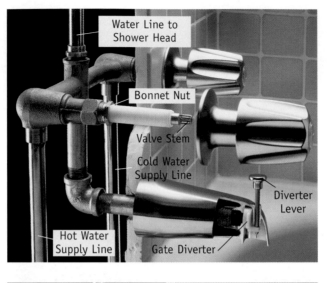

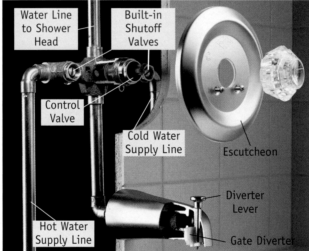

Both two-handle and single-handle faucets use a gate diverter operated by a pull lever or knob on the tub spout. Gate diverters rarely need repair, but it does happen. If the pull lever breaks, comes loose, or refuses to stay up, replace the entire tub spout.

## Replacing a Tub Spout

**1.** To remove the old spout, look under it for a small access slot, which indicates that it's held in place by an Allen screw. If it has one, remove the screw with an Allen wrench, then slide the spout off.

**2.** If there's no access slot, unscrew the spout itself. Use a pipe wrench or insert a large screwdriver, hammer handle, or 2" dowel into the spout and turn counterclockwise.

**3.** Spread pipe joint compound or wrap Teflon tape on the threads of the spout nipple and attach the new spout. If you use a pipe wrench, wrap the jaws with masking tape or fold a cloth around the spout to avoid scratching the finish.

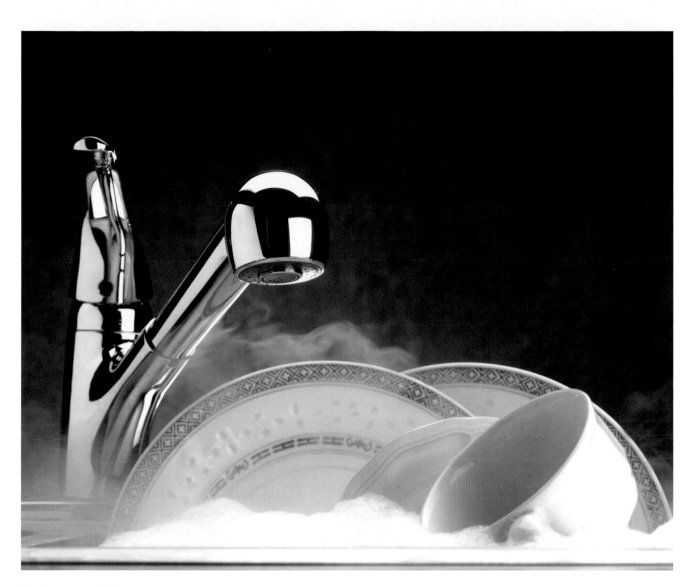

# Water Heaters

Water heaters are pretty simple devices. In gas models, hot water leaves the tank through the hot water outlet, and cold water enters through the dip tube. As the water temperature drops, the thermostat opens the gas valve, and the pilot flame lights the gas burner. Exhaust gases are vented through the flue.

If your gas water heater is not producing hot water, first check to see if the pilot light is out. Relight if necessary (see page 153).

An electric water heater has one to two heating elements mounted in the side wall of the tank. When the water temperature drops, the heating elements turn on. Simple.

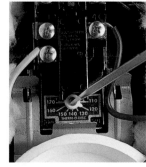

If your electric water heater is not producing hot water, make sure the power is on, then reset the thermostat and set the temperature between 120° and 125° or to "L" for low.

If you still don't get hot water, flush the water heater to remove sediment (see page 139). Sediment can cause corrosion and reduce efficiency.

If these simple procedures don't fix the problem, then your water heater may need more extensive repair. Contact an experienced plumber.

If you find water on the floor around your water heater, check to see if the pressure-relief valve is leaking. If it is, try lowering the temperature setting. If the valve continues to leak, test the valve by lifting the lever and letting it snap back. The valve should allow a burst of water into the drain pipe. If it doesn't, the valve needs to be replaced.

⚠ **If the water heater itself is leaking**, replace it immediately—this means that the inner tank has rusted through. If it gives way, the resulting flood of scalding hot water could cause serious injury and major property damage.

## To Relight a Pilot Light

**1.** Make sure the gas is on, then turn the gas cock on top of the control box to the PILOT position.

**2.** Remove the outer and inner access panels covering the burner chamber. Light a match and hold the flame next to the end of the pilot gas tube inside the burner chamber.

**3.** While holding the match next to the end of the pilot gas tube, press the reset button on the control box. When the pilot flame lights, continue to hold the reset button for one minute. Turn

the gas cock to the ON position. Reattach the inner and outer access panels, and keep them in position—operating the water heater without the panels can allow air drafts to extinguish the pilot light.

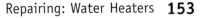

# Repairing Showerheads

When the water from the showerhead starts to spray off to the side, it's time to clean the showerhead. Wrap the jaws of an adjustable wrench or channel-type pliers with masking tape, then unscrew the swivel ball nut. Next, unscrew the collar nut.

Clean the outlet and inlet holes of the showerhead with a thin wire—a paper clip works nicely—then flush the head with clean water. Also soak the showerhead in hot vinegar to remove calcium and hard-water deposits from within the head.

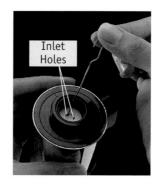

Inlet Holes

O-Ring

If a pivoting shower head won't stay in position, or if it leaks, checks the O-ring that seals the pivot head against the swivel ball. If this O-ring is worn, replace it with a new O-ring lubricated with heatproof grease.

✔ If the showerhead isn't too badly clogged, you may be able to clean it the easy way: Fill a small plastic bag with white vinegar and fasten it around the showerhead, using a rubber band. Let the showerhead soak in the vinegar for an hour or so, and the problem should be solved.

# Pipe Problems

Plumbing pipes are sometimes noisy, which typically is pretty easy to fix. The trick is to keep them from vibrating against other building materials.

Burst pipes are more complicated, but if you live in a cold climate, you should know what to do in case of emergency.

## Quieting Noisy Supply Pipes

**Pipes that bang** against studs or joists can be quieted with pieces of foam rubber pipe insulation. If you can, locate the offending pipe and wrap it with a section of pipe insulation.

**Loose pipes** may also bang or rub against joists and pipe hangers, creating annoying sounds. Make sure the pipe hangers are secure, and use pieces of pipe insulation to cushion the pipes.

If pipe insulation doesn't deaden the noise, you may have to install an air chamber, which is a vertical length of pipe installed in the supply line. The air chamber provides a cushion of air to absorb the shock wave caused by the sudden stop of flowing water, known as "water hammer." Consult a certified plumber to determine if an air chamber is necessary.

## Patching Leaky Pipes

If a pipe should burst, immediately turn off the water at the main shutoff valve. You'll need to call a plumber to make the permanent repair, but you can make a temporary repair with a sleeve clamp repair kit.

After the water main is off, allow the pipe to drain completely. Smooth any rough edges at the rupture

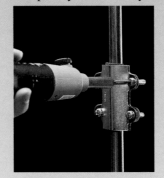

with a metal file. Place the rubber sleeve of the repair clamp over the rupture, sandwich it with the two metal repair clamps, and tighten the screws with a screwdriver. Open the water supply and watch for leaks. Retighten screws if necessary.

Remember: This repair is temporary. Replace the ruptured section of pipe as soon as possible.

# Clogs

## *Bathroom Sinks, Tubs, and Showers*

Most clogs are caused by soap and hair, and they're easy to remove. First, pull out the drain stopper. Some lift out 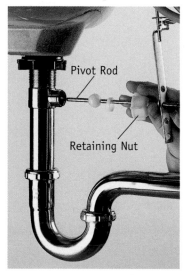 directly, others need to be turned counter-clockwise.

Some stoppers are connected to the pivot rod; you have to remove the retaining nut to release the pivot rod and free the stopper.

Once you get the stopper out, remove anything you find in the drain—a long tweezer or a Kelly clamp works really well for this. You can even use a bent piece of stiff wire—a wire hanger will do—to snag soap and hair clogs.

If the drain's still clogged, it's time to plunge. The goal here is to break up the clog so the pieces can move on through the pipes. To do that, you need suction power, and lots of it. Stuff a wet rag into the sink overflow opening to eliminate air flow; run a little petroleum jelly around the lip of your plunger to create a good seal against the sink.

Put the plunger cup over the drain and run enough water into the sink to cover it. Quickly move the plunger handle up and down six or eight times. Remove the plunger and see what happens. If the water drains but you're not quite there yet, repeat the plunging process. If nothing seems to be happening, it's time to remove the drain trap.

☑ If you drop something valuable down a sink drain, don't panic. And don't run the water. The trap holds standing water and—sometimes—the lost item. Remove the trap (see page 157) and check for the lost item. You might get lucky.

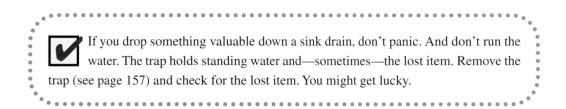

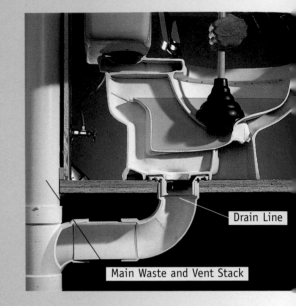

Drain Line

Main Waste and Vent Stack

Drain traps contain standing water, that's their job. (The water seals the trap to keep sewer gases from getting into your house.) When you take the trap off, that water will spill out. If you've put any chemicals down the drain, they're going to spill out, too. Protect yourself with rubber gloves and eye protection.

Put a bucket under the drain trap. Use channel-type pliers to loosen the slip nuts on the trap bend. Unscrew the nuts by hand and slide them away from the connections. Pull off the trap bend. (That water we mentioned will spill out now. Be ready.)

Slip Nuts

Fixture Drain Line

Trap Bend

Remove any debris, then clean the trap bend with a toothbrush or small wire brush.

Check out the slip nut washers—replace them if they're damaged or worn. Put the trap bend back in place and retighten the slip nuts.

## Clogged Toilets

For best results, place the cup of the plunger over the drain opening and rapidly plunge up and down 15 to 20 times. Slowly pour a bucket of water into the bowl to flush debris through the drain. Repeat as needed.

If plunging doesn't clear the clog, push the plunger down over the drain opening to create a vacuum, then quickly pull it up. This may suck the clog free.

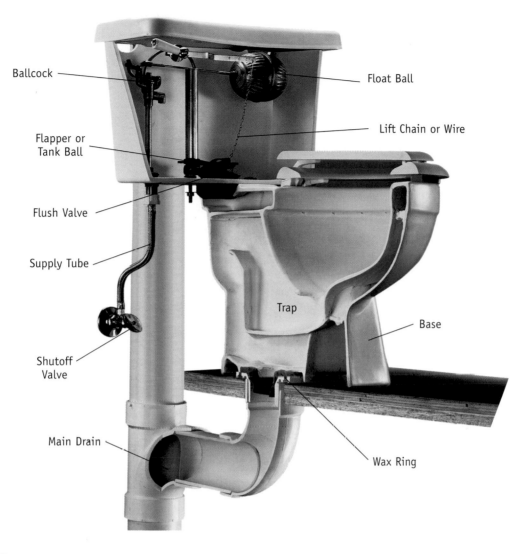

Ballcock

Float Ball

Lift Chain or Wire

Flapper or
Tank Ball

Flush Valve

Supply Tube

Trap

Base

Shutoff
Valve

Main Drain

Wax Ring

# *Toilets*

Many common problems with standard toilets can be resolved with a few minor adjustments. However, before you can make any repair, you need to be able to identify the parts and know how they work.

When you push the *handle*, the *lift chain* or *lift wire* raises a rubber seal, which is called either a *flapper* or a *tank ball*. Water in the tank rushes down through the *flush valve* opening, in the bottom of the tank, into the *toilet bowl*.

Waste water in the bowl is forced through the trap into the *main drain*. When the toilet tank is empty, the flapper seals the tank, and a water supply valve, called a *ballcock*, refills the toilet tank. The ballcock is controlled by a *float ball* that rides on the surface of the water. When the tank is full, the float ball automatically shut off the ballcock.

# Fixing a Running Toilet

A running toilet can waste 20 or more gallons of fresh water each day. Loosely translated, that means a higher water bill for you.

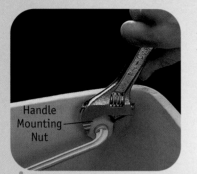

**1.** The first step toward a fix is to jiggle the handle. If the sound of running water stops, then either the handle or the lift chain (or lift wires) need to be adjusted.

If the handle sticks, remove the tank cover and clean the handle mounting nut. The nut has reverse threads; loosen it by turning clockwise.

**2.** Adjust the lift chain so it hangs straight with 1/2" of slack. Hook the chain in a different hole, if necessary. Replace broken chains.

**3.** For toilets without lift chains, Adjust the lift wires so that the wires are straight and operate smoothly when the handle is pushed.

**4.** If jiggling the handle does not stop the running water, take a look inside the tank. If the float ball is touching the side of the tank, bend the float arm to reposition it away from the tank wall. Another problem could be a leaky float ball: unscrew the float ball and shake it gently. If there is water inside, replace the ball.

**5.** If the water still runs after these adjustments, check the overflow pipe. If water flows into the overflow pipe, you'll need to adjust or repair the ballcock (see pages 160 to 161).

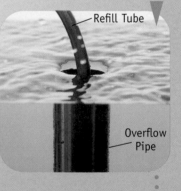

**6.** If water doesn't flow into the overflow pipe, clean or repair the flush valve.

# Adjusting a Ballcock

Ideally, the water level in the toilet tank should be ½" below the overflow pipe. A simple adjustment to the ballcock allows you to raise or lower that water level in the tank. But, of course, there are four styles of ballcock, each with its own (simple) adjustment method.

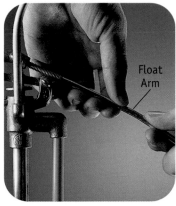

A **traditional plunger-valve ballcock** uses a brass plunger attached to the float arm and ball. Bend the float arm up to raise the water level; bend it down to lower the level.

Float Arm

A **float cup ballcock** is also made of plastic. To raise the water level, pinch the spring clip on the pull rod, and move the float cup upward on the ballcock shank. To lower the level, move the cup downward.

Shank
Pull Rod
Float Cup
Spring Clip

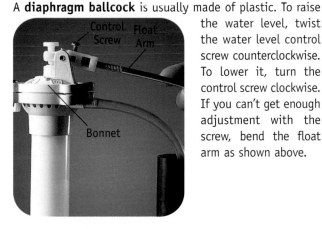

A **diaphragm ballcock** is usually made of plastic. To raise the water level, twist the water level control screw counterclockwise. To lower it, turn the control screw clockwise. If you can't get enough adjustment with the screw, bend the float arm as shown above.

Control Screw
Float Arm
Bonnet

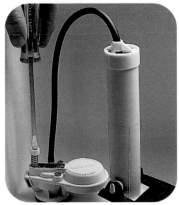

A **floatless ballcock** controls the water level with a pressure-sensing device. To raise the water level, turn the adjustment screw clockwise, half a turn at a time. To lower it, turn the screw counterclockwise.

✔ Before you spend hours fussing with a malfunctioning ballcock, check the replacement cost of a toilet tank. Standard tanks can be purchased—with all-new mechanisms installed—for astonishingly low prices, often as little as $20.

# Replacing a Ballcock

Ballcocks are reliable, but if they do develop problems, they're fairly inexpensive, and easy to replace.

**1.** Shut off the water and flush the toilet to empty the tank. remove any remaining water with a sponge. Use an adjustable wrench to disconnect the supply tube coupling nut and the ballcock mounting nut, then remove the old ballcock.

Loosen the shank lock ring on the new ballcock, and adjust the shank until the top of the ballcock is an inch from the top of the tank. Retighten the shank lock ring until it locks in place.

**2.** Attach a cone washer to the new ballcock tailpiece and insert the tailpiece into the tank opening.

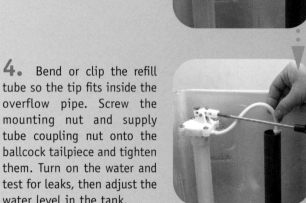

**3.** Line up the float arm socket so the float arm passes behind the overflow pipe. Attach the float arm to the ballcock, then attach the float ball to the float arm.

**4.** Bend or clip the refill tube so the tip fits inside the overflow pipe. Screw the mounting nut and supply tube coupling nut onto the ballcock tailpiece and tighten them. Turn on the water and test for leaks, then adjust the water level in the tank.

# Fixing a Leaky Tank Ball or Flapper

**1.** Turn off the water supply and flush the toilet to empty the tank. Lift the tank ball or unhook the flapper. Gently scrub the inside of the valve seat and rim with emery paper. Line up the tank ball by loosening the screws holding the guide arm, and position the arm directly over the valve seat.

If the flapper or tank ball is soft or cracked, replace it.

**2.** Straighten the vertical lift wire on the tank ball assembly. The ball should rise and fall smoothly when you trip the lever. Turn on the water, let the tank refill, and flush to test.

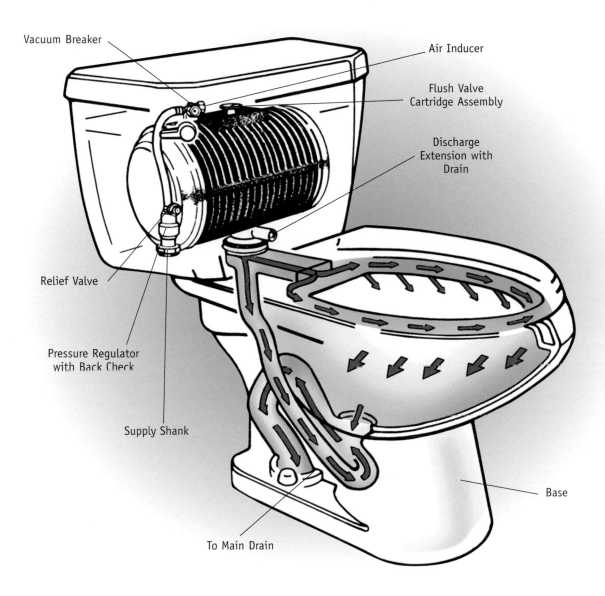

Vacuum Breaker

Air Inducer

Flush Valve
Cartridge Assembly

Discharge
Extension with
Drain

Relief Valve

Pressure Regulator
with Back Check

Supply Shank

To Main Drain

Base

## Repairing a Pressure-Assisted Toilet

Pressure assisted toilets rely on pressure (between 20 and 80 PSI) rather than water volume to create an adequate flush. The handle is connected to a flush rod that pushes an actuator on the flush valve cartridge to start the flush.

Insufficient water supply can cause many problems in a pressure-assisted toilet—it may run constantly, have a weak flush, or not flush at all.

**To check the water pressure**, turn off the water at the shutoff valve and flush the toilet. Use an adjustable wrench to disconnect the water supply tube from the tank. Place the end of the supply tube in a five-gallon bucket, open the shutoff valve all the way for 30 seconds, then measure the amount of water in the bucket. For the toilet to operate properly, there should be more than a gallon of water.

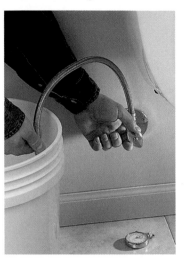

If there is less than a gallon of water, your water supply pressure is probably low. Call your plumber or your local water utility for ways to improve water pressure.

If the water pressure is fine but the **toilet runs constantly**, remove the supply assembly from the tank hole and inspect the shank screen. If necessary, clean the screen with a soft brush dipped in vinegar.

Next, **check the actuator adjustment.** The rod shouldn't interfere with the flush. Empty the system by flushing the toilet. Remove the rod and the flush valve cartridge and check the O-rings for wear. If necessary, replace the cartridge.

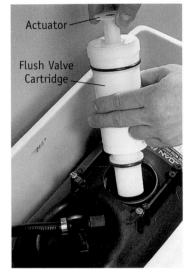

Actuator

Flush Valve Cartridge

To reset the cartridge in the grooves, rotate it two turns counter-clockwise, then turn it clockwise until it fits tightly. Don't over-tighten it. Turn on the water supply and let the tank refill. If water continues to run beyond the refill, depress the actuator. If this stops the flow, tighten the valve cartridge in quarter turns until the water stops. If the water continues to flow when you press the actuator, loosen the cartridge in quarter turns until the water stops.

Rod

**If water flow is weak,** flush the toilet by depressing the actuator, then, when the unit begins the flush cycle, carefully raise the actuator to flush debris from the system.

# Fixing a Leaky Toilet

When you see water leaking around a toilet, find and resolve the problem, pronto. If you don't, water will penetrate the layers of the floor, damaging the subfloor and even the floor joists. Not "a good thing."

**1.** First, make sure all connections are water-tight. Use a socket wrench to tighten the tank bolts, and an adjustable wrench to tighten the ballcock mounting nut and the supply tube coupling nut. Go easy and don't overtighten anything; you can crack the toilet tank.

Ballcock Mounting Nut

Supply Tube Coupling Nut

Tank Bolt

**2.** If water seems to seep out from around the base of the toilet, especially during or just after flushing, the wax ring is probably worn or broken. To check it, add a few drops of food coloring to the tank water and flush. If colored water appears on the floor, you can be fairly sure that is the problem. Also check the tank and the toilet for cracks. Cracks cannot be repaired. You need a new toilet.

**3.** If you find that either the wax ring or the toilet itself needs to be replaced, call a certified plumber for repair estimates.

If the leak seems to be coming from the tank, check the spud washer, a soft disc between the tank and the base. If that washer is hardened or deteriorated, it should be replaced. It's a pretty simple matter to remove the tank, replace the washer, and reinstall the tank.

## Fixing a Broken Toilet Seat

Trust us, they break. (Don't ask.) Luckily, a broken toilet seat is easily replaced.

**1.** Remove the old bolts, using a socket wrench. If the old bolts are rusted (very likely), spray them with penetrating oil and wait a few minutes. If that doesn't work, use a rotary tool with a metal-cutting disc to cut them away. Wear safety goggles, long sleeves, and a dust mask for this job.

**2.** Remove the old bolts and old toilet seat, then clean the toilet bowl with a damp cloth. Set the new seat in place and push the bolts through the hinges and bowl. Install the washers and nuts, and tighten by hand.

# electricity

*I'll bet Einstein turned himself all sorts of colors before he invented the lightbulb.*

**HOMER SIMPSON**

You don't have to be Einstein to work with your electrical system, but it helps to be a little better informed than Homer Simpson. So we've filled this chapter with the basic information you need to clean, maintain, and repair the electrical fixtures and devices in your home.

You'll even find some advice on that perennial question about changing a light bulb.

## With this chapter you'll . . .

- Learn how your electrical system works so you can maintain it safely.

- Fix or replace old light fixtures, receptacles, and switches.

- Clean hard-to-reach electrical fixtures quickly and easily.

# electricity

## THE WAY IT WORKS

Electricity turns a lot of people off. What we mean is, many homeowners refuse to touch anything electrical beyond switches, receptacles, and lightbulbs. Although it's good to be cautious, almost anyone who knows and follows safety precautions and uses common sense can safely work on their electrical system. And even if you're not going to delve into its inner workings, you should recognize the basic parts and understand the fundamental nature of this system.

**Large power plants** located in all parts of the country use turbines turned by water, wind, or steam to generate electricity. The plants send electricity to large "step-up" transformers that increase the voltage to half a million volts or more. Electricity flows easily through high-voltage transmission lines.

When the electricity reaches its destination, "step-down" transformers called **substations** reduce the voltage so electricity can be distributed along street lines.

On **utility power poles**, smaller transformers further reduce the voltage to ordinary 120-volt current for household use.

Lines carrying current into your house run either underground or overhead and are attached to a post called a *service head*. Most homes built after 1950 have three wires running to the service head: two power lines, each carrying 120 volts of current, and a grounded neutral wire. Power from the two 120-volt lines may be combined at the service panel to supply power to 240-volt appliances, like clothes dryers or electric water heaters.

(Some older homes have only two wires running to the service head, one 120-volt line and a grounded neutral wire. This older two-wire service isn't adequate for today's homes and should be upgraded by an electrical contractor.)

Incoming power passes through an electric meter that measures consumption. The power then enters the service panel, where it's distributed to circuits that run throughout the house. The service panel contains fuses or circuit breakers that shut off power to the individual circuits if there's a short circuit or overload. High-powered appliances—like microwave ovens—usually are plugged into their own individual circuits to prevent overloads.

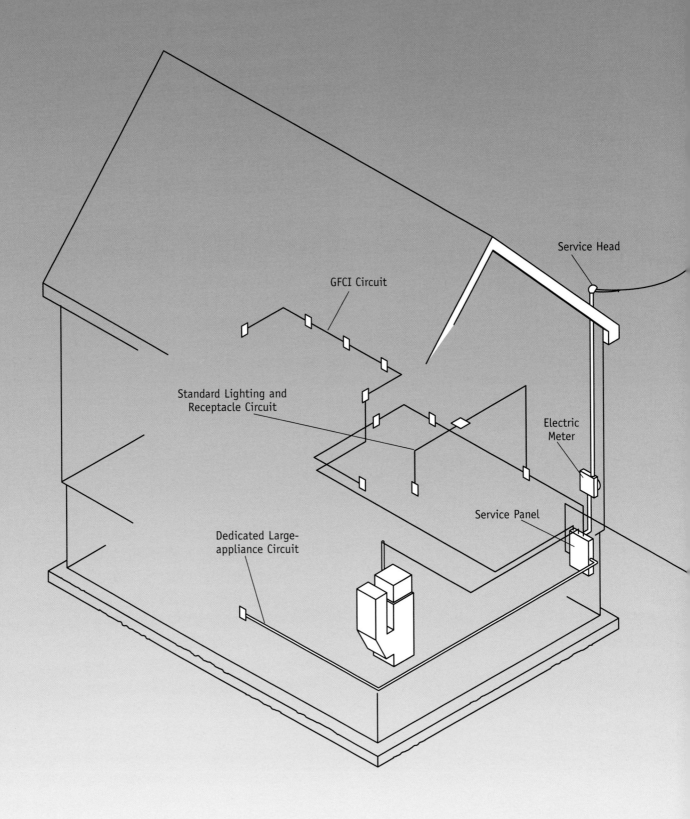

Service Head

GFCI Circuit

Standard Lighting and
Receptacle Circuit

Electric
Meter

Service Panel

Dedicated Large-
appliance Circuit

# The Flow of Electricity in Your Home

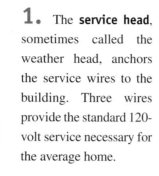

**1.** The **service head**, sometimes called the weather head, anchors the service wires to the building. Three wires provide the standard 120-volt service necessary for the average home.

**2.** The **electric meter** measures the amount of electricity consumed. It usually is attached to the side of the building and connects to the service head. A thin metal disc inside the meter rotates when power is used. The electric meter belongs to your utility company. If you suspect it isn't functioning properly, contact the power company right away.

**3.** The **main service panel**, sometimes called a fuse box or breaker box, distributes power to individual circuits. Fuses or circuit breakers protect each circuit from short circuits and overloads. Fuses and circuit breakers also are used to shut off power to individual circuits while repairs are made.

**4.** **Electrical boxes** enclose wire connections. According to the National Electrical Code, all wire splices or connections must be contained entirely in a plastic or metal electrical box.

**5.** **Receptacles**, sometimes called outlets, provide plug-in access to electricity. A 125-volt, 15-amp receptacle with a grounding hole is the most typical receptacle in systems installed after 1965. Most receptacles have two plug-in locations and are called duplex receptacles.

**6.** **Switches** control electrical current passing through hot circuit wires. Switches can be wired to control light fixtures, ceiling fans, appliances, and receptacles.

**7.** **Fixtures** are directly connected to the electrical system. They usually are controlled with wall switches.

**8.** A **grounding wire** connects the electrical system to the earth through a grounding rod. If there's an overload or short circuit, the grounding wire lets excess electrical power find its way harmlessly to the earth.

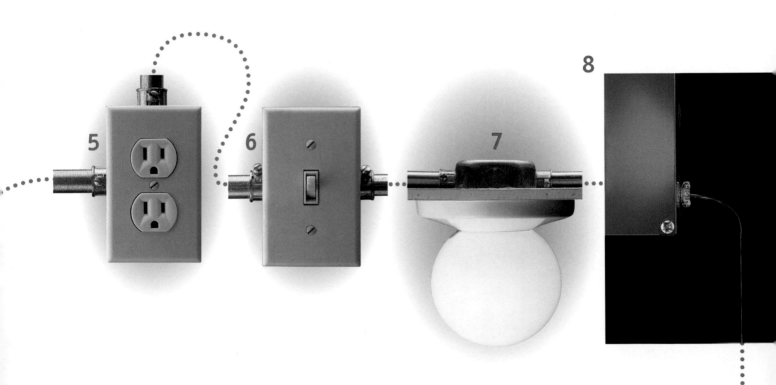

# Cleaning & Maintaining

*How does one clean an electrical system? Carefully.*

*Only a few parts of an electrical system actually need to be cleaned. Light fixtures and appliances quickly come to mind, but did you know that even switches and receptacles can do with a good dusting now and then? Let's start there.*

## Switches & Receptacles

Too much dust and debris inside a switch or receptacle box creates a fire hazard. Particles—particularly lint or sawdust—floating in a small, enclosed space can be ignited by even a tiny spark. Avoid problems by cleaning out the electrical boxes every couple of years.

Turn off the circuit at the service panel. Remove the switchplate or receptacle cover and carefully vacuum inside the box, using a plastic or rubber crevice tool. When you're finished vacuuming, check for loose wires or other signs of faulty connections. Replace the cover and restore the power.

At the beginning of each month, test your GFCI outlets.

Ground-fault circuit interrupter (GFCI) receptacles protect against electrical shock caused by faulty appliances or worn cords or plugs. A GFCI can sense small changes in current flow and shut off the power in as little as $\frac{1}{40}$ of a second. You can identify them by the test and reset buttons on the cover.

GFCIs are now required in bathrooms, kitchens, garages, crawl spaces, unfinished basements, and outdoor receptacle locations. They work best when they're wired to protect only themselves, but they sometimes protect a series of receptacles, switches, and light fixtures. It's worthwhile to find all the GFCIs in your home and identify the devices each one protects.

To test a GFCI, press the TEST button. Plug a lamp or other small device into the receptacle: It shouldn't work. Now press the RESET button: The device should work again. If a GFCI fails this test, replace it or hire an electrician to do it for you.

Older homes may not have any GFCIs. If your house doesn't, add them (it's easy) or hire an electrician to do it for you. This is important: GFCIs protect your home and family.

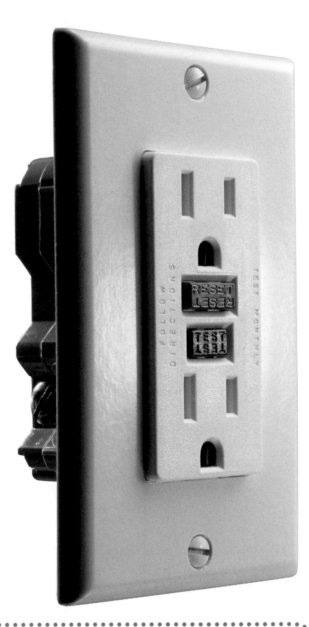

As long as we're on the subject of switches and receptacles, let's talk about **keeping the faceplates clean**. Shut off the circuit before you begin. You're going to be using at least a little liquid here, and liquid and electricity do not mix. You can use a slightly dampened cloth, a cleaning pad like Mr. Clean Magic Eraser, or a paper towel and spray cleaner. Even with the circuit shut off, don't spray any water or cleaner directly onto a switch or toward a receptacle. Dampen your rag, pad, or paper towel, then wipe off the faceplate and surrounding wall. When the switches and receptacles are dry, restore the power.

# Fixtures

The word *illuminate* means "to make luminous or shining." You simply can't make a room luminous or shining (illuminate it, in other words) with light fixtures that are less than sparkling clean.

Start with a good dusting. If you can't reach the top of a hanging fixture, try a lamb's wool duster on a long handle. Dust hanging fixtures often, especially in the kitchen and areas open to the kitchen. When dust particles get mixed with airborne grease, they form a film that can be difficult to remove.

Globe and bowl lights are notorious for collecting bugs and other debris. Clean them each time you replace a light-bulb—more often if you use long-life bulbs. Turn the fixture off and leave it for a few minutes before you begin. Light bulbs, globes, bowls, and hardware get quite hot.

**Bowl lights** typically have a nipple at the center of the bowl that you unscrew in order to remove the bowl and gain access to the bulbs.

The edges of some **globes** have slots that fit into tabs on the fixture base. To remove a globe, align the slots and tabs, and pull down. To replace it, line up the slots and tabs, push the globe into place, then twist until it's secure (usually an inch or so beyond the tab).

Compact fluorescent bulbs last up to ten times longer than incandescents. Designed to work in standard lamps and fixtures, these bulbs pay for themselves through increased energy efficiency.

Other globes are held in place by setscrews spaced around the edges. Loosen the screws to free the globe. Make sure you've got a good grasp on the globe before loosening even the first screw.

**Chandelier globes** often are held in place with spring clips. To remove a globe, pinch the spring clips together and lift. To replace it, pinch the spring clips together and set-

tle the globe into position before gently releasing the clips.

Wash glass globes or bowls in a vinegar and water solution, about a cup of vinegar to a gallon of water. Dry thoroughly with a lint-free cloth. You can use a spray cleaner if you prefer, but never spray any liquid toward hot glass, such as lightbulbs or fixture globes.

 Speaking of lightbulbs, it can't be avoided—we have to talk about changing them. No lawyer or blonde jokes, please.

Turn off the light and let it cool. Remove the globe, bowl, or cover. Grasp the bulb and turn gently to the left. Align the new bulb in the socket, and turn it to the right.

From time to time, a bulb breaks off in the socket. It has happened to almost every veteran homeowner, and most have a special remedy. It doesn't matter whether you choose a tennis ball, bar of soap, or potato, all old favorites. What does matter is that you use a pliable object that doesn't conduct electricity. Let's say you choose a bar of soap. Press the soap down onto the broken glass until it's seated securely enough to be used like a handle. Turn the soap to remove the bulb.

Cleaning **chandelier crystals** can be a real challenge . . . or not, depending on how you go about it. Here's one easy way: Cover the floor beneath the chandelier with a drop cloth or clean newspaper. Mix ¼ cup of ammonia with ¾ cup of white vinegar in a small jar. Hold the jar under each crystal in turn, and dip the crystal into the cleaning

solution. Let the crystals drip dry, and they'll sparkle like Lucy in the Sky.

**Ceiling fans** can be a challenge, too. The blades attract dust and grease, especially in kitchens, and they're not exactly positioned conveniently. For everyday dusting, a lamb's wool duster on a long handle works well. Once a season, you've got to get up close and personal with those blades, though.

Turn the fan off. (Shut off the circuit if there's anyone else in the house.) Set up a ladder within safe reach. Clean each blade with a slightly dampened cloth, then dry it. If the fixture hasn't been cleaned for a while, you may have to use a solution of liquid dish soap. Depending on the material of the blades, you may be able to follow up with a coat of paste wax, which helps the blades repel dust and grease in the future. (Read and follow the manufacturer's recommendations.)

If this is a fan/light combination, change the lightbulbs while you're up there. Fresh bulbs may save you another trip up the ladder to replace a bulb that burns out in a day or a week. Use the old bulbs in table lamps that are easy to reach.

And, if your fan blades were wobbly or noisy— or if you want to change the air-flow direction—you should attend to that before you climb down from the ladder. We show you how on page 218.

**Wall sconces** can generally be kept clean with regular dusting of shades or globes, but occasionally you'll want to wash glass parts with a solution of vinegar and water (see page 175) and polish any metal with a gentle metal polish or another polish recommended by the manufacturer.

**Fabric shades** on fixtures or lamps gather dust almost as quickly as glass. Most of the time, dusting them with a soft-bristled paint-brush puts things right.

Occasionally, shades end up with finger-prints or other dirty marks, and removing them is a more delicate operation. It's deli-cate, but not hard . . . kind of fun, in fact.

## Cleaning a Fabric Shade

**1.** Mix ½ cup of liquid dish soap, ½ teaspoon of ammonia, a teaspoon of vinegar, and a quart of warm water. Beat the mixture with a whisk or a hand mixer until it froths up like a cappuccino.

**2.** Carefully sponge the foam—just the foam—onto the shade. Wipe it off with a damp cloth and check your progress.

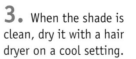

**3.** When the shade is clean, dry it with a hair dryer on a cool setting.

# Service Panels

Many people refer to the service panel as the fuse box or breaker box. No matter what you call it or whether it uses fuses or breakers, the panel protects the electrical system from short circuits and overloads. And it's ingenious.

Most service panels installed before 1965 use **fuses**. Inside each fuse is a current-carrying metal ribbon. If a circuit is overloaded (exceeding its capacity for carrying power), the metal ribbon melts and stops the flow of power.

Screw-in plugs protect the 120-volt circuits for lights and receptacles. Cartridge fuses protect 240-volt appliance circuits and the main shutoff of the service panel.

Most service panels installed after 1965 contain **circuit breakers**. Each circuit breaker has a permanent metal strip that heats up and bends when voltage passes through it. If a circuit is overloaded,  the metal strip inside the breaker bends enough to "trip" the switch and stop the flow of power.

Single-pole circuit breakers protect 120-volt circuits, and double-pole circuit breakers protect 240-volt circuits. Amperage ratings range from 15 to 20 amps.

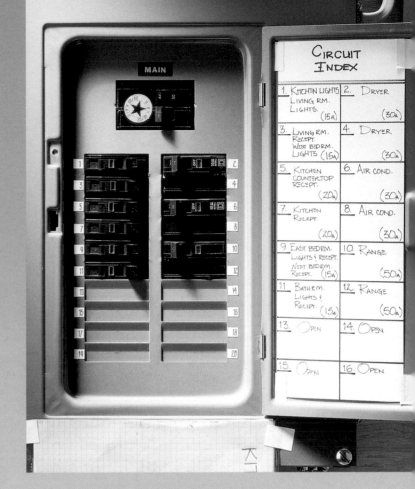

Each fuse or breaker protects one circuit—that is, one set of switches, receptacles, and fixtures. It makes life much, much easier if you know exactly which devices are controlled by each fuse or breaker. You may find a map or chart inside the door of the service panel identifying the devices on each circuit. If not, it's a good idea to make one.

One at a time, shut off the circuits and try switches and receptacles until you've figured out which ones are on that circuit. This isn't as difficult as it sounds—all the devices on one circuit will be in the same general area of the house. An experienced homeowner or an electrician can help you with this if necessary.

The service panel depends on good conductivity, and you can help ensure that. Every three months or so, check it.

**If the system has fuses,** check for signs of rust on individual fuses and in the panel itself. If a fuse is slightly rusty, replace it. If you notice signs of corrosion in the panel itself, consult an electrician.

**Test GFCI breakers** by pushing the TEST button. The breaker should trip to the OFF position. If it doesn't, call an electrician—the breaker needs to be replaced right away.

**If the system has breakers**, turn each one off and back on. You should feel a firm click when you press the switch back to the ON position. If the breaker doesn't click into place or the lever feels at all loose, consult an electrician.

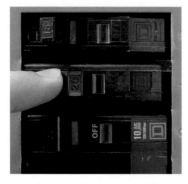

In older systems with circuit breakers, sometimes two 120-volt breakers are joined to create a 240-volt breaker. If you have a system like this, **check the tie rods** when you're checking out the service panel. Make sure each tie rod is secure and the breakers are working together. If not, call an electrician right away.

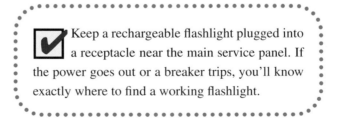

✔ Keep a rechargeable flashlight plugged into a receptacle near the main service panel. If the power goes out or a breaker trips, you'll know exactly where to find a working flashlight.

## Blown Fuses and Tripped Circuits

When a fuse blows or a circuit breaker trips, it's usually because there are too many fixtures and appliances drawing power through the circuit. Move some of the appliances to another circuit, then replace the fuse or reset the breaker.

If the fuse blows or the breaker trips again immediately, there may be a short circuit in the system, and it's time to call an electrician.

 When working at the service panel, wear rubber-soled shoes and stand only on dry floors.

## Fuses

If the lights go out or an appliance plugged into a receptacle stops working, go to the service panel. (Take a flashlight if the lights are  out in that area.) Check out the fuse for the circuit—it should be a plug fuse. If the window in the fuse is discolored (left), there was a short circuit in the system. If the metal ribbon inside the fuse is cleanly melted, the circuit was overloaded. Either way, it has to be replaced.

Unscrew the fuse, touching only the insulated rim of the fuse. Replace it with a fuse that has the same amperage rating. This is important: A fuse has to match the circuit's amperage rating. Never replace a fuse with one that has a larger rating.

If a large electric appliance stops working or you've lost power in the whole house, check the cartridge fuses.

Grip the handle of the fuse block and pull sharply to remove it from the panel. Use a fuse puller to take the individual cartridge fuses from the block. Put the probe of a continuity tester on one end of the fuse and touch the alligator clip to the other. If the tester glows, the fuse is good. If the tester doesn't glow, replace the fuse. Make absolutely sure the new fuse matches the circuit's amperage rating.

## Breakers

Open the service panel and find the tripped breaker. The lever on a tripped breaker will be either in the OFF position or in a position between ON and OFF.

Reset the breaker by pressing the lever all the way to the OFF position, then pressing it to the ON position.

If a circuit breaker trips over and over even though the demand for power isn't excessive, the mechanism inside the breaker may be worn out. Call an electrician to inspect and replace it if necessary.

# Repairing Wiring

*Most people get nervous just thinking about their home's electrical system, much less the idea of actually making repairs to it. But don't be so easily scared off; most wiring repairs involve reconnecting loose wires or installing a replacement part.*

## Wiring Basics

**Testing for power:** The two most important steps in any wiring project are shutting off the power at the main service panel, then testing to confirm that the power is definitely off. (See page 184.)

**Stripping wire:** Use a combination tool to strip insulation from wires.

**Connecting to screw terminals:** Form a C-shaped loop in the end of each wire, using a needlenose pliers, then hook the wires around the screw terminals in clockwise loops. Tighten the screws with a screwdriver.

**Using push-in fittings:** Use the strip gauge as a guide for stripping the wires. Insert the stripped wires into the push-in fittings. When fully inserted, no bare copper should be visible. To remove, push a small nail or screwdriver into the release opening next to the wire and pull out the wire.

**Using wire connectors:** Connect two or more wires together with a wire connector. Strip ½ inch of insulation from the wires. Hold the wires parallel, insert them into the connector, and screw the connector clockwise until it's snug.

**Pigtailing wires:** A pigtail is simply a short piece of wire that is the same gauge and color as the circuit wires. Use a pigtail to connect two or more wires to a single screw terminal or to lengthen short circuit wires.

# Receptacles

Household receptacles have no moving parts to wear out, so they'll usually last for many years without a problem. The problems that do crop up are mostly caused by loose wire connections, by faulty lamps or appliances, or by plugs and cords. Other common problems include old receptacles that are in poor condition, that lack grounding, or that no longer hold plugs firmly.

Household receptacles provide two types of voltage: normal (110, 115, 120, 125 volts) and high voltage (220, 240, 250 volts).

You can easily make most repairs to normal-voltage receptacles yourself, but repairing high-voltage receptacles is a job for a professional.

The most common receptacle is a **grounded duplex receptacle**. Each half has a long (neutral) slot, a short (hot) slot, and a U-shaped grounding hole that ensures that the connection between the receptacle and plug is polarized and grounded for safety.

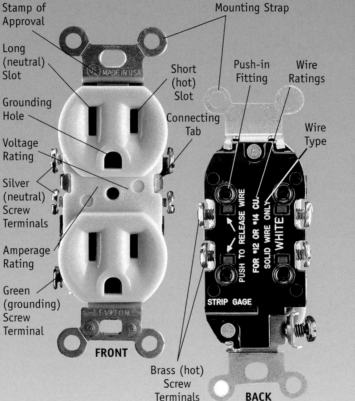

Stamp of Approval
Long (neutral) Slot
Grounding Hole
Voltage Rating
Silver (neutral) Screw Terminals
Amperage Rating
Green (grounding) Screw Terminal
**FRONT**

Mounting Strap
Short (hot) Slot
Connecting Tab
Push-in Fitting
Wire Ratings
Wire Type
Brass (hot) Screw Terminals
**BACK**

The second is the **polarized two-slot receptacle**, commonly used in homes built before 1960. Two-slot receptacles have no grounding wire attached to the receptacle, but the box may be grounded through the cable. These are no longer widely available.

Another common receptacle is the **ground-fault circuit interrupter (GFCI)**. A GFCI receptacle protects against electric shock by shutting off the power when it senses small changes in current flow. If you suspect problems with GFCI receptacles, contact a certified electrician. (See page 173 for maintaining GFCIs.)

Receptacles are marked with ratings for maximum volts and amps. The most common receptacle is marked 15A, 125V. When replacing a receptacle, make sure to check the amp rating of the circuit at the main service panel and buy a receptacle with the same rating.

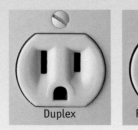

Duplex
Polarized 2-slot

GFCI

A problem at one receptacle may affect others in the circuit. If the cause of a faulty receptacle is not readily apparent, check the other receptacles in the circuit.

# Receptacles

During repair or replacement work, you'll often need to test receptacles for various reasons. An inexpensive neon circuit tester makes it easy to perform the tests. The tester has a small bulb that glows when electrical power flows through it. When using the tester, be careful not to touch the metal probes.

## Testing for Power

**1.** Before any repair, test for power to make sure that live voltage is not reaching the receptacle while you're working on it.

After turning off the power at the service panel, place one probe in each slot of the receptacle. If the tester glows, return to the main service panel and shut off the right circuit. If it doesn't glow, move on to the next test.

**2.** Remove the coverplate and pull the receptacle from the box without touching the wires. Touch one probe to the brass screw terminal and the other to the silver screw terminal across from it. If there are wires connected to both sets of terminals, test both sets. If the tester glows, there is power in the receptacle, and you need to shut off the correct circuit at the main service panel.

# Testing for Grounding

Test for grounding to plan receptacle replacements. This test will indicate how an existing receptacle is wired and whether a replacement should be a two-slot polarized, a grounded duplex, or a GFCI receptacle. Power to the circuit must be on when testing a receptacle for grounding.

To test a **grounded duplex receptacle**, insert one probe into the U-shaped grounding hole and the other in the short (hot) slot. The tester should glow. If it doesn't, move the probe from the short (hot) slot to the long (neutral) slot. If the tester glows, the hot and neutral wires are reversed. If the tester doesn't glow in either position, the receptacle isn't grounded correctly.

must be free of paint, dirt, and grease. If the tester glows, the receptacle is grounded. If it does not glow, place one probe in the long (neutral) slot and touch the other to the screw. If the tester glows, the receptacle box is grounded but the hot and neutral wires are reversed. If the tester doesn't glow, the box is not grounded.

**Plug-in testers** are also available for testing three-slot receptacles. With the power on, insert the tester into the suspect outlet. The three colored lights on the face of the tester will light up in different combinations, according to the outlet's problem. A reference chart comes with the tester, often printed on the tester itself.

To test a **two-slot polarized receptacle** for grounding, place one probe in each slot. The tester should glow. If it doesn't, there is no power to the receptacle.

Place one probe of the tester in the short (hot) slot and touch the other to the coverplate screw. The screw head

## Testing for a Hot Wire

Finally, **test for a hot wire** if you need to confirm which wire is carrying live voltage. With the power off at the service panel, carefully separate the ends of all the wires and spread them out so that they aren't touching each other or anything else.

Restore the power to the circuit at the main service panel. Touch one of the probes of the tester to each of the wires while holding the other probe on the grounded metal box or the grounding wire entering the box from the source. If the tester glows, the wire is hot. Turn off the power at the service panel again before continuing to work.

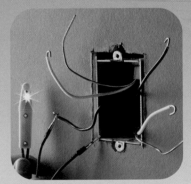

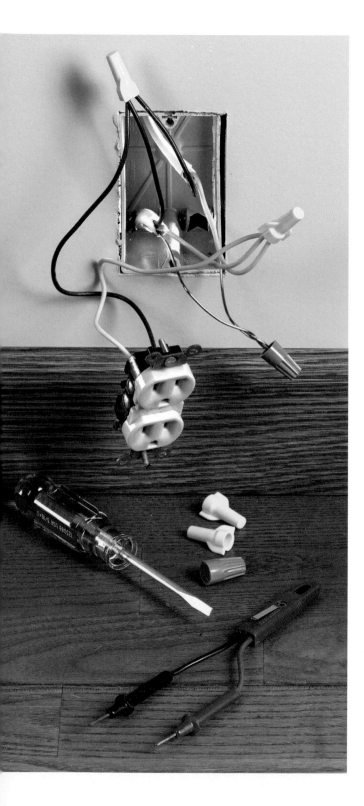

## Repairing Receptacles

**1.** Turn off the power at the service panel, then test the receptacle for power, using a neon circuit tester (see page 184).

Remove the coverplate and the mounting screws. Carefully pull the receptacle from the box, without touching any bare wires. Confirm that the power is off, using the neon circuit tester. If there are wires attached to both sets of screw terminals, test them both. If the tester glows, return to the service panel and turn off the correct circuit.

**2.** Inspect the bare wire ends. If they're darkened or dirty, disconnect them one at a time, and clean them with fine sandpaper.

**3.** Reconnect the wires and tighten all the connections. Be careful not to overtighten or strip the screws.

Vacuum out the receptacle box if it's dirty or dusty (see page 172), then reinstall the receptacle and restore the power at the main service panel. If it still doesn't work, check the other receptacles in the circuit before replacing it.

# Replacing Receptacles

**1.** Test the receptacle for grounding (see page 185) to find out how it's wired. If it's a GFCI, simply replace it with a new GFCI. If it's a grounded two-slot or grounded duplex receptacle, you can replace it with a new grounded duplex.

If the test indicates that the hot and neutral wires are reversed, be sure to install the wires correctly for the replacement receptacle.

Check the amp rating for the circuit at the main service panel, and buy a replacement receptacle with the correct amperage rating.

**2.** Turn off the power at the main service panel, then test the receptacle for power using a neon circuit tester (see page 184). Test both ends of a duplex receptacle. Remove the coverplate and mounting screws, then carefully pull the receptacle from the box, without touching the wires. Use the neon circuit tester to confirm that the power is off.

Label each wire for its location on the receptacle screw terminals. Disconnect the wires and detach the old receptacle.

**3.** Connect each wire to its respective screw terminal on the new receptacle. (See 188 to 189 for common configurations.) Tighten all the screw connections, taking care not to overtighten or strip the screws.

**4.** Carefully tuck the wires back into the box and install the receptacle. Reattach the coverplate and turn on the power. Test the receptacle with the neon circuit tester to make sure it works.

## GFCI Receptacles

In circuits that aren't grounded, a GFCI receptacle can be installed in place of a standard duplex receptacle to improve safety. GFCI is required by code in bathrooms, kitchens, garages, crawl spaces, unfinished basements, and outdoor receptacle locations. Call a certified electrician if the electrical circuits in any of these locations don't have GFCI protection.

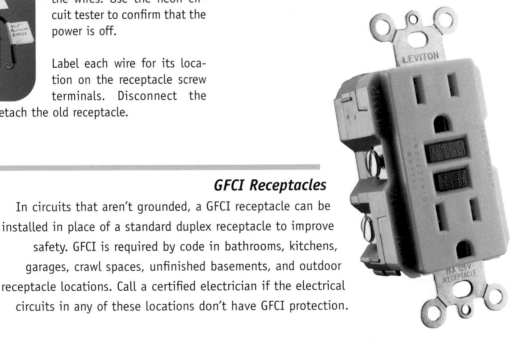

# Wiring Configurations

A 125-volt grounded duplex receptacle can be wired in a number of ways. Common wiring configurations include:

**Middle-of-run wiring:** Two cables enter the box. The black hot wires are attached to the brass screw terminals, and the white neutral wires are connected to the silver screw terminals. The grounding wires are pigtailed to the grounding screw on the receptacle and to the grounding screw on the metal box, if present.

**End-of-run wiring:** One cable enters the box. The black hot wire is attached to a brass screw terminal, and the white neutral wire is connected to a silver screw terminal. The grounding wire is pigtailed to the grounding screw on the receptacle and to the grounding screw on the metal box, if present.

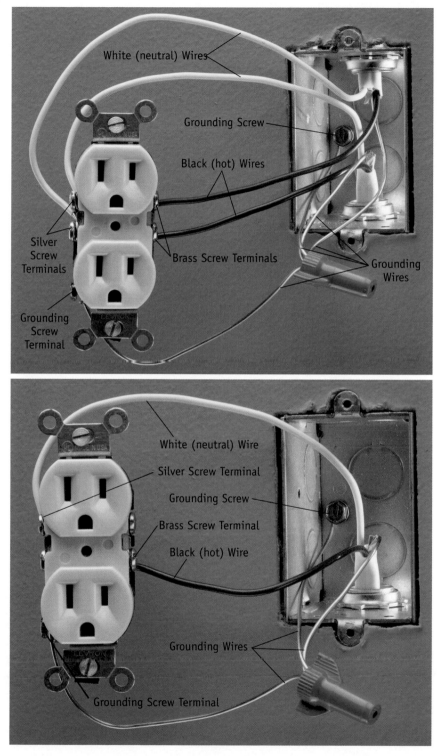

White (neutral) Wires

Grounding Screw

Black (hot) Wires

Silver Screw Terminals

Brass Screw Terminals

Grounding Wires

Grounding Screw Terminal

White (neutral) Wire

Silver Screw Terminal

Grounding Screw

Brass Screw Terminal

Black (hot) Wire

Grounding Wires

Grounding Screw Terminal

**Silver Screw Terminal**

**Connecting Tab Intact**

**Grounding Screw Terminal**

**White (neutral) Wire**

**Grounding Screw**

**Brass Screw Terminal**

**Black (hot) Wire**

**Connecting Tab Removed**

**Red (hot) Wire**

**Grounding Wires**

**Single cable entering the box indicates end-of-run wiring**

**Brass Screw Terminal**

**Black (hot) Wires**

**Silver Screw Terminal**

**White (neutral) Wires**

**Two cables entering the box indicates middle-of-run wiring**

**Split-circuit receptacle:** Each half of the receptacle is wired to a separate circuit, so it can accommodate two high-wattage appliances without overloading the circuit. The hot wires (black and red) are attached to the brass screw terminals, and the connecting tab or fin between the brass terminals is removed. The white wire is attached to a silver screw terminal, and the connecting tab on the neutral side remains intact. The grounding wires are pigtailed to the grounding screw on the receptacle and to the grounding screw on the metal box, if present.

**Two-slot receptacle:** Often found in older homes, these receptacles have no grounding wire attached to the receptacle. The black hot wires are connected to the brass screw terminals, and the white neutral wires are pigtailed to a silver screw terminal.

Two-slot receptacles may be replaced with grounded duplex receptacles, but only if a means of grounding exists at the receptacle box.

**Consult an electrician** if you need to install a grounded duplex receptacle where there is no grounding or if you want to replace a two-slot ungrounded receptacle with a receptacle of another type.

## Switches

Since the average light switch is turned on and off more than 1,000 times a year, it's not surprising that the wire connections tend to loosen and the parts tend to wear out. What is surprising is that it doesn't happen more often.

A typical wall switch has a movable metal arm that opens and closes the electrical circuit. Problems can occur if the screw terminals aren't tight or if the metal arm inside the switch wears out. If a fuse blows or a circuit breaker trips when the switch is turned to the ON position, a loose wire may be touching the metal box. Other symptoms of this kind of problem include overheating or buzzing in the switch box.

The methods for repairing or replacing a switch vary slightly, depending on the switch type and its location along an electrical circuit. Individual switch styles may vary from manufacturer to manufacturer, but the basic switch types are universal.

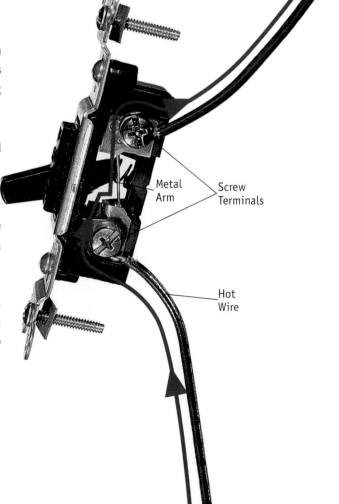

Metal Arm

Screw Terminals

Hot Wire

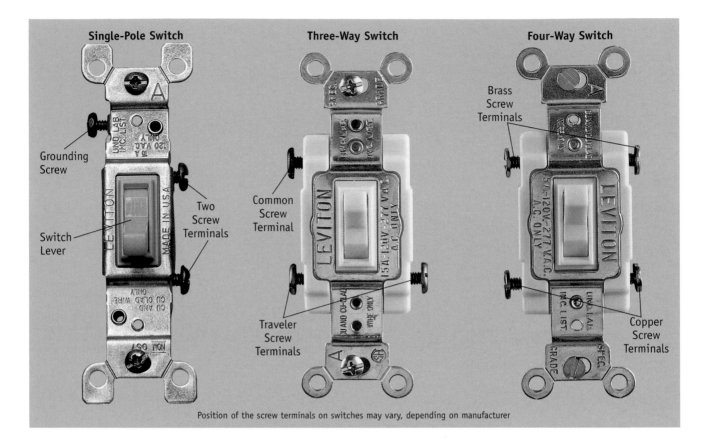

**Single-Pole Switch**

Grounding Screw

Switch Lever

Two Screw Terminals

**Three-Way Switch**

Common Screw Terminal

Traveler Screw Terminals

**Four-Way Switch**

Brass Screw Terminals

Copper Screw Terminals

Position of the screw terminals on switches may vary, depending on manufacturer

There are three kinds of wall switches: **Single-pole switches** control lights from one location. **Three-way switches** control lights from two locations. **Four-way switches**, combined with a pair of three-way switches, control lights from three or more locations. Identifying these switches is easy: count the number of screw terminals.

A **single-pole switch**, the most common type of wall switch, has two screw terminals and a grounding screw. These switches are used to control lights, appliances, and receptacles. The switch lever usually has ON/OFF markings.

A **three-way switch** has three screw terminals. The dark screw is the common screw terminal, to which connects the hot wire in the circuit. The two lighter-colored screw terminals are the traveler screw terminals. The traveler

terminals are interchangeable, so there's no need to label the wires connected to them. Three-way switches are always installed in pairs and are used to control a set of lights from two locations. The levers do not have ON/OFF markings.

A **four-way switch** has four screw terminals paired by color, typically copper and brass. In a typical installation, two pairs of color-matched wires are connected to the four screw terminals, matching the wires to the screw terminals by color. For example, if you connect a red wire to one of the brass screw terminals, make sure the other red wire is connected to the other brass screw terminal. Four-way switches do not have ON/OFF markings and are always installed between two three-way switches.

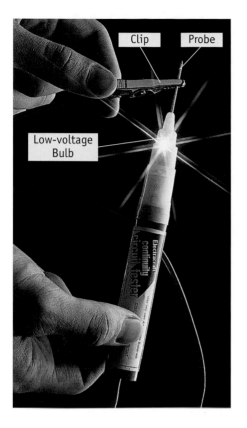

Clip | Probe

Low-voltage Bulb

**Single-pole switches:** Attach the clip to one of the screw terminals, then touch the probe to the other terminal. If the switch is good, the tester will glow when the switch lever is in ON, but not glow when in OFF.

**Three-way switches:** Attach the clip to the dark common screw terminal, then touch the probe to one of the traveler terminals. The tester should glow when the switch lever is in one position, but not both. Touch the probe to the other traveler screw terminal. The tester should glow only when the switch lever is in the position opposite from the positive test on

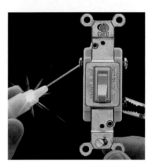

the first traveler screw terminal. Because three-way switches are installed in pairs, you should inspect both switches to find the source of the problem.

## Testing Switches

Troubleshooting problems with switches requires a continuity tester, which detects any break in the metal pathway in the switch. Before each use, always test the continuity tester by attaching the clip to the metal probe. If the tester doesn't light up to signal a connection, the battery or the bulb needs to be replaced.

If the continuity tester shows a switch to be faulty, replace it with a new switch.

Some specialty switches, like dimmers and electronic switches, can't be tested for continuity.

**Four-way switches:** Touch the probe and clip to each pair of screw terminals. (A-B, C-D, A-D, B-C, A-C, B-D). The test should show continuous pathways between two pairs of screw terminals. Flip the switch lever to the opposite position, and repeat the test. Continuous pathways should exist between different pairs of screw terminals. If the switch is good, the tester will show a total of four continuous pathways between screw terminals—two pathways for each lever position.

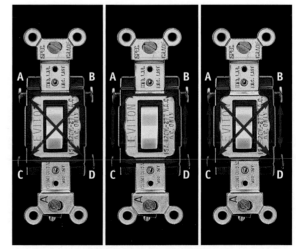

# Repairing & Replacing Switches

If a switch is faulty, replace it with one that has the same number of screw terminals as the old switch. (The location of the screws may vary, but this doesn't affect how a switch works.) The following project shows how to wire a single-pole switch located at the end of a circuit:

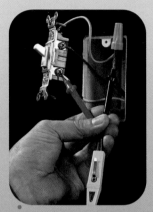

**1.** Turn off the power to the circuit at the service panel. Remove the switch coverplate and the switch mounting screws. Carefully pull the switch from the box; do not touch any bare wires or screw terminals until you've tested for power with a neon circuit tester.

**2.** When you're sure the power is off, disconnect the circuit wires and remove the switch. If the wires are broken or nicked, use a combination tool to clip them off and strip about ³/₄" of wire to expose new copper. If the ends look darkened or dirty, clean them with fine sandpaper.

**3.** Test the switch for continuity (see page 192). If the switch is faulty, replace it.

To reinstall a switch, connect the wires to the screw terminals. Tighten the screws firmly, but don't overtighten them or strip the screw threads.

**4.** Remount the switch, carefully tucking the wires into the box; then reattach the switch coverplate. Restore the power to the switch at the service panel.

## Installing a Dimmer Switch

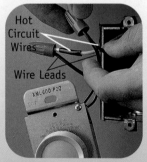

Hot Circuit Wires

Wire Leads

Replacing a regular switch with a dimmer is easy. Shut off the power to the circuit, test and remove the switch, and, if necessary, label the circuit wires (see above). Straighten the circuit wires and clip the ends, leaving about ¹/₂" of bare wire exposed. Using wire connectors, join the wire leads on the dimmer switch with the circuit wires; the switch leads are interchangeable and can be attached to either of the two circuit wires.

A three-way dimmer has an additional wire lead, called a common wire. Attach it to the wire that was attached to the darkest screw terminal.

Common Circuit Wire

Common Lead

## Additional Switch Wiring Configurations

When two cables are running into the electrical box, the switch is located in the middle of the circuit. Each cable has a white and a black circuit wire, as well as a green or a bare-copper grounding wire.

When installing a **single-pole switch**, connect the hot black wire to the screw terminals. Join the neutral white wires together with a wire connector. Pigtail the grounding wires to the grounding screw on the switch.

When it comes to **three-way switches**, the wiring changes slightly. When the switch is located at the end of a circuit, one cable enters the box. However, that cable contains a third circuit wire, color-coded red. Connect the black wire to the common screw terminal, and the white and red wires to the traveler screw terminals. Pigtail the grounding wires to the grounding screw on the switch or to the grounding screw on the metal box, if present.

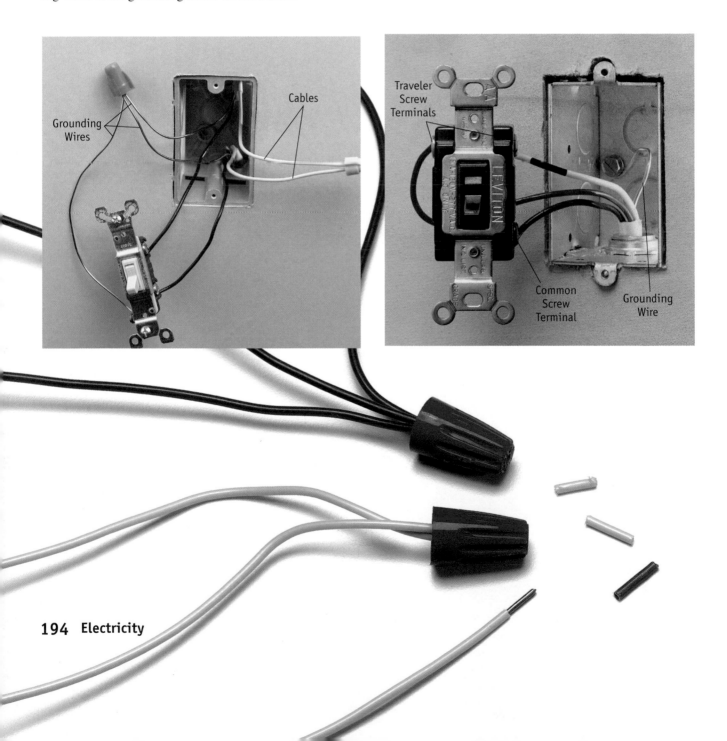

When a **three-way switch is in the middle of a circuit**, one of the cables contains two wires while the other contains three. Connect the black wire from the two-wire cable to the dark common-screw terminal. Connect the red and black wires from the three-wire cable to the traveler screw terminals. Join the white neutral wires together with a wire connector. Pigtail the grounding wires to the grounding screw on the switch or to the grounding screw on the metal box, if present.

**Four-way switches** are always located in the middle of a circuit. Four wires attach to the switch: Connect one pair of same-colored wires to the copper-screw terminals and the other pair of same-colored wires to the brass-screw terminals. Join the third pair of wires with a wire connector. Pigtail the grounding wires to the grounding screw on the switch or to the grounded metal box. Some four-way switches have a wiring guide to help simplify installation.

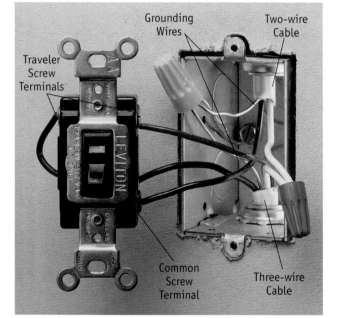

Traveler Screw Terminals

Grounding Wires

Two-wire Cable

Common Screw Terminal

Three-wire Cable

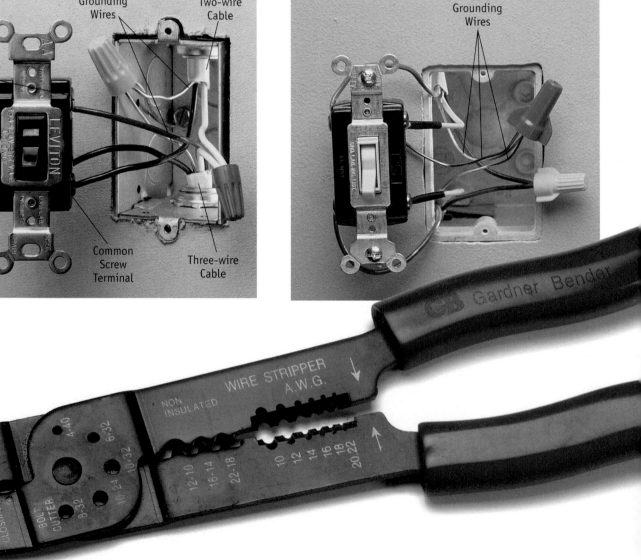

Grounding Wires

# Incandescent Light Fixtures

If a hard-wired light fixture continues to fail even after the bulb has been replaced, and you've determined that the switch isn't the source of the problem (see pages 192 to 195), remove the fixture and test the socket.

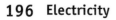 Damage often occurs to light fixtures when lightbulbs that have a wattage that is too high for the fixture are used. Always use a lightbulb with a wattage rating that is the same as or lower than the rating indicated on the fixture.

## Testing a Socket

**1.** Before starting, turn off the power to the circuit at the main service panel. Remove the shade or globe and the lightbulb. Remove the mounting screws that secure the fixture, then carefully pull the base away from the box. Test for power with a neon circuit tester: Touch one probe to the green grounding screw, then insert the other probe into each wire connector. The tester should not glow. If it does, turn off the power to the correct circuit at the service panel.

**2.** Disconnect the fixture base by loosening the screw terminals. (If the fixture has wire leads instead of terminals, remove the fixture base by unscrewing the wire connectors.)

**3.** To test the socket, use a continuity tester. First, attach the tester's clip to the hot terminal (or black lead wire) and touch the probe to the metal tab in the socket. The tester should glow. Next, attach the clip to the neutral terminal (or white lead) and

touch the probe to the threaded portion of the socket (as shown). The tester should glow. If the tester doesn't glow for either test, the fixture is bad and should be replaced. If it does glow, try improving the connection with the bulb by prying up the metal tab slightly and cleaning the threads of the socket with fine sandpaper.

---

Continuity testers rely on batteries to generate current to test the metal pathways running through electrical fixtures or switches. Before using a tester, test it.

Touch the tester clip to the metal probe. The tester should glow. If it doesn't, the battery or lightbulb is dead and needs to be replaced.

---

# Replacing an Incandescent Fixture

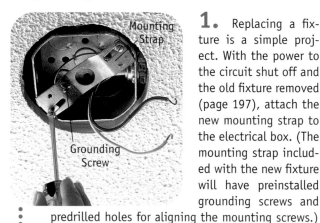

Mounting Strap

Grounding Screw

**1.** Replacing a fixture is a simple project. With the power to the circuit shut off and the old fixture removed (page 197), attach the new mounting strap to the electrical box. (The mounting strap included with the new fixture will have preinstalled grounding screws and predrilled holes for aligning the mounting screws.)

Circuit Wires

Wire Leads

**2.** Use wire connectors to connect the white lead to the white circuit wire and the black lead to the black circuit wire. Also attach the grounding wire to the green grounding screw on the mounting strap. If there is more than one grounding wire, pigtail the wires to the grounding screw (see page 182).

**3.** Attach the new fixture base to the mounting strap, using the provided mounting screws or mounting nut.

**4.** Install a lightbulb with the right wattage rating, then attach the light shade or globe. Finally, restore the power at the service panel.

# Repairing Track Lighting Fixtures

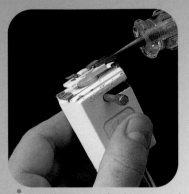

**1.** When a track light fails, first tighten or replace the bulb. If it still doesn't work, clean the contacts. Turn off the power to the circuit at the service panel and use a neon tester to confirm that the power is off. Let the fixture cool, then turn the lever to release the fixture from the track. Use fine sandpaper to clean the track contacts, then bend them up slightly with a screwdriver (as shown).

Remove the bulb. Scrape any corrosion you find on the socket contact tab. Pry it up slightly to improve its contact with the bulb. Screw the bulb back in, replace the fixture in the track, and restore the power.

Fixture Stem

**2.** If the bulb still doesn't light, turn off the power to the circuit and remove the fixture again. Let it cool then test the socket. Loosen the screws on the fixture stem and take the stem apart. Also unscrew the socket from the shade and remove the socket from its mounting. Attach the clip of a continuity tester to the brass track contact and touch the probe to the black wire connection at the socket terminal. Then, attach the clip to the silver track contact and touch the probe to the white wire connection. The tester should light in both tests. If it doesn't, replace the socket.

**3.** To replace the socket, loosen the terminal screws and remove the old wires from the contact pins, then pull the old socket and wires from the shade. If the wires are held in an insulating sleeve, reuse it with the new socket wires.

**4.** Thread the new socket wires through the hole in the shade and both parts of the stem. Strip ¼" of insulation from the wire ends; twist each end so the strands are tight, feed it into a ring connector, and crimp the connector with a combination tool. Attach the black wire to the brass contact pin and the white wire to the silver contact pin, and tighten the terminal screws. Finally, reassemble the fixture, replace it in the track, and restore the power.

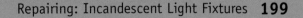

# Fluorescent Light Fixtures

Fluorescent fixtures are relatively trouble free, and the tubes typically last about three years.

Flickering, partial lighting, and discolored ends are all signs that a tube needs to be replaced.

**1.** First, rotate the tube to make sure it is seated properly in the sockets. If that doesn't work, turn off the power to the fixture at the service panel and test to confirm that the power is off. Rotate the tube a quarter turn in either direction and slide it out of the sockets.

**2.** Insert the new tube so that the pins slide fully into the sockets, then twist it a quarter turn in either direction until it's securely locked. Reattach the diffuser cover and restore the power.

Older fluorescent fixtures may have a small cylindrical device, called a **starter**, near one of the sockets. When you replace the tube, also replace the starter. Push it slightly and turn it counterclockwise to remove it.

Fluorescent fixtures are generally inexpensive. Rather than repair a fixture that hums, has chipped sockets, or has a noticeable black substance around the ballast, replace it with a new one.

⚠ Fluorescent tubes contain a small amount of mercury. Never break them, and contact your local environmental agency for disposal instructions.

## Replacing a Fluorescent Fixture

**1.** Turn off the power to the circuit at the service panel. Remove the diffuser, tubes, and coverplate. Test for power using a neon circuit tester: Touch one probe to the grounding screw and insert the other probe into each connector. The tester should not glow.

**2.** Disconnect all the circuit and grounding wires. Loosen the cable clamp that holds the circuit wires. Unscrew the fixture from the wall or ceiling and carefully remove it. Take care to support the fixture as it comes loose.

Cable Clamp

**3.** Position the new fixture, threading the circuit wires through the knockout opening in the back. Screw the fixture in place so it's firmly anchored to the framing members. Following the wiring diagram included with the new fixture, connect the circuit wires to the fixture wires using wire connectors. Tighten the cable clamp that holds the circuit wires. Finally, attach the new coverplate, install tubes, and attach the diffuser before restoring the power.

# HVAC

*Ah get born keep warm.*

BOB DYLAN

Or as another lyric from *Subterranean Homesick Blues* tells it, "You don't need a weatherman to know which way the wind blows." You do need this chapter, though, to help you understand how your heating, ventilation, and air-conditioning (HVAC) system controls the flow of air and the temperature of your home.

On the following pages, you'll learn how to keep your heating, ventilation, and air conditioning systems in peak condition so that your home is warm in the winter, cool in the summer, and fresh all the time. This chapter will help you get there.

## With this chapter you'll . . .

- Learn how your heating and cooling systems work and when to perform basic maintenance.

- Fine-tune your systems for maximum efficiency.

- Clean your vents, ducts, and appliances to keep your house clean, dry, and mold-free

# HVAC

## THE WAY IT WORKS

A well-maintained heating, ventilation, and air conditioning system—HVAC—controls and maintains the temperature and humidity inside your house, regardless of what the weather may be outside.

HVAC is generally thought of as one system, but it's made up of three parts that work together to make a home comfortable and functional.

**Heating:** In most houses, heating begins at a furnace or boiler, where heat is released from burning fuel and transferred to air or water. The air or water is then circulated through a series of ducts or pipes to registers, radiators, or convectors that warm the individual rooms. Although the appearance and technology of heating systems vary widely, they all operate on a simple principle. Heat is generated at a central source and is dispersed to to your rooms through some medium (air, steam, or water), traveling through a channel (pipes or ducts). At the termination points, registers or radiators release the heat into living spaces. Return lines bring cool air, water, or vapor back to the furnace or boiler for reheating.

An appliance that supplies heat to an air transfer system is called a *furnace*. One that heats water or makes steam is called a *boiler*. Another type of appliance, known as a *heat pump* works as both an air conditioner and a furnace, using refrigerant to direct heat into or out of your home.

Your furnace or boiler may be in the basement, in a closet or utility room, or in the attic. Heat pump units are usually outside the house.

Natural-gas-fired appliances are connected directly to the gas utility pipelines. Natural gas or propane is primarily methane, which burns more cleanly than oil. It's colorless and odorless in its natural state, so utility companies add a distinctive odor to it so you can smell even small leaks.

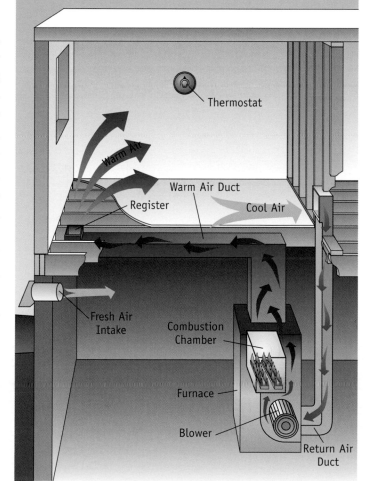

Thermostat

Warm Air

Warm Air Duct

Register

Cool Air

Fresh Air Intake

Combustion Chamber

Furnace

Blower

Return Air Duct

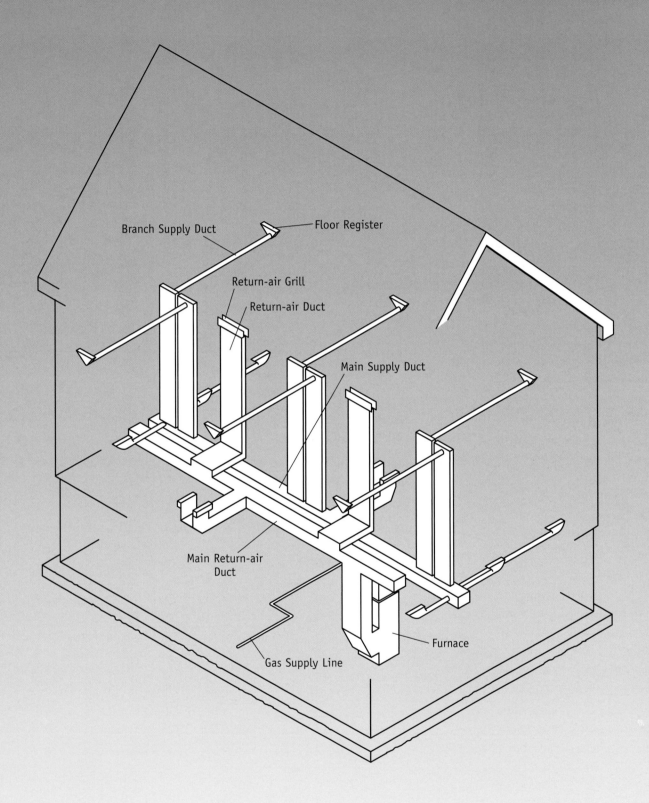

Branch Supply Duct

Floor Register

Return-air Grill

Return-air Duct

Main Supply Duct

Main Return-air Duct

Gas Supply Line

Furnace

Oil- and propane-fired heating systems draw fuel from refillable tanks. The tanks may be in the basement, a crawl space, or outside the house, connected to the boiler or furnace by a pipe. If the tank is inside, it should be at least 7 feet away from the heating appliance.

Electric furnaces cost less to purchase than other furnaces and are cheaper to install, but electricity can cost up to three times as much as other fuels for the same amount of heat. Electric furnaces produce heat cleanly because there is no combustion in the unit. Compared to oil- and gas-burning furnaces, they're nearly maintenance free.

**Ventilation** introduces a supply of fresh air into the house and can help regulate both temperature and humidity. Without proper ventilation, the air in a house can get stale, mold can develop, and gases such as radon and carbon monoxide can rise to dangerous levels. To provide proper ventilation, local codes usually require exhaust and appliance ventilation. In new construction, many local codes also require a heat exchanger.

Electric exhaust vents in bathrooms and kitchens carry moisture and airborne grease directly outdoors. Experts estimate that not using a kitchen exhaust fan spreads up to six quarts of grease throughout your home in just one year. Unventilated bathrooms retain so much moisture that mold can develop on the walls and ceilings—an unhealthy situation, to be sure.

In some older homes, vent fans exhaust into the attic, a serious problem that should be corrected immediately.

Self-circulating kitchen fans are virtually useless; they should be replaced with fans that vent to the outdoors.

All fuel-burning heating appliances, including furnaces and water heaters, need an adequate supply of air for combustion. In newer or tightly sealed homes, furnaces, water heaters, fireplaces, and other fuel-burning appliances must have sealed combustion chambers that draw air directly from the outdoors. In older homes, these appliances can safely draw combustion air from the indoor air around the appliance as long as the immediate spaces around the appliances are open.

**A heat exchanger** uses a blower fan and ductwork to exhaust stale interior air to the outside while, at the same

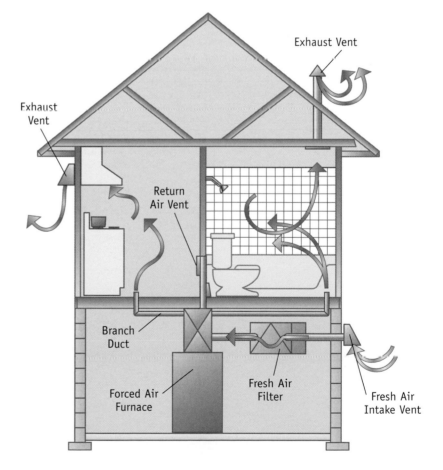

Exhaust Vent

Exhaust Vent

Return Air Vent

Branch Duct

Forced Air Furnace

Fresh Air Filter

Fresh Air Intake Vent

time, drawing in fresh outside air. Two sets of parallel ducts inside the heat exchanger allow the incoming fresh air to absorb the heat of the outgoing moist air. Heat exchangers are also used to reduce radon problems in basements.

**Central air-conditioning units** are, in essence, two-part refrigerators, with a cooling unit (evaporator) installed inside the furnace and a heat transfer unit (condenser) mounted outdoors.

When the thermostat turns the system on, refrigerant flows through a network of copper pipes, picking up heat from air blowing over the evaporator coil located inside the furnace. The refrigerant then flows outside to a compressor where it's forced into a liquid state. A condenser coil then releases the heat from the refrigerant.

Homes with hot-water or steam heating systems and no furnace ductwork can be centrally air conditioned using a ductless system. Instead of ducts, small tubes run between the outdoor condenser and several indoor evaporator units, forming a closed-loop cooling system. The cooling units look like window-mounted air conditioners, but they're much quieter because the compressor is outside.

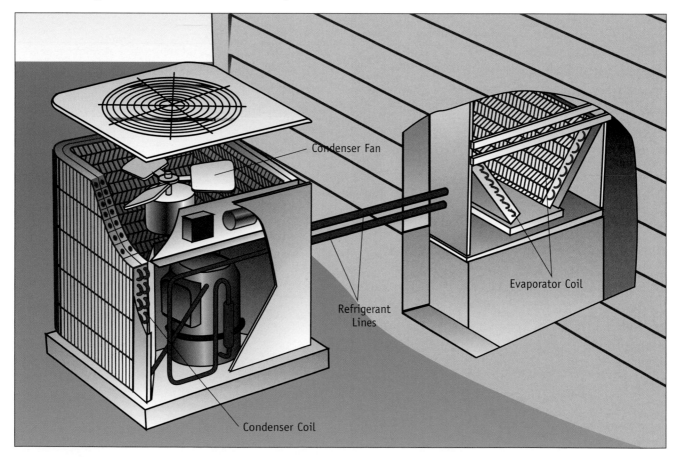

Condenser Fan

Evaporator Coil

Refrigerant Lines

Condenser Coil

# Cleaning & Maintaining

*Cleaning and maintaining an HVAC system is mostly a matter of changing or cleaning filters and keeping ductwork clean. In this section, we'll show you how to balance your dampers from one season to the next, too.*

Before we discuss cleaning and maintenance, there are some important healthy and safety issues to consider when it comes to your HVAC system.

**Asbestos:** Until the 1970s, asbestos was used in many ways throughout a home—in insulation, drywall joint compound, resilient floor tiles, and soundproofing materials, to name a few. Many older HVAC systems have asbestos insulation on steam pipes, boilers, or furnace ducts. Door gaskets on older furnaces, wood stoves, and coal stoves may contain asbestos, as may artificial ashes and embers in older gas fireplaces.

The mere presence of asbestos isn't dangerous. As long as it's left completely alone, asbestos won't harm you. When disturbed, it can release microscopic fibers that cause skin irritation or respiratory problems, including lung cancer. Don't touch or handle materials containing asbestos. If the material has been disturbed or appears to be loose or crumbling, consult a specialist. You'll find them listed in the phone book under "asbestos abatement."

**Pollens, viruses, bacteria, and other respiratory and skin irritants** may not seem related to heating and cooling systems, but some types of microorganisms grow in areas that are poorly ventilated or insulated. Maintaining your HVAC system reduces your family's exposure to these irritants.

**Carbon monoxide (CO)**, a by-product of combustion, is a common health hazard. CO poisoning can be fatal. Leaks in exhaust flues, chimneys, gas ranges, woodstoves, and fireplaces are potential sources of CO. Protect yourself and your family: Keep an eye out for potential problems and have your furnace or boiler inspected every two years.

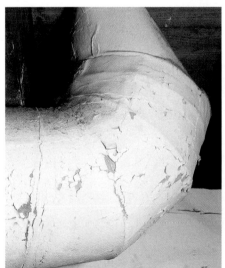

⚠️ 📱 **Damaged asbestos insulation** on ductwork (left) should be inspected and remedied by a certified asbestos abatement specialist. Do not touch or disturb damaged asbestos insulation.

# Forced Air

The most common method of home heating is what's known as "forced air." In this system, air is warmed by a furnace and is then blown, or forced, into ducts that carry it throughout the house.

**Filters:** On its way into the furnace, air passes through filters designed to trap dust, pollen, and other airborne particles that would otherwise be recirculated by the system. These filters need to be cleaned or replaced according to the manufacturer's specifications and should be inspected once a month. Check the manufacturer's recommendations for specific instructions.

**Drain tubes and condensate traps:** Condensation is removed from the system through drain lines or removable condensate traps. It's important to keep these lines or traps functioning properly—if not, moisture can build up inside the heat exchanger and restrict the flow of gas.

Clean the drain line once a year by disconnecting it from the furnace and running water from a garden hose through the line to flush it out. If the drain line is black plastic, remove it at a connection point, then reattach it when it's clean. If the line is white (meaning it's made of PVC), you'll need to reconnect it to the unit with a coupling.

If your system has a condensate trap, clean it out at the beginning of the winter season. Just remove the trap and flush it with water. Check the trap throughout the heating season and dump the water as necessary.

## Changing Furnace Filters

**1.** To change the filters, find the filter compartment and take off the access cover. Its location depends on the type of furnace and the style of filter. Many styles fit into a slot between the return air duct and the blower; a few are found inside the main furnace compartment; electrostatic filters are installed in a separate unit attached to the furnace.

**2a.** **Standard filters:** Slide the filter out of its compartment, taking care not to catch it on the sides of the blower housing. Hold the filter up to a light. If it appears dirty or blocks the light, replace it with a new one.

**2b.** **Electrostatic filters:** Wash the filters with cool water and a soft scrub brush or run them through a light, gentle cycle in the dishwasher. Do not use the dry cycle. Let the filter air dry, then return it to its compartment.

## *Forced Air* (continued)

**Vent pipes:** Check the vent pipes and furnace unit for signs of corrosion. The condensation produced by the furnace is very acidic and will corrode metal quickly. If any pipes are leaking, don't try to seal them—they have to be replaced.

**Air intake:** Make sure the areas around the air intake and exhaust are free and clear. If anything—plants, bushes, snow, leaves, or other debris—blocks the intake and exhaust, the furnace will shut down. Remove anything that could reduce the airflow, and keep the area clear throughout the season.

Many systems have air intakes that run inside the house—a large aluminum tube connected to a metal flue in the existing chimney. These tubes need to be clear. Make sure they're connected properly and not obstructed.

**Humidifiers:** Furnace humidifiers, attached to the furnace's warm-air or return-air duct, increase the humidity inside your home. When well maintained, they make your home more comfortable, but they can spread mold spores and other unpleasant things if they're not kept clean (see page 211).

If your furnace has a drum-style humidifier, clean the evaporator pad monthly and replace it at the end of each heating system. For a drip-style humidifier, inspect the humidifier monthly and replace the evaporator pad at the end of every heating season (see page 211).

## Maintaining a Drum-style Humidifier

**1.** Shut off the power to the furnace at the service panel and turn off the water at the supply valve. Loosen the nuts or release the clips that hold the humidifier cover in place. Remove the cover and lift out the drum by holding both ends.

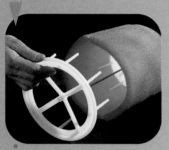

**2.** To separate the pad from the drum shaft, remove the clip on the center spindle and pull apart the two pieces of the drum shaft. Soak the pad in a 3:1 mixture of white vinegar and water for about an hour, then rinse and wring it out. If it's still hard or appears damaged, get a new one. Install the clean or new pad and replace the drum.

**3.** Restore power and water to the system. Measure the depth of the water and compare that to the manufacturer's recommendations. If the owner's manual isn't available, check the side of the tray wall for a line that shows where the water level generally sits. If you're not sure, run the humidifier and make sure the pad dips into the water and comes up wet during each rotation.

To adjust the water level either up or down, loosen the screw on the float mount. To raise the water level, raise the float height and then retighten the screw. To lower the level, lower the float, then retighten the screw. Wait 30 minutes and check the water level and evaporator pad again.

**4.** If water leaks from the supply tube fitting, tighten the nut with an open-end wrench.

## Maintaining a Drip-style Humidifier

**1.** Shut off the power to the furnace and turn off the water supply. Slide your finger under the plastic water outlet and lift up to pop off the outlet. Remove the distribution tray from the assembly by pushing down on the tray while pushing out on the plastic frame.

**2.** Use a chisel to scrape out any mineral deposits from the V-shaped notches on the tray.

**3.** Slide the evaporator pad from the frame. Twist and flex the pad to loosen any deposits, then use a putty knife to scrape them away. If the pad itself crumbles, replace it.

**4.** Disconnect the drain hose. Flex it, then flush it with cold water. Reassemble the humidifier and reattach the drain hose. Restore the power and the water supply.

# Balancing a Forced-Air System

Most forced-air systems have dampers within the ducts that let you control how much air flows to various parts of the house. They are separate from the registers used to manage airflow within each room. Adjusting the dampers one at a time ensures that rooms farthest from the furnace receive enough warm air and that rooms closest to the furnace don't get too hot. This is called "balancing" the system.

Balancing a forced-air system is relatively easy, but it takes time—often several days—to fine-tune your adjustments. Start at the furnace and follow the ductwork until you locate the dampers. When a damper handle or wing nut is parallel to the duct, it's wide open, which allows maximum airflow. When the handle is perpendicular to the duct, it's closed, which restricts airflow as much as possible. If your system doesn't have dampers or needs more dampers than it has, consult an HVAC specialist about adding them.

To balance the system, set the thermostat at a comfortable temperature. Close the dampers that lead to the room with the thermostat. Wait a few hours, and go to the rooms that are farthest from the furnace. If those rooms are too warm, leave them until later, when more dampers are open; if they're too cold, ask an HVAC

professional to increase the blower speed on the furnace. Check the other rooms for comfort and adjust dampers accordingly. After each damper adjustment, wait a few hours for the air temperature to stabilize.

Once you're satisfied with the amount of air and heat each room receives, use a permanent marker on each duct to indicate the correct setting for each damper. Repeat the process in the summer for air conditioning and make a second set of marks to indicate the correct damper settings for cooling.

# Electric Baseboard Heaters

Baseboard heaters are clean and efficient, but fairly expensive to operate. In severe climates, they're typically used to provide supplemental heat in rooms that don't stay warm for some reason. Most heater units are wired to a 240-volt circuit, which means both black and white wires are "hot" and carry voltage. Other baseboard heaters run on 120 volts and are wired directly to a circuit or plugged into a standard receptacle.

Baseboard heater fins often get clogged with dust and debris, which restrict air flow through the fins and decrease the heater's output. To clean the fins, first unplug the unit if it's plugged into a receptacle, or shut off the power to the circuit at the service panel. Let the heater cool down.

## Cleaning a Baseboard Heater

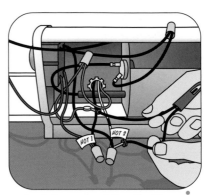

**1.** If the heater is hard-wired, remove the control box cover and use a neon circuit tester to make sure the power is off. Insert one probe of the circuit tester into the wire connector of the black "hot" wire, and touch the other probe to the grounding screw on the heater casing. If the heater is wired to a 240 volts, also insert the tester probe into the white "hot" wire connector and touch the other probe to the grounding screw. Finally, insert a probe into each of the "hot" circuit wire connectors. If the tester glows for any of the tests, the power is still on. Return to the service panel and shut off the correct circuit.

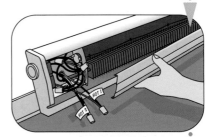

**2.** Remove the front panel from the baseboard heater.

**3.** Use a vacuum cleaner and a nozzle attachment or a dry rag and a dry, soft-bristle brush to clean dust and dirt from the element.

**4.** Use a needlenose pliers to straighten badly bent fins. Don't worry if some are slightly bent; it won't effect the heater's operation.

# Hot-Water Systems

Hot-water and steam-heat systems, also known as *hydronic* systems, rely on a boiler-type furnace that typically burns natural gas or oil and delivers hot water or steam to room radiators or convectors.

To keep hot-water systems operating quietly and efficiently, release any trapped air by bleeding them once a year. During the heating season, bleed individual radiators or convectors again if they stay cold when the boiler is running.

## Cleaning & Painting Radiators

To clean radiators, use a vacuum to pick up the heavy dust and, if necessary, a dust wand to clean the hard-to-reach areas between the fins. Then simply wipe down the radiator with warm water and a little detergent.

If you plan to paint a radiator, first turn off the heat to the unit by closing its valve and let it cool down for at least 24 hours.

Lightly sand the radiator and wipe away the dust with a damp cloth or sponge. Allow the unit to dry thoroughly, then prime any bare areas with a metal primer. (Primer protects the radiator from rust and helps the paint hold.)

Most latex interior paints are safe to use on radiators, although there are also specialty radiator paints available. Start with the interior surfaces and work your way to the outer surfaces. A bendable paint tool makes this job easier; it can be shaped to fit the fins of the radiator.

Once the radiator is painted, let it dry fully before turning the radiator on again. You'll probably notice a paint smell when the radiator heats up. This is normal and will go away quickly.

# F.A.Q.

**Q** *I'm planning to paint my radiators and want them to blend into the room. Does it matter what color I use?*

**A** Believe it or not, the color you choose to paint a radiator will affect its heat output. Dark colors, especially black, absorb and radiate more heat than lighter colors. Before settling on a paint color, get a sense for how well the radiator heats the room. If adjusting the radiator doesn't change it's performance, choose your paint colors accordingly: dark colors to enhance heat output, light colors to decrease it.

By the way—another way to greatly increase the amount of heat radiated back into a room is to install a piece of reflective aluminum or sheet metal behind each radiator.

## Bleeding Hot-Water Radiator Systems

With the boiler running, start with the radiator that's highest in the house and farthest from the boiler. Place a cloth under the bleed valve and open the valve

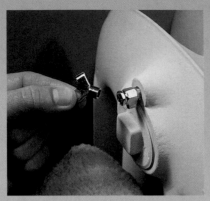

slowly. Close the valve as soon as water squirts out. Some bleed valves have knobs, which open with a half turn; others must be opened with a screwdriver or valve key, available at hardware stores.

Steam radiators have automatic bleed valves. To clear a clogged bleed valve, close the shutoff valve at the radiator and let the unit cool. Unscrew the bleed valve and clear the valve orifice with a fine wire or needle.

## Bleeding Hot-Water Convector Systems

Older convector systems may have bleed valves on or near the convectors. Bleed these convectors as you would radiators.

Most modern convector systems don't have bleed valves, but you can bleed the entire system by attaching a hose at the boiler.

Locate the hose bib where the return water line reaches the boiler. Close the gate valve between the bib and the boiler. Attach a short section of hose to the bib and put the end in

a bucket of water. Open the valve on the bib while adding water to the boiler. Add water by opening the supply valve (located on the supply pipe, usually the smallest

pipe in the system). Flush the system until no air bubbles come out of the hose in the bucket. Open the gate valve to bleed any remaining air. Close the hose bib before restarting the boiler.

# *Fireplaces*

Many homes contain fireplaces or woodstoves—often chosen as much for decorative purposes as for their ability to provide supplemental heat. An annual inspection and cleaning will help these systems run more efficiently and safely. Wood-burning fireplaces should be professionally cleaned at least once a year.

## Inspecting & Cleaning a Wood-burning Fireplace

**1.** Open the flue and look up through it—you should be able to see a shaft of light from above. If the firebox is too small for a clear view, use a bright flashlight and a mirror for the inspection. If the flue is dirty or blocked, have it professionally cleaned.

**2.** Once you know the flue is clear, test the damper lever or chain controls to make sure the damper seals tightly. (The damper helps control the draft—how fast air goes up the chimney—and determines the rate at which the fire burns.)

**3.** If the damper doesn't open or close completely, open it as far as you can and clear the area around its edges on all sides with a stiff-bristle brush (an old toilet brush will do). Also scrub the firebox, then use a wet-dry vacuum to clean up all the debris within the firebox.

# Maintaining a Gas Fireplace

Inspect your gas fireplace before each burning season. Check to see whether there has been any change in the flame's shape or color or whether soot has formed on the logs or windows. If so, contact your gas supplier to find out if the gas composition has changed.

**1.** Before doing any maintenance work, turn off the gas and electrical power and let the unit cool down.

Remove any logs or stones and the burner. Take them outside and clean them with a soft-bristle nylon brush. Next, scrub the firebox and vacuum out the dust.

Turn off the pilot light, then use a dry cloth to clean the pilot nozzle and burner assembly. Then turn on the pilot light and make sure it burns properly.

**2.** Inspect the vents to make sure they're clear and placed properly. Some fireplaces have more than one vent inside the firebox—one at the top and one at the base. If your fireplace has an external vent, make sure it is clean and clear.

**3.** Finally, clean the viewing glass using a nonammonia household cleaner and warm water. Replace the logs, stones, and burner in their exact locations. Restore the power and the gas, and turn on the flame—make sure the fire burns properly and that you don't smell any gas.

Properly adjusted gas fireplaces have blue flames with yellowish tips and don't produce any soot.

If your flames don't match that description, adjust the primary air shutter, usually located on the control panel. If the flames still don't look right, consult a specialist.

# Ventilation

In addition to drawing fresh air into your home, good ventilation keeps air circulating and moves exhaust gases from appliances to the outside. Keeping each element of your home's ventilation system working smoothly can improve your health, reduce heating and cooling costs, and enhance the comfort of your home.

Always shut off the power to any fan or unit at the main service panel before performing any maintenance work.

**Ceiling fans:** Wobbling fan blades reduce the fixture's efficiency. To balance them, tighten all the screws that secure the blades and blade brackets to the fixture.

Next, check the blade angle by measuring each blade's distance from the ceiling. To make adjustments, gently bend the blade bracket until the misaligned blade is the same distance from the ceiling as the other blades.

If the wobble remains, place counterweights on the blades. Purchase a blade balancing kit at a hardware store or home center, and follow the kit manufacturer's instructions.

**Exhaust fans:** Exhaust fans last longer if the filter is kept clean. Remove the grill and filter, and clean the filter with lots of warm water and liquid detergent. Also wipe down the fan blades, if necessary. If the fan or motor is damaged or worn out, have it replaced.

**HEPA air filters:** High efficiency particulate air (HEPA) filters are an excellent, though expensive, way to maintain indoor air quality. Very little maintenance is required. Periodically vacuum the outside screens and change the

filter according to the manufacturer's specifications— every three to five years is common.

✔ You can stay comfortable while using less heat and air conditioning if you make full use of your ceiling fan. In the summer, set the fan to draw warm air up. In the winter, set the fan to force warm air down. You'll save 4 to 8 percent on cooling costs for every degree you raise the thermostat in hot weather, and 1 to 2 percent for every degree you lower the thermostat in cold weather.

**Air-to-air exchangers:** An air-to-air exchanger supplies fresh air with minimal heat loss. It can eliminate many of the airborne irritants and pollutants common in superinsulated homes. These units require little maintenance.

Clean the air filter every one to three months. Some filters are disposable and can simply be replaced, while most new units have washable fil-

ters that can be cleaned with mild soap and water. Let the filters dry before reinstallation.

Clean the heat exchanger core, sometimes called the "heat recovery core," once a year. Remove the heat exchanger by sliding out the metal rods that hold the top plate in place.

Clean the plates in the exchanger with cool water and mild detergent, then rinse thoroughly with clear water. (Hot water and strong

detergent can damage some heat exchangers.) Once the plates are dry, reinstall them.

If there is a condenser tray, empty it periodically and clean it out with mild soap and water. Several times a year, make sure the air intake screen on the exterior of the house is clean and free of debris. In cold weather, make sure ice doesn't form on the screen.

## Ventilation *(continued)*

**CO detectors:** Carbon monoxide (CO) is one of the most commonly encountered and deadly poisons found in homes—and the most preventable. Electronic CO detectors take samples on a recurring basis and alert you when CO content changes or rises to dangerous levels.

Test CO detectors at least once a month, following the manufacturer's instructions. Replace CO detectors and batteries according to the manufacturer's instructions (usually every five years). Also make sure detectors are not covered by draperies or obstructed by furniture. Use CO detectors that are UL (Underwriters Laboratories) approved.

Along with installing plug-in CO detectors (below) on each floor of your house, you can help prevent CO poisoning by having combustion appliances checked annually, by checking chimneys for proper caulking and intact mortar, and by installing automatic door closers between living spaces and attached garages.

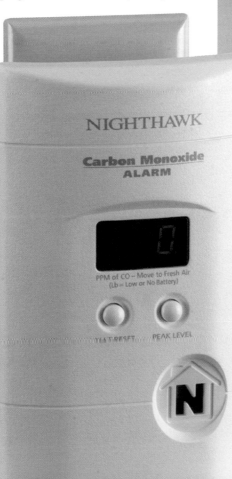

## Testing for Carbon Monoxide

Carbon monoxide test kits can detect lower levels of CO than some of the electronic detectors.

**1.** Snap the sensor button into the hole on the front of the plastic badge.

**2.** Write the date on the badge, then stick it to a hard, flat surface in the test area, away from cleaners, solvents, or direct sunlight. If carbon monoxide is present, the sensor will turn gray or black within 15 minutes. Even if the sensor darkens slightly, it indicates a dangerous amount of carbon monoxide. Contact a certified professional to inspect for CO leaks in your home.

## Roof Ventilation

Roof vents are openings in the attic or in the soffit. They're designed to let moisture and excess heat escape. One common roof vent will ventilate 150 square feet of attic space, 300 square feet if the attic has vapor barriers.

Vents also transfer heat. In the summer, a poorly ventilated roof can cause your room temperatures to rise because hot air gets trapped in the attic. Proper venting can drop attic temperatures by 40°F or more. And in the winter, vents keep the roof cold, which prevents ice dams.

 Inadequate attic ventilation causes all sorts of problems, not the least of which—if you live in a cold climate—is ice dams. If ice builds up at the edges of the roof, it gets pushed up under the shingles where it melts and runs down to the nearest convenient spot, often  a nearby ceiling. The time to resolve attic ventilation problems is *before* your living room ceiling starts leaking.

If you need to add ventilation, consult an expert. Check the phone book under "Roofing," or search the Internet for roofing specialists in your area.

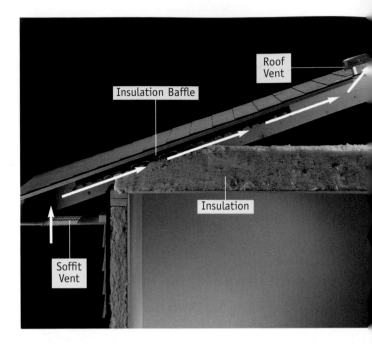

Roof Vent

Insulation Baffle

Insulation

Soffit Vent

# F.A.Q.

**Q** *I understand that roof vents get rid of moisture inside the house, but where does that moisture come from and why do I need to get rid of it?*

**A** Everyday living—showers, cooking, even breathing—releases water vapor into the house. If the roof's not ventilated properly, that vapor condenses into moisture that collects on the attic insulation and roof framing, making the insulation less efficient and eventually rotting the framing lumber, situations you definitely want to avoid.

# Central Air Conditioning & Heat Pumps

Central air conditioners and heat pumps operate on the same basic principles, so most of their maintenance needs are the same. You can do the routine maintenance yourself; however, repairs that involve discharging a capacitor, checking refrigerant levels, and adding refrigerant should be done by a heating and cooling specialist.

Before doing any maintenance work, shut off the power at the unit's disconnect switch and at the main service panel. Then remove the top and side access panels.

## Maintaining a Condensing Unit

**1.** Remove any debris from inside and around the condenser coil, fan, and motor. Remove dirt and debris from the outer fins and coils using a soft-bristle brush and a garden hose.

**2.** Carefully straighten bent fins, using a fin comb. Most fin combs have a number of sides with different tooth widths and spacings. Match the teeth with the fins before you begin.

**3.** Make sure all fan blades are fastened securely and rotate smoothly. If a fan blade is bent, do not try to fix it—have the entire fan assembly replaced.

**4.** A condensing unit must always be level to operate properly. Check the unit for level both lengthwise and widthwise. If the unit isn't level in either direction, you can make slight adjustments if the unit has adjustable feet or by placing wood shims under the feet. If major adjustments are in order, you may need to hire a mudjack professional to repair or replace the slab.

# Room Air Conditioners

Though room air conditioners require little maintenance, regular cleaning can help keep them working efficiently for quite some time. Switch off the power and unplug the unit before cleaning it.

**Clean the filter** once a month during the cooling season. Remove the front access cover, then remove the filter and inspect it. If the filter is damaged, replace it, otherwise wash the filter with a mild deter-  gent, following the directions on the label. Let the filter dry completely before reinstalling it.

With the unit removed from the window or wall sleeve, remove the back panel. Gently **clean the condenser fins**, using the soft brush attachment on a vacuum. Straighten any bent fins, using a fin comb.

The **drain hole** on most room units is located on the outside, with a drain pan usual-  ly found just below the condenser coils. Use a sponge or rag to soak up any water found in the pan. Inspect the drain hole to make sure it's clear and remove any blockage by wiping the area with a clean cloth.

If you can, remove and **wash the drain pan**. Otherwise, flush it with equal parts bleach and water to discourage algae growth.

# Evaporative Chillers

Also known as "evaporative coolers," evaporative chillers are popular in hot, dry regions. Though chiller units are mechanically simple, they require careful maintenance. Check the filters, pads, reservoir, and pump twice a month during the cooling season. Replace the pads once a year—twice a year if you have hard water.

And remember: before doing any maintenance, always switch off the power at the service panel and shut off the water supply to the chiller.

Maintenance starts with draining the reservoir. Attach a garden hose to the drain fitting on the lower edge or bottom of the unit, then unscrew the overflow tube inside the reservoir and

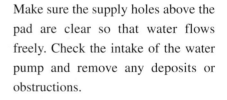

Reservoir

Evaporative Pad

Garden Hose

allow all the water to run out. When done, replace the overflow tube and remove the hose.

Next, use a mild detergent to clean dirt and grease from the fan blades and louvers.

Make sure the supply holes above the pad are clear so that water flows freely. Check the intake of the water pump and remove any deposits or obstructions.

Finally, as you turn the water supply back on, watch the float valve for leaks. If you encounter any problems with the chiller unit, contact a heating and cooling specialist.

# Repairing HVAC Systems— When to call for help

When regular cleaning and maintenance don't solve a problem, it may be time to call in the pros. But how do you know when you've done all you can?

Before contacting a professional, inspect the failing system or appliance to make sure you haven't forgotten anything. The first thing to do is make sure you've restored the power or turned the water supply back on. It sounds obvious, but this gets overlooked all the time.

As you continue with your inspection, begin with the easiest items and work to the more difficult. More often than not, it's the simplest, most obvious things that are at the root of a problem—an unlit pilot light or an improperly installed filter, for example.

Collect as much information as you can to help zero in on the source of the problem. Take notes. You don't have to write down every detail, but jot down anything that looks or sounds suspicious. The more information you have on hand, the easier it will be for an HVAC technician to assess and repair the problem.

Finally, take the time to check the warranties on failing HVAC appliances such as furnaces and air conditioning units. Depending on the terms and conditions of the warranty, repairs on the appliance may be covered, which could save you some serious money.

When it comes to health and safety issues, always contact a certified HVAC specialist:

➤ If you smell natural gas or suspect a gas leak, take immediate action. If the smell is faint, turn off the gas supply at the main supply valve and leave the house. If the smell is strong, leave the house immediately. In either situation, contact your gas company from outside the house.

➤ If material containing asbestos has been disturbed or appears to be loose or crumbling, don't touch or handle the material. Consult an asbestos abatement specialist.

➤ If you find leaks in exhaust flues, chimneys, furnaces, gas ranges, wood stoves, fireplaces, or any other potential carbon monoxide source, have them repaired immediately.

To find certified HVAC specialists in your area, look in the phone book under "HVAC" or "Heating and Cooling."

# appliances

*Machines seem to sense that I am afraid of them. It makes them hostile.*

**SHARYN MCCRUMB**

Modern homes include a wide range of appliances—machines designed to simplify the work of daily living. Sometimes they actually do simplify our lives; sometimes they don't.

If we're afraid of them, appliances can seem hostile, but there's no reason to fear. In this chapter, we'll show you how to keep them in good working order. All you really need is a good measure of preventive maintenance, a dash of knowledge, and a dab of common sense.

Well, that and the phone numbers for good repair people in case of true emergencies.

## With this chapter you'll . . .

- See how your major appliances work.

- Keep your appliances clean so they'll last longer.

- Learn how to perform minor maintenance so your appliances will run safely and efficiently.

# appliances
## THE WAY THEY WORK

Even with all the advances in technology, the basic tasks of running a household haven't changed much in this new millennium. Like generations before us, we store food; prepare, serve, and clean up after meals; clean and dry our clothing. The major difference is that today, appliances do the heavy lifting for us. With the press of a button, a dishwasher or clothes washer fills with water and scrubs our dishes or our clothing. Refrigerators belch forth ice and store our food at constant, safe temperatures.

And what do those appliances require in return for all that convenience? Usually not much more than some tender lov-

ing care—basic cleaning and maintenance. Appliances do break down, of course, but if you're not an expert, it's better to call a service person when major problems arise. You may void your warranty if you attempt repairs on your own.

One repair note: If an appliance stops working, check the main service panel. If a breaker has tripped, reset it. If a fuse has blown, replace it with a fuse of the same amperage. (See page 178 for more.) If the breaker trips or the fuse blows again immediately, call a service person—the appliance may have a short in its wiring.

**Dishwashers:** A standard dishwasher slides into the cabinets and is fastened in place with screws. It easily can be pulled out to be repaired or replaced.

Water comes into the dishwasher through a supply hose and gets pumped up into rotating arms that spray the dishes. When the cycle is finished, the water exits through the drain hose and enters the waste plumbing system at the sink drain, first passing through the garbage disposal, if there is one.

**Clothes washers:** A washing machine includes plumbing, electrical, and mechanical systems. Plumbing pipes deliver and remove water; electrical devices control the switches, timer, and motor; mechanical parts drive the agitator and tub. The chemical action of detergent combined with the physical action of the tub cleans the clothes.

**Clothes dryers:** Standard dryers include a motor, a tumbler, a blower, a timer, and a heating element (electric) or a burner (gas). As the motor drives the tumbler, air enters the dryer through a vent, passing the heating element or burner before being blown into the tumbler. The air is then forced through the lint screen and vented outdoors.

**Refrigerators:** A refrigerator has five basic parts: a compressor, two sets of heat-exchanging coils, an expansion valve, and the refrigerant. Compression raises the temperature and pressure of a refrigerant, such as ammonia. The first set of heat-exchanging coils helps disperse the heat of that pressurization. As the refrigerant cools, it moves through an expansion valve and into the second set of heat exchanging coils, flowing from a high-pressure zone to a low-pressure zone. Under less pressure, the refrigerant expands and evaporates, absorbing heat and cooling the food compartments. Each time the refrigerator kicks on, it's going through this cycle.

**Ranges, ovens, or cooktops:** An electric range, oven, or cooktop is a collection of heating elements controlled by switches, a timer, and a thermostat. Basically, electricity surges through the burners or heating element to bring it to a temperature determined by the thermostat.

A gas range, oven, or cooktop is much the same, except that it's a collection of gas burners lighted by a pilot light, electronic igniter, or electrically heated glow bar.

# Cleaning & Maintaining

*Clean, well-maintained appliances are not only more pleasant to use, they're more energy efficient and longer lasting. No appliance—from a dryer to a refrigerator—can operate efficiently when its coils, air intake, or exhaust is clogged by layers of dust and lint. Even simple parts like water supply hoses for a clothes washer need a little attention now and then, and it's much easier and less expensive to do preventive maintenance than damage control.*

## Dishwashers

Dishwashers are exposed to many sources of germs and bacteria, which can lead them to smell a little funky now and then. Once a year or so, **give your dishwasher a once-over**—clean out the strainer, clean the spray arms, and run an extra cycle with detergent but no dishes.

Begin by shutting off the power to the dishwasher at the service panel. Remove the strainer and wash it out. If necessary, use a soft scrub brush to remove any stubborn residue.

(Note: Removing the strainer will be easier in some models than others. At a minimum, you'll need to take out the dish rack and remove any screws holding the strainer in place. At most, you'll have to remove the spray arm to reach the strainer. Read and follow manufacturer's directions.)

A **leaky dishwasher** usually isn't a complete disaster, but it can become one if you ignore it. The door catch is sometimes the culprit, other times it's the gasket around the door. Check both if you notice water on the floor in front of the machine.

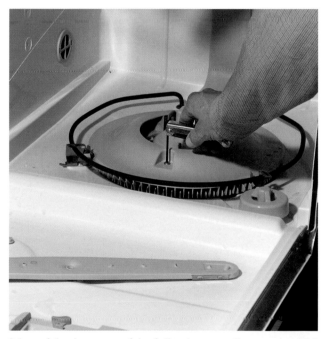

Most of the time, one of the following remedies on page 231 will solve the problem. If not, it's time to call a service person. It's possible that a hose—or even the tank itself—has cracked.

## Cleaning a Dishwasher

**1.** With the power still shut off, remove the dish rack and unscrew the spray tower. Remove the screw holding it in place and lift off the spray arm. Spray arms have tiny holes that can get clogged with minerals from the water as well as with food debris. Cleaning out these holes helps the dishwasher maintain peak efficiency. Use a toothpick, paper clip, or small wire to unclog the holes on both sides of the spray arm. Rinse it off and reassemble all the parts—strainer, spray arm, spray tower, and dish rack.

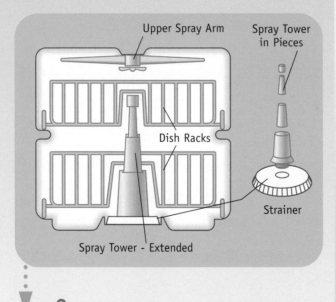

Upper Spray Arm

Spray Tower in Pieces

Dish Racks

Strainer

Spray Tower - Extended

**2.** Turn the power back on. With the dishwasher still empty, add dishwashing detergent and run a cycle.

## Fixing a Leaky Dishwasher

**1.** Start by checking the gasket—the rubber strip running around the inside edge of the door. If it appears to be in good condition, the door catch may need to be adjusted. Loosen the retaining screws, reposition the catch, and retighten the screws.

**2.** If the gasket is damaged, replace it. Shut off power to the dishwasher at the service panel. Pull out the bottom dish rack, and use a screwdriver to pry up the tabs or loosen the retaining screws holding the gasket in place. Take the old gasket to a hardware or appliance store and buy an identical replacement. Have your dishwasher's model number handy, too, in case they need to order the gasket.

**3.** Soak the new gasket in warm soapy water to make it more pliable. Starting at the center of the door, press or slide the gasket into the track. If there are screws or clips, refasten them as you go.

# Clothes Washers

A washer's tub is frequently exposed to water, dirt, bacteria, and chemicals—quite a recipe for unpleasant odors in a closed container. To keep the tub clean and fresh, run an unloaded cycle with hot water, detergent, and bleach once a month. To help top loaders stay clean, leave the lid open when the machine isn't being used.

The rubber gasket that seals the door of a front-loading machine needs to be cleaned periodically. A gentle scrubbing with a nonabrasive cleaner will keep mildew and other buildup at bay.

Flexible hoses at the back of the unit connect the washer to the water supply pipes. Because these hoses are constantly exposed to water pressure, they require attention. Over time they can become brittle and worn and have been known to burst or crack, flooding the laundry area and beyond.

Inspect the hoses every few months and replace them as necessary. Generally, the hoses have threaded connections that you tighten onto the water supply lines and the connections to the washer, but read and follow manufacturer's directions.

A standard load of laundry should dry in about 40 minutes. If your drying times are a lot longer but you know the dryer is heating properly and is vented correctly, check the washer's spin cycle. Fill the washer with water, then set the dial for the final spin. Let the washer spin for 90 seconds, then open the lid to see if all the water has drained out. If not, the drain hose may be clogged or kinked—call a service person for repairs.

Coming home to find a broken hose or overflowing machine and a deluge would be an unpleasant surprise indeed. Make it a habit to finish the laundry before leaving the house.

And just to be safe, turn off the water supply before vacations or other extended absences. Problems are rare, but those hoses are always under pressure from the water supply (whether the machine is running or not), and it's better to be safe than sorry.

# Clothes Dryers

Dryers differ in many ways, but every version combines two things: a heat source and lots of lint. This flammable combination makes maintenance absolutely essential—an unmaintained dryer can be a serious fire hazard.

There may be many versions, but every dryer has a lint collection system and a vent. Clean the lint screen before each load and clean the vent hose and outlet at least once each season.

**To clean the vent outlet**, go outside and make sure that nothing is clogging it. There should be at least 12 inches

between the outlet and the ground or any other obstructions, and it should have a swing-out damper to prevent backdrafts and keep out wildlife.

**Electric dryers:** Remove lint from inside the dryer once a year. First, unplug the dryer or shut off the power to the circuit. Disconnect the exhaust vent at the back and pull the dryer away from the wall. Take off the back panel and carefully use the brush attachment on a vacu-

um cleaner to remove dust and lint from inside the dryer. Clean out the vent hose, then reassemble everything and put the dryer back in place.

 **Cleaning a gas dryer** is a more delicate operation—moving it can rupture a gas line. Instead of doing it yourself, call a service person to clean your dryer once a year.

 Every dryer should be vented to the outdoors. If you find that yours is not, hire a carpenter or contractor to install a vent outlet as soon as possible.

About a gallon of water is dispersed with every load of laundry you dry. Released indoors, that much moisture could cause mildew and other problems.

# *Refrigerators*

Forget dust bunnies. The condenser coils under and on the back of a refrigerator develop dust *buffalos*. And all that dust isn't merely unattractive and unhealthy, it's expensive. The dust actually insulates the coils and makes it difficult for the refrigerator to operate efficiently. **Cleaning the coils** every season saves energy and helps the refrigerator last longer.

**1.** Pull the refrigerator away from the wall and unplug it. Use a brush attachment on a vacuum to remove dust and lint from the coils at the back.

**2.** Remove the panel at the bottom of the refrigerator. (On most units, the panel is held in place by snaps or small screws.) Use a crevice attachment on a vacuum to clean the coils.

**3.** Most refrigerators have a drain pan beneath the coils to catch the water when the compartments defrost. Carefully remove this pan and empty the water, then clean and disinfect the pan before replacing it.

**4.** Clean the floor, then plug in the refrigerator and push it back into place.

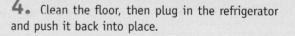

*Once a week, throw away all expired food and wash out the inside of the refrigerator with a solution of baking soda and warm water—about half a cup of baking soda to a gallon of water.*

Refrigerator doors are sealed with rubber gaskets. If those gaskets get brittle or develop cracks, cold air leaks out and the system has to work overtime to keep the compartments cool. **Replacing a gasket** isn't difficult, but it takes planning and a little patience.

Before you take the old gasket off, buy the new one. You really don't want to get the old one off and find out the new one has to be ordered, which is often the case. Locate the model or serial number of your unit and call a parts supplier or appliance dealer to find an exact replacement for the gasket.

**1.** First, soak the new gasket in warm water for half an hour to make it more pliable.

**2.** Unplug the refrigerator. Working on one side of the door at a time, pry up the edge of the gasket and remove the screws that hold the retaining strip in place. Pull the gasket from the door.

**3.** Align a new section of gasket on one side. Insert the retaining strip, replace the screws, and partially tighten them.

**4.** Replace the gasket on the three remaining sides, then check the door's alignment. Adjust the gasket if necessary, then tighten the screws securely.

# Ovens, Ranges & Cooktops

Wash the cooktop with dishwashing liquid and hot water. For stubborn spills, apply a paste made from baking soda and water. Let the paste sit on the spill for about five minutes, then wipe it away. Rinse the area with a 3:1 solution of water and white vinegar. Run the burner drip pans through the dishwasher.

The self-cleaning feature of modern ovens has almost eliminated the messy job of cleaning the oven. Almost, but not quite. Before running the cycle, remove the racks and wash them by hand. Use a plastic scraper to remove any burned-on deposits, then wipe off the walls and floor of the oven. Follow manufacturer's instructions to lock the door and start the cycle. When the oven has cooled, wipe the walls and floor once again.

Here's an easy way to get burned-on deposits off of oven racks: Put the racks in a large plastic bag, like a garbage bag. Pour some ammonia onto a rag, add the rag to the bag, and seal it. Put the bag outside and let it sit for several hours or overnight. Afterward, wash the racks in hot water—those deposits should come off quite easily.

**Gas cooktops and ovens** are very reliable, but to operate efficiently, they have to be kept clean, with all the burner holes open.

Electric burners and heating elements occasionally burn out, but most are easy to replace. If none of the burners is working, the problem probably is at the service panel (a tripped breaker or blown fuse) rather than with the appliance.

If only one burner is affected, the burner itself is probably to blame. Check to see how the burner is attached to the stove. Most modern burners simply plug in to the stove. In that case, lift the burner, remove the chrome ring, and pull the burner free.

Take the burner to an appliance store and buy an exact replacement. Plug in the new burner, and you should be all set.

Other types of burners are fastened with screws. In this case, call a service person to replace the burner.

When a burner or the oven won't light, check the pilot light—it's probably out. If you're using propane, check the tank—it may need to be refilled. If the pilot light is the culprit, relight it.

You may notice a slight smell of gas as you relight the pilot light. Leave the oven door open and open a window or find other ways to provide ventilation. If the smell is more than slight, shut off the main gas valve right away. Don't use a phone or touch any electrical switches. Call the utility company from outside the house.

# basements

*It was the best place to be, thought Wilbur, this warm, delicious cellar. . . .*

E. B. WHITE

When you think of a basement, is it with the kind of fondness that Wilbur, the pig from E. B. White's classic *Charlotte's Web*, has for the cellar? If not, it's time to take action, and this chapter can help. We'll show you how to keep your basement clean, dry, and in good repair. The rest—the warm and delicious part—is up to you.

## With this chapter you'll . . .

- Learn all about what's holding your house up—the foundation.

- Find out how to grade your yard so your basement stays clean and dry.

- See why the way to keep water out of your basement is to keep leaves out of your gutters.

# basements
## THE WAY THEY WORK

Over 75 percent of all basement wall foundations are built with either poured concrete or concrete blocks. In old or very new homes, however, you may find other materials, each with its own maintenance needs.

**Poured concrete** is the strongest foundation material—a poured concrete foundation has an expected life span of about 200 years. If your basement walls are a solid mass and you can see the texture of the wood or metal forms that shaped the wet concrete, you have a poured concrete foundation. In older homes, some walls that look like solid concrete are actually rubblestone that's been finished with a concrete or mortar topcoat.

The walls and floors of a poured concrete foundation appear to be one unit, but there's a joint between the bottom of the walls and the slab (called an isolation joint) that lets the walls and the slab expand and shift independently. Without this joint the walls or floors could crack or buckle, but it's an easy place for water to get in. If water seeps into a poured concrete basement, this joint is the first thing to check.

**Concrete block** foundations, constructed with large hollow blocks held together by mortar, have a life expectancy of about 100 years. One glance at an exposed basement wall tells you whether you have a concrete block foundation. Cracks in the mortar joints are not serious and can be repaired by packing the joint with new mortar. Cracks in the blocks themselves can be more serious—especially if they are growing—and should be evaluated by professionals.

**Rubblestone and brick** basements are found only in very old residences. Like block, cracks in the mortar are natural but cracks in bricks or stones themselves should be evaluated by a professional.

**Wood** foundations are inexpensive and easy to construct, even during cold weather. If you have a wood foundation, watch for signs or stress of rot.

Most foundations have some sort of protection from soil moisture so it doesn't build up and seep into the house.

**Drain tile** is a common moisture guard in newer homes. Drain tiles are actually perforated pipes that are laid near the footings at the base of the foundation. The area around the tile is filled with gravel, and water filtering down through the soil finds its way into the drain tile, which moves water to a storm sewer or drainage pit.

In many houses, a **sump pump** removes water from the drainage pit. The pump senses water in the pit (called a sump) and automatically turns on. The pump then forces the water up through a pipe, out of the house, and away from the foundation. When the water level gets low enough, the pump shuts off. In some homes, especially older ones, the sump pit is located in a central location. In newer homes, where drain tile below the slab directs water to the sump, the pit is often located in a corner of the basement. In wet regions, sump pumps are required in new construction, but they're not necessary in dry climates.

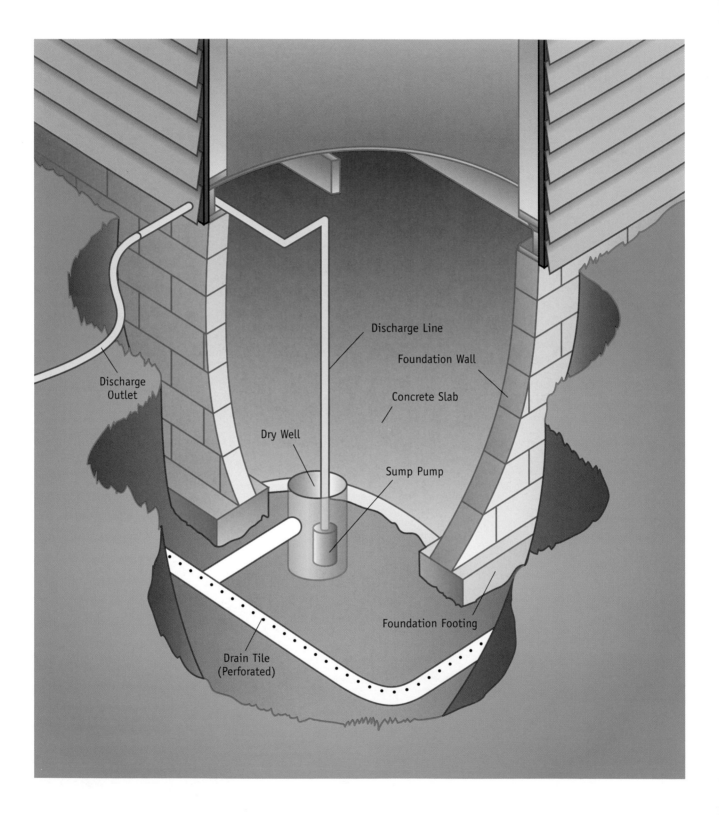

Discharge Line

Foundation Wall

Concrete Slab

Discharge
Outlet

Dry Well

Sump Pump

Foundation Footing

Drain Tile
(Perforated)

# Cleaning & Maintaining

*In many ways, cleaning and maintaining the basement is much like cleaning and maintaining any other part of the house. The major difference is that, since basements are exposed to the surrounding soil, moisture is a constant concern. In fact, whether it's sealing surfaces, filling cracks, or adjusting the soil grade around the house, much of the care of a basement involves the containment or control of moisture.*

## Cleaning Concrete

Plain concrete isn't lovely under most circumstances, but stains make it look unkempt. You can remove most stains with commercial-grade concrete cleaner or one of several consumer products marketed for this purpose. If you use these chemicals, read and follow the directions carefully. Make sure there is adequate ventilation in the area, and wear proper protective equipment such as safety glasses, acid-proof gloves, and a respirator. When diluting the chemicals, slowly pour them into the water rather than adding the water to the chemical, which could cause splashing and splattering.

**Efflorescence,** a powdery crust created by the buildup of mineral salts on masonry surfaces, can be removed with a stiff-bristle brush. Oxalic acid crystals dissolved in water remove iron stains, and smoke stains can be removed with a mixture of ammonia and water.

# *Basement Walls & Floors*

To protect against moisture and help prevent stains, it's a good idea to seal basement walls and floors with a water-proof masonry sealer, concrete coating, or masonry paint.

## Protecting with Sealer

Waterproof masonry sealer helps eliminate moisture from minor seepage. Sealer products are sold in powder form and contain cement. These products must be mixed with water and applied to damp walls.

**1.** To begin, clean the walls with household cleaner and a wire brush. Then rinse thoroughly with clear water and a sponge. Mix the sealer, following the manufacturer's instructions, and apply it to damp walls using a stiff-bristle paintbrush. Make sure to cover the surface—and any mortar joints—completely. After the sealer has dried, apply a second coat.

## Protecting with Concrete Coating

For poured concrete or concrete block walls with an abundance of cracks and fissures, add a layer of concrete coating. Make sure to fill all holes or cracks larger than ⅛ inch before applying the coating (see pages 245 to 246).

**1.** To mix the coating, combine 1 part cement with 2½ parts moist, loose mortar sand. Add water until it resembles a stiff plaster.

**2.** Scrub the walls with a wire brush and rinse them clean with water and a sponge. With the walls still wet, apply a ¼"-thick coat of the mixture with a trowel.

**3.** Allow the coat to dry, then scratch the surface with the teeth on a paint roller cleaning tool. After 24 hours, apply a second coat. After another 24 hours, mist the wall with water twice a day for three days.

## Protecting with Paint

Waterproof masonry paint helps keep minerals in concrete, brick, and block surfaces from leeching through the paint and hardening into a white, dusty film (called efflorescence). Masonry paint is available in stock colors, and can be mixed with a tint base for custom colors.

**1.** As with any paint job, thoroughly prepare the surface. Scrub the wall using a wire brush or a drill with a wire-wheel attachment. Then rinse the walls clean with water and a sponge.

**2.** After the walls have dried, apply masonry primer with a stiff-bristle paint-brush. Allow the primer to dry completely.

**3.** Finally, mix and apply the masonry paint according to the manufacturer's instructions.

# F.A.Q.

**Q** *Help! Every time it rains very much, there's water in my basement. What can I do?*

**A** 95 percent of all wet-basement problems occur because water pools near the foundation. The cause can usually be traced to cracks in foundation walls, failing gutters or downspouts, or an improperly graded yard. Seal any cracks in the walls, repair all gutters and downspouts, and make sure your yard is graded correctly. If that doesn't solve the problem, consult an expert.

## Filling Cracks in Concrete Floors

**A-B1.** To repair cracks of any size, you need to create a good bonding surface for the patching material. Remove loose masonry from the crack using a chisel and wire brush. Clean all dust and debris with a hand vacuum.

**A2.** **For small cracks** (less than 1/4" wide), apply gray-tinted concrete caulk to seal the crack. Smooth it level with the floor using a putty knife.

**B2.** **For larger cracks**, use a cold chisel to create a backward-angled cut (called a "keyhole" cut) that's wider at the base than the surface and no more than 1/2" deep.

**B3.** Apply a thin layer of bonding adhesive, and then fill the crack with a pourable crack filler or fortified patching cement using a trowel.

# Filling Holes in Concrete

The quickest method for **sealing small holes** in concrete is to fill them with gray-tinted latex masonry caulk. If the hole is more than 1" deep, stuff a piece of fiberglass insulation into the hole to provide a base for the caulk.

**Repair larger holes** using latex bonding agent and a concrete patch product. Clean the hole with a wire brush and remove the dirt and debris from the hole with a vacuum. Coat the edges of the hole with latex bonding liquid. Mix the concrete patch following the manufacturer's instructions. Pour the mixture into the hole and smooth it with a flexible knife.

# Filling Cracks in Concrete Walls

Minor, stable cracks in concrete foundation walls can be repaired rather easily, but larger fractures and cracks that continue to expand over time are signs of a major structural problem.

**1.** To determine if a foundation crack is stable, you need to monitor it over the course of several months, particularly over the fall and spring seasons. Draw marks across the crack at various points, noting the length as well as its width at the widest gaps. If the crack moves more than $1/16$", consult a building engineer or foundation specialist.

**2.** To repair a stable crack, use a cold chisel to widen it. Make a keyhole cut (see page 245 for a detailed picture). Cut no more than $1/2$" deep. Clean out the crack with a wire brush. Fill the crack with expanding foam to help seal out moisture.

**3.** Finally, mix hydraulic cement according to the manufacturer's instructions, and apply it to the crack in layers no more than $1/2$" thick. Work from the bottom to the top. The patch should be slightly higher than the surrounding area. Feather the cement with the trowel until it's even with the surface and allow to dry thoroughly.

# Grading

An improper grade can direct water toward, rather than away from, the foundation of your house and can cause water to seep through basement walls. To remedy the problem, you'll need to regrade the soil so that it has a gradual slope away from the house of about ¾" per horizontal foot.

**1.** Drive a pair of stakes into the soil, one at the base of the foundation, and another at least 8 ft. out into the yard in a straight line from the first. Attach a string with a line level to the stakes and adjust the string until it's level. Measure and flag the string with tape at 1-ft. intervals.

Measure down from the string at the flags. Use these measurements as guidelines for adding or removing soil to create a correct grade. Starting at the base of the house, add soil to the low areas until they reach the desired height. Using a garden rake, evenly distribute the soil over a small area. Measure down from the tape markings as you work to make sure that you are creating ¾" per foot pitch.

**2.** Add or remove soil as needed, working away from the house until the soil is evenly sloped. (Topsoil can be purchased from and delivered by a soil contractor.) Use a hand tamp to lightly compact the soil.

**3.** After all the soil is tamped, use a grading rake to remove any rocks or clumps. Starting at the foundation, pull the rake in a straight line down the slope.

**4.** Repeat the process, working on one section at a time until the entire area around the house is graded.

# Downspouts & Gutters

Wet basements can usually be traced to roof gutters and downspouts that are plugged, rusted through, or not diverted away from the house.

## Extending Downspouts

The simplest option for extending downspouts is to attach a new length of downspout pipe to the existing downspout. Cut the new length of downspout pipe with a hacksaw and attach it to the existing downspout with a gutter elbow.

Other accessories include swing-up elbows to allow the outlet pipe to be lifted, roll-up sleeves that fit snugly on the end of the downspout and automatically unroll when the gutters channel water, or splash blocks to help direct runoff water from your house.

## Cleaning Gutters

You should clean gutters and downspouts at least twice a year, so that rain falling on the roof is directed well away from the foundation.

**Use a trowel** to remove leaves, twigs, and other debris.

**Repair any leaks or holes** as soon as possible, and make sure that the water from the downspouts is directed *away from the house.*

**Flush out clogged downspouts** with water. Wrap a large rag around a garden hose and insert it into the top of the downspout opening. Arrange the rag so it fills the opening of the downspout, then turn on the water full force. When the clog breaks up, water will gush out the bottom of the downspout.

You can also clean plugged downspouts with a **drain auger**. To help prevent clogs in the future, install strainers and shield gutters with mesh gutter guards that match the size and style of your gutters.

## Rehanging Gutters

**Gutters should angle toward the downspouts** so water travels freely rather than standing in the gutters, promoting rust. Check the slope of your gutters with a level and adjust the hangers if necessary.

**To rehang sagging gutters**, mark the fascia by snapping a chalk line that follows the correct slope (usually ¼" per 10 ft. toward the downspouts). Remove the hangers near the sag and lift the gutter. Replace the hangers, shifting their locations slightly and making new holes. Add hangers, if necessary, to evenly distribute the gutter's weight.

## Sealing Leaky Metal Gutters

Small leaks and minor damage often can be repaired with easy-to-use gutter repair products. Use **gutter caulk** to fill small holes and seal minor leaks.

To **seal a leaky gutter joint**, disassemble it by removing the screws or drilling out the rivets. Scrub the damaged area with water and a stiff-bristle brush, and allow to dry completely. Apply caulk to the joining surfaces, then reassemble the joint with new fasteners.

**For temporary repairs** to gutters with minor damage, use a gutter patching kit, following the manufacturer's instructions.

## Patching a Metal Gutter

**1.** Clean the area around the hole with a stiff-bristle brush. Scrub it with steel wool or an abrasive pad to loosen residue, then rinse it with water.

**2.** Apply a ⅛"-thick layer of roofing cement evenly over the damage, spreading the roofing cement a few inches beyond the hole on all sides.

**3.** Cut a patch from a piece of flashing. Use the same type of metal (usually aluminum or galvanized steel) as the gutter. Bend the patch to fit inside the gutter, and press it in the roofing cement. Feather out the excess cement so it lies flat and won't cause damming.

# Sump Pumps

There are two basic types of pumps: **pedestal** and **submersible.** A pedestal pump has its pump motor mounted above the sump pit so it won't get wet, while the submersible pump's motor is designed to operate underwater. Basic maintenance is the same for both models.

Test your sump pump prior to the rainy season or every few months if it is used more frequently. Slowly add water to the pit to start the pump. If the motor runs but the water drains slowly or not at all, then the inlet screen may be clogged.

If your power fails often during severe storms—the times when the pump is needed the most—consider installing a battery backup for the sump pump. Pump alarms are also available to alert you if the system fails.

## Servicing a Sump Pump

**1.** Always shut off the power at the breaker box or unplug the pump before working on the unit. Clear any debris you can from the floor of the pit.

**2.** Remove the inlet screen from the sump pump and flush with clear water.

**3.** If the pump motor doesn't start, check the motor reset switch. If that's not the problem, check the float activation switch—move the float up and down to clean dirty switch contacts and to activate the motor.

**4.** If the pump still fails to start, the motor may be worn out, which means the pump will have to be replaced (see page 251).

# Replacing A Sump Pump

If you've cleaned and serviced a sump pump and it still won't start, replace it. Installation is the same for both pedestal and submersible sump pumps.

**1.** Remove the old pump from the sump pit, disconnect the discharge line from the drainpipe, and clean the pit thoroughly. Connect a new discharge line to the discharge outlet on the new sump pump using a compression clamp or the fitting recommended by the pump manufacturer.

**2.** Connect the new discharge line to the drainpipe check valve. For best results, the drainpipe should be the same size as or larger than the discharge line.

(Note: A check valve keeps water from draining back into the pit and typically must be installed within 2 ft. of the pump. If there isn't already a check valve in the discharge line, install one following the valve manufacturer's instructions, or hire a plumber to install the valve.)

**3.** Drill a ⅛" relief hole in the discharge line 2" above the pump discharge outlet but below the check valve and within the sump pump pit. The relief hole allows trapped air to escape to prevent air-locking the pump.

**4.** Place the new pump against the sump pit wall so the float switch faces the center.

**5.** Adjust the float switch as recommended by the manufacturer. Test the pump to make sure it operates properly. Make any necessary adjustments.

# details

*To keep a lamp burning we have to keep putting oil in it.*

**MOTHER TERESA**

Details—such as pest control, proper handling of hazardous materials, and seasonal maintenance routines—are the figurative oil that we put into our homes to keep them burning, or running properly.

Without continual attention, details such as these can become small problems and—eventually—even large ones. But by establishing and adhering to simple, effective routines, you can keep the home fires burning.

## With this chapter you'll . . .

- Stop bugs and small animals from becoming unwelcome houseguests.

- Know exactly when to perform routine maintenance.

- Understand what repair people and contractors are talking about (or at least you'll be able to look it up in the glossary after they leave).

# Pest Control

*While they are annoying and just plain creepy, not all pests pose any real risk to you or your home. In fact, some actually help: ladybugs and ladybird beetles eat the bugs that destroy your plants; lacewings eat a number of destructive bugs, including insect eggs; and spiders eat the bad bugs you don't want around (unfortunately, they eat the good ones, too). Other helpful insects include lightning bugs, dragonflies, and praying mantises.*

However, there are a number of pests that can cause you potentially serious health problems and even compromise the structural integrity of your home. A fungus that grows on bat and bird droppings causes a respiratory disease called histoplasmosis; hantavirus is spread through mouse droppings; and cockroach feces are strongly linked to the rising asthma rates in children. And let's not forget about termites—these charming insects actually eat wood and can severely damage or weaken structural framing members.

The first step in combating pest infestation is to find the source of the problem. Examine the outside walls of your house—from the foundation up to the roof—and seal any cracks or holes that could allow insects or other pests inside. Pay particular attention to trails leading up to a crack or hole—more than likely, they are favorite and oft-used entrances for pests.

Gable vents are a common a entry point for birds and bats. Place screening or $1/2$-inch mesh hardware cloth over these on either the inside or outside. Seal gaps between soffits and walls with trim molding, and trim any tree or shrub branches that touch or come close to the house or roofline. If you have a wood-burning stove or fireplace, store wood away from the house. Woodpiles are havens for insects and other creatures.

It is best to leave any bird or bat droppings undisturbed. If you must clean the area, moisten the droppings first so they do not release dust. Do not use a shop vacuum to clean up droppings, as the filter will not catch the fungal particles and will thus spread them. If you choose to vacuum the area, use only a vacuum with a HEPA filter. Wear a respirator and disposable rubber gloves and wash all clothing in hot water immediately afterward.

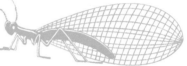

Lace Wing

Spider

Praying Mantis

Ladybug Beetle

Whenever you clean up mouse droppings or nesting materials, wear a respirator and disposable rubber gloves. Be careful not to touch your eyes, nose, or mouth with the gloves. Dispose of the gloves after use.

It may not be possible to remove cockroach feces and shed cuticles because they tend to collect in hard-to-reach crevices. It's best to focus on eliminating the roach infestation. Because roaches do not like traveling in the open, an effective deterrent is to caulk or seal all potential travel paths. Use expanding foam to seal around all plumbing and utility line openings. Use clear or paintable caulk to seal around cabinets where they meet each other and the walls, and to seal baseboards where they meet at the floor and the wall. Eliminate the roaches by using bait stations or baiting gel. Don't use fogging devices, as these chemicals degrade interior air quality and are no more effective than bait stations. Prevent roach infestations by removing all food waste immediately and keeping surfaces clean. Follow these same techniques for handling ant infestations.

Dry, pest-free lumber will last for centuries, but wood attacked by rot or termites can be destroyed in short order. Framework at the foundation is the most vulnerable because it's so close to the ground. Act quickly if that lumber is damp or you suspect termites.

If you have reason to suspect termites, probe into the lumber with a penknife and flashlight. Termites destroy lumber by eating it from the inside out: Boards can be nearly hollow and still look fine on the surface.

**Subterranean termites** avoid light and open air. This common species tunnels up from the ground directly into the wood. They also can create tunnels up foundation walls to reach wood framing.

**Damp-wood termites** live along the Pacific Coast. They damage only moisture-soaked wood.

**Dry-wood termites**, present in warm climates, bore directly into above-ground wood then cover their tracks by plugging their holes.

**Carpenter ants** are found in many of the same regions as termites, and the two are easily confused. Ants nest in wood but don't feed on it; so they do less damage than termites.

Call a reputable exterminator if you find insects. Most insecticides are very dangerous and difficult to apply. Rot can be just as damaging, but it's easier to guard against. Plug leaks, keep exterior caulk in good shape, and make sure the house is adequately ventilated.

If you wind up with critters nesting in your home, immediately contact a pest- control specialist or your local animal control department. These individuals are trained to remove animals humanely and can provide information for preventing future pest problems.

Elbowed Antennae
Straight Antennae
Slender Waist
Ant
Termite
Broad Waist

# Maintenance Schedule

*Grandma was right—a stitch in time really does save nine. If you never quite figured out what that means, let me explain. It's Grandma-speak for "Taking care of small problems today keeps them from becoming bigger problems tomorrow." And it works. For example, missing caulk is no big deal—a couple of dollars and 30 minutes takes care of it. But if you ignore missing caulk until water has damaged your siding or window or door frames, you've got expensive—and time-consuming—problems on your hands.*

The best way to keep your home in prime condition is to perform routine maintenance inspections throughout the year. The following pages will help you remember the elements of your home that need to be inspected regularly.

Items that you should inspect monthly include air filters and the batteries in your smoke and carbon monoxide detectors. You may not need to clean or replace these items every time you inspect them, but frequent checks will draw your attention to problems before they become serious.

Seasonal inspections and repairs are designed to address typical wear and tear, as well as damage due to freeze and thaw cycles, summer heat, and other weather conditions.

Make each of your inspections as soon as weather permits. You'll be glad to have them completed, and you'll avoid working outdoors or in attics and other semiexposed areas in harsh weather.

# Monthly

**Smoke and carbon monoxide detectors:** Test units for power by depressing the test button and waiting for the alarm to sound.

**Fire extinguishers:** Check the tank pressure. If the pressure is low, replace the extinguisher or have it recharged.

**Bathroom walls and floors:** Check grout and caulk joints for cracks, crumbling, and mold (pages 44 to 45 and 84 to 85).

**Water supply lines and shutoff valves:** Inspect hoses, pipes, and tubes supplying water to appliances and plumbing fixtures. Also inspect and test shutoff valves to ensure proper operation (page 137).

**House drains:** Inspect plumbing fixtures and appliance drains for leaky connections (page 136). Clean and deodorize sink drains with warm water, chlorine bleach, and powdered laundry detergent (pages 136).

**Whirlpool:** Flush the water pump system to remove mineral deposits, oils, and bacteria (page 134).

**GFCI receptacles:** Test the trip mechanism by pushing the TEST button (page 173).

**Ceiling fans:** Thoroughly clean the blades (page 176). If the fixture wobbles, tighten the fastening hardware and balance the blades (page 218).

**Furnace filter:** Inspect the filter for buildup of particles. Clean a soiled filter or replace it, according to the manufacturer's instructions (page 209).

**Furnace humidifiers:** For drum-style humidifiers, clean the evaporator pad and adjust the water level if necessary (page 211). For drip-style humidifiers, inspect the system and remove mineral deposits as necessary (page 211).

**Furnace:** Remove dust and debris from the air intake fan. Lubricate the blower motor every two months.

**Air exchanger:** Inspect and clean or replace the filter (page 219).

**Air conditioner and heat pump:** Check the condenser unit for level and remove leaves, branches, and other debris from the fan and coils (page 222 to 223).

**Clothes washer:** Run an unloaded cycle with hot water, detergent, and bleach. Inspect door gaskets and hoses periodically and replace them if necessary (page 232).

**Clothes dryer:** Clean the flexible ventilation duct at the back of the dryer to remove accumulated lint (page 233).

# Spring

**Windows:** Clean all windows and test their operation. Make adjustments as necessary; repair damaged units (pages 100 to 103).

**Doors:** Clean all doors and hardware and test their operation. Make adjustments or repairs as necessary (pages 110 to 112).

**Garage doors:** Where necessary, tighten hinge screws and other hardware, realign locks and lock bars, and adjust misaligned tracks. Clean and lubricate the rollers, door tracks, locks, cable pulleys, hinges, and the chain and track of chain-driven automatic door openers (page 117).

**Weatherstripping:** Inspect weatherstripping around doors and windows for wear. Feel for drafts (pages 106 to 107 and 114 to 115).

**Dampers:** Open or close dampers to balance the flow of forced air for the season (page 212).

**Chimney:** Inspect the masonry and flashing. Clean the flue to remove creosote buildup (page 216).

**Boiler (oil-burning type only):** Replace the oil filter.

**Air conditioner and heat pump:** Ask a professional to inspect the refrigerant level. Clean the condenser fins and coils and check the fan blades (page 222).

**Exhaust and bath fans:** Clean filters, grills, or blades to maximize air flow (page 219).

**Thermostat:** Inspect the wires and remove dust and grime from the bimetal coil. Check the unit for level.

**Insulation:** Add insulation in areas where existing protection proved insufficient during the winter months.

**Roof:** Inspect the roof for damaged or missing shingles. Check flashing and joint compound for wear and cracking.

**Attic:** Check rafters and roof sheathing for signs of moisture. Feel around vents to check for airflow.

**Crawl spaces:** Inspect framing members for moisture and rot. If the space is inadequately ventilated, contact a ventilation contractor.

**Basement:** Check for moisture on foundation walls. Inspect beams, posts, floor joists, and sill plates for water or stress damage.

**Gutters:** Clean gutters and downspouts. Check for loose connectors and leaky joints. Make sure that long runs are straight and sloped properly toward the downspouts (pages 248 to 249 ).

**Sump pump:** Test the unit and clean out the sump pit prior to the rainy season or every two months if used more frequently (pages 250 to 251).

# Summer

**Windows:** Check for leaks, wood rot, and moisture buildup.

**Dampers:** Open or close dampers to balance the flow of forced air for the season (page 212).

**Furnace or boiler:** Drain the system to flush accumulated sediment (page 209).

**Room air conditioner:** Clean the filter and clear the drains monthly (page 223).

**Evaporative chiller:** Replace the pads. Drain the reservoir and check the filter, pads, and pump twice a month (page 224).

**Foundation:** Inspect outside walls for deterioration. Seal and repaint where needed (pages 243 to 246). If necessary, regrade the soil to redirect water drainage (page 247).

**Concrete walls and structures:** Check for cracks and deterioration. Repair mortar joints and replace damaged bricks. Caulk or patch stucco walls.

**Roof and exterior walls:** Pressure-wash the surfaces to remove dirt and debris.

**Exterior siding:** Repair damaged areas and touch up chipped or peeling paint.

**Walkways, driveways, and concrete surfaces:** Inspect for cracking, crumbling, frost heave, and other common problems.

**Septic tank:** Ask a professional to inspect the tank and pump it if necessary.

# *Fall*

**Weatherstripping:** Inspect the materials around doors and windows for wear and feel for drafts. Replace the weatherstripping where necessary (pages 106 to 107 and 114 to 115).

**Storm windows:** Repair any damaged windows. Tighten and lubricate the fastening hardware (page 108).

**Storm doors:** Tighten and lubricate fastening hardware, and adjust the closer as necessary (page 116).

**Garage doors:** Replace worn or damaged weatherstripping (page 117).

**Outdoor faucets:** Remove garden hoses, close indoor shutoff valves, and open faucets to drain trapped water.

**Water heater:** Drain the tank to remove accumulated sediment. Test the pressure relief valve (page 139).

**Heat registers:** Clean the register to maximize airflow.

**Baseboard heater:** Clean the element to increase heating efficiency and prevent burning odors (page 213).

**Radiators and convectors:** Bleed air from the hot water system (page 215).

**Dampers:** Adjust the flow of forced air to accommodate specific rooms for the season (page 212).

**Vent Pipes:** Check for corrosion and replace any damaged sections (page 210).

**Furnace:** Clean and lubricate the blower motor. Inspect the drive belt, pilot light, and burner flame. Use clear water to flush out the drain line and the condensation trap (page 209). Make sure the air intake and exhaust are free of debris and obstructions (page 210).

**Furnace humidifiers:** Replace the evaporator pad for both drum-style (page 211) and drip-style humidifiers (page 211).

**Fireplace and wood stove:** Inspect and clean the flue, damper, and firebox (page 216). If necessary, have the chimney cleaned by a certified chimney sweep.

**Air exchanger:** Inspect and clean the exchanger core and condenser tray (page 219).

**HEPA filters:** Clean the outside screens, then inspect the filter and replace it if necessary (page 219).

**Exhaust and bath fans:** Clean the filters, grills, and blades to maximize airflow (page 219).

**Heat pump:** Clean the condenser fins and coils. Check the fan and lubricate the motor (page 222).

**Dryer vents and service pipes:** Check the caulk around all the openings around dryer vents or service pipes entering your basement. If the seal isn't solid, clean out the old caulk thoroughly and replace it, using a good-quality silicone caulk.

**Gutters:** Clean the gutters and downspouts. Check for loose connectors and leaky joints. Make sure long runs are straight and sloped properly toward the downspouts (pages 248 to 249).

**Foundation sill plates:** Check for any gaps and seal them using plastic or foam backer rope. Sealing these gaps will also provide a barrier against insects and other pests seeking entry into your house.

# *Winter*

**Smoke and carbon monoxide detectors:** Replace batteries on battery-operated and battery-backup units.

**Emergency supplies:** Check emergency items, such as a radio, batteries, flashlights, stored water, and food, candles, and matches. Stock the first-aid kit.

**Unglazed tile:** Test tile sealer and reseal if necessary (page 85).

**Tile grout:** Test existing grout sealer and reseal grout lines if necessary (page 85). Make sure to remove and replace damaged grout prior to resealing (pages 55 and 93).

**Windows and doors:** Check for drafts during cold or windy periods. As a temporary solution, install plastic sheeting or a shrink-wrap product to block drafts for the remainder of the season.

**Water softener:** Inspect the brine line and injector screen for sediment buildup every two years.

**Electrical boxes:** Shut off the breaker to the circuit, then vacuum out the electrical boxes (page 172). Check for loose wire connections when done.

**Home air quality:** Check windows for moisture buildup and bathroom ceilings for mold and mildew.

**Dampers:** Adjust the flow of forced air to accommodate specific rooms for the season (page 212).

**Roof:** Check for ice dams and record their locations (page 221).

**Dishwasher:** Clean out the strainer and the spray arms and run a cycle an extra cycle. Also inspect the door gasket for leaks (pages 230 to 231).

**Clothes dryer:** Remove lint from inside electric units (page 233). For gas dryers, call a service person to clean the unit.

**Refrigerator:** Clean the condensor coils on the bottom and back of the unit, and drain, clean, and disinfect the condensor drain pan (page 234). Inspect the door gasket and replace if necessary (page 235).

# Glossary

**Air exchanger** – also known as a heat-recovery ventilator; a device that draws fresh air into a forced-air heating/cooling system, warming the air as it enters the system by passing it across metal tubes containing warm air.

**Alkyd** – a synthetic resin used in oil-based paints. "Alkyd" paint is another name for oil-based paint.

**Amperage** – Also: "amps"; a measure of the rate at which electricity is forced into a circuit. Amperes = wattage ÷ voltage.

**Ash pit** – collection area for ash dumped through the grate in a fireplace.

**Ballcock** – a valve that controls the water supply entering a toilet tank.

**Baseboard** – a wide trim molding, typically made of wood, fastened along the bottom of interior walls.

**Base shoe** – a strip of wood trim with two flat sides and a curved front that is typically installed along flooring in front of a baseboard.

**Batt insulation** – insulation, typically fiberglass, supplied in rolls and often used as a household insulation material.

**Bleed valve** – a valve on a room radiator or convector used to release air from a hot-water heating system.

**Blocking** – a piece of solid lumber spanning a cavity between framing members to add strength or retard the spread of fire.

**Building code** – the set of formal regulations used to dictate construction standards in a community.

**Carbon monoxide** – an odorless, colorless gas produced during fuel combustion that can cause dizziness, headaches, and death.

**Caulk** – a pastelike substance, usually containing silicone, used to seal joints. Caulk is waterproof and flexible when dry and adheres to most dry surfaces.

**Cement** – also called portland cement; the component that hardens masonry mixtures when mixed with water; a blend of lime, silica, alumina, iron, and gypsum.

**Concrete** – a mixture of portland cement, gravel, and sand. Concrete structures may be reinforced internally with iron bars or mesh.

**Condenser** – a component of an air-conditioning or heat-pump system that condenses a refrigerant to a liquid state, causing it to cool as it releases heat to the air.

**Continuity** – the uninterrupted flow of electrons from one point to another in an electrical circuit or appliance.

**Crazing** – fine cracking in the finish coat of paint or on the surface of concrete, caused by uneven shrinkage during the drying process.

**Damper** – a device installed on most forced-air and hot-water systems as a means of controlling the flow of water or air to various parts of the system.

**Diverter** – a valve that stops the supply of water to one fixture and redirects it to another fixture. Commonly found in sink fixtures with a sprayer attachment or bathtub fixtures with a shower attachment.

**Downspout** – the vertical tubing of a gutter system, which extends from the gutter to the ground.

**Drip edge** – a metal strip that protects the edges of the lowest roof shingles and helps divert water away from the house.

**Drywall** – also called "wallboard" or "Sheetrock"; flat 4 × 8 panels made of gypsum and covered with several layers of paper. Used for most interior wall and ceiling surfaces in newer homes.

**DWV** – "drain-waste-vent"; the part of the plumbing system that removes waste from a house.

**Eaves** – the portion of the lower end of a roof that overhangs the exterior walls.

**Element** – a fine metal coil used in electric furnaces and heaters to generate heat by creating resistance to the flow of electrons.

**Escutcheon** – a decorative metal cover plate used to conceal the entry point of a pipe in a wall or floor surface.

**Evaporative chiller** – a type of air cooler, found mainly in hot, dry regions, that uses evaporation of water to dampen and cool the air.

**Evaporator** – a component of an air conditioner or heat pump that cools air by blowing it across a coil through which a chilled refrigerant flows.

**Faced insulation** – batt insulation (see Batt insulation) with an outer layer, often made of kraft paper or foil, that serves as a vapor barrier.

**Facing** – any material used as a veneer to cover an inferior surface and improve appearance.

**Fascia** – a wide board nailed across the ends of the roof rafters. The fascia holds the outside edge of the soffit.

**Fin** – one of a series of plates in a convector or electric heater that disperses heat to the surrounding air.

**Firebox** – the area of a fireplace where fire is contained.

**Flapper** – a rubber seal in a toilet that controls the flow of water from the tank to the bowl.

**Flashing** – aluminum or galvanized-steel sheeting cut and bent into various sizes and shapes. Used to keep water from entering joints between roof elements and to direct water away from structural elements.

**Four-way switch** – a switch installed between a pair of three-way switches. Four-way switches do not have ON/OFF markings and make it possible to control a single fixture or set of lights from three or more locations.

**Framing member** – a common term for a single structural element of a construction framework, such as a stud, joist, truss, beam, or rafter.

**Frost heave** – the upward movement of structural footings caused by the expansion of the ground as it freezes.

**Frost line** – the depth to which frost penetrates the ground in winter. The depth differs depending on the climate of the region.

**Furring strip** – narrow strips of wood or other material attached to a solid surface to create a flat or level foundation for a finish surface.

**GFCI** – "ground-fault circuit interrupter"; a receptacle designed to detect minute changes in current—as in a short circuit—and to interrupt the flow by shutting off power before the short can cause injury. GFCI receptacles are required by code in many parts of the house.

**Grade** – the slope of landscaping; generally grades are built up to direct water away from a house.

**Ground** – a pathway for conducting electricity between the earth and an electrical circuit or device. On a switch, receptacle, or electrical box, the screw or terminal to which a ground wire (usually green or uninsulated) normally is connected.

**Grout** – a fluid cement product used to fill spaces between ceramic tiles or other crevices.

**Heat exchanger** – the area of a furnace where heated gases are used to heat air that will circulate throughout the house.

**Heat pump** – a reversible air-conditioning system that extracts heat from the air for heating or cooling purposes.

**High-voltage circuit** – a 240-volt circuit (see Voltage).

**Hot** – carrying live voltage, as in an electrical circuit. In NM cable (see NM cable), the hot wires are usually black or red.

**Impeller** – the grinding mechanism in a food disposer, consisting of two metal teeth fixed to a rotating metal disk powered by the motor.

**Jack** – the female part of an electrical connection that receives a probe or plug to complete a circuit.

**Joist** – horizontal framing member secured to beams or wall frames to support floor and ceiling surfaces. Ceiling joists are smaller than floor joists.

**Jumper wire** – a wire used to bypass the water meter and ensure an uninterrupted grounding pathway.

**Laminate flooring** – flooring made of a synthetic surface bonded to a fiberboard core.

**Limit control** – a heating element that switches an electric heater off if it reaches too high a temperature.

**Line voltage** – the voltage that comes directly from a household circuit without being reduced by a transformer.

**Low voltage** – voltage produced by a transformer that reduces standard household current to 12 to 24 volts for powering doorbells, telephones, some lighting, and many thermostats.

**Molding** – a strip of wood or other material used to cover construction joints or decorate functional elements of a building.

**Mortar** – a mixture of portland cement, lime, and sand used to bond the bricks or blocks of a masonry wall.

**Neutral** – a wire or terminal in an electrical circuit that is designed to return current to its source. A neutral wire is usually coated with white insulation.

**NM cable (nonmetallic cable)** – standard modern-day cable for indoor use, with either two or three individually wrapped wires (plus a bare copper ground) encased inside.

**On center** – a construction layout term used to describe the measurement or spacing from the center of one member to the center of another member.

**Pilot light** – a flame on an oven, furnace, water heater, or other heating device; used to ignite fuel when there is a call for heat.

**Plaster** – a wall material made of a mixture of gypsum, sand, and water that is troweled wet over lath or mesh; common in older houses, plaster is very hard and durable.

**Plenum** – a central duct exiting a furnace and leading to branch ducts that extend to various sections of a home.

**Plumb** – a carpentry term meaning perfectly vertical. The outer bubble gauges of a level are used to inspect for plumb.

**Polarized plug** – a type of plug with a long and a short slot designed to keep electrical current directed along the proper wires for safety.

**PVC** – "polyvinyl chloride"; rigid plastic material that is highly resistant to heat and chemicals. Used for drain-waste-and-vent piping.

**Radon** – a colorless, odorless, naturally occurring gas that can cause illnesses.

**Rafters** – the diagonal structural members of the roof that create the roof's slope.

**Resilient flooring** – flooring made of sheets or tiles of vinyl or linoleum.

**Ridge** – the horizontal line along the high point of a peaked roof. The ridge is created by the ridge beam, which joins the top ends of the rafters.

**Riser** – the vertical part of each step in a set of stairs; risers are attached to the stringers and link adjacent treads.

**Saddle valve** – a plumbing fitting that is clamped to copper supply pipe; uses a hollow spike that pierces the pipe to divert water to another supply line.

**Sash** – the frame that encases the glass panes of a window.

**Sash cord** – found in older windows, a rope connecting the window sash to a weight inside the window frame. The cord travels on a pulley that rotates as the window is opened or closed.

**Service panel** – a panel of fuses or circuit breakers from which electrical current is directed to various household circuits.

**Sheathing** – a layer of plywood or other sheet goods covering the wall or roof framing of a house. Also: the protective outer layer of nonmetallic electrical cable, made of plastic or woven fibers.

**Sheet vinyl** – a flooring material made from vinyl and other plastics in the form of sheets that are 6 ft. or 12 ft. wide and approximately $1/8$" thick.

**Sill plate** – a $2 \times 4$ or $2 \times 6$ board attached flat to the top of the foundation to anchor the framing above.

**Single-pole switch** – a switch designed to serve as the exclusive switch for a light or fixture. The labels ON and OFF are marked on the switch.

**Soffit** – the covering that attaches to the fascia and exterior wall to enclose the underside of the roof eaves.

**Solenoid** – a switch that uses electricity passing through coiled wires to create a magnetic field that moves a metal cylinder into position to complete a circuit.

**Spalling** – chipping or flaking of a brick or block surface, caused by weather changes, freezing water, or other forces.

**Spline** – a flexible rubber cord used to hold screening in a frame. Also: a narrow piece of wood or metal used for strengthening joints.

**Stack** – the main vertical drain line in a home plumbing system, designed to carry waste from the branch drains to a sewer line.

**Strike plate** – a metal plate with a curled front edge that is fastened to a door jamb to receive the live-action bolt of a doorknob mechanism.

**Stringers** – the structural members of a staircase that extend diagonally from one floor to another and support the stair treads and risers.

**Stucco** – a cement-based plaster used to cover exterior walls. Installed in three layers over strips of wood lath or metal mesh.

**Stud** – a vertical framing member in a wall. In house construction, studs are typically $2 \times 4$ boards spaced 16" apart.

**Subfloor** – plywood or 1" lumber decking nailed across the tops of the floor joists to create the foundation of the floor surface.

**Thermocouple** – a safety device found in gas appliances that automatically shuts off the gas supply if the pilot light goes out.

**Three-way switch** – a switch used in applications in which two switches control the same fixture or set of lights. Three-way switches are always installed in pairs and do not have ON/OFF markings.

**Transformer** – a device that receives the line voltage in a household circuit and reduces it to a specific low-voltage rating.

**Trap** – also called a P-trap, a curved section of pipe used in most household drains. The trap holds standing water that prevents sewer gases from backing up into the house.

**Tread** – the horizontal platform of each step in a set of stairs. Treads are supported from below or at the ends by stringers.

**Trim** – any decorative molding used for ornamentation or to conceal construction seams.

**Underlayment** – a layer of plywood or other material laid over the subfloor to create a smooth surface for a floor finish.

**Valley** – the junction between two sloping roof surfaces.

**Voltage** – a measure of the pressure with which electricity is forced through a wire or cable. In North America, most household circuits are 120-volt circuits. Heavy appliances may require a 240-volt circuit. Voltage = wattage ÷ amperes.

**Waste vent** – an open-ended pipe that ventilates a plumbing drain line, allowing waste water to travel through the drain system without getting stopped by trapped air.

**Wattage** – a measure of the rate at which electricity is consumed. Wattage = voltage × amperes.

# Metric Equivalents

| Inches (in.) | ¹⁄₆₄ | ¹⁄₃₂ | ¹⁄₂₅ | ¹⁄₁₆ | ⅛ | ¼ | ⅜ | ⅖ | ½ | ⅝ | ¾ | ⅞ | 1 | 2 | 3 | 4 | 5 | 6 | 7 | 8 | 9 | 10 | 11 | 12 | 36 | 39.4 |
|---|---|---|---|---|---|---|---|---|---|---|---|---|---|---|---|---|---|---|---|---|---|---|---|---|---|---|
| Feet (ft.) | | | | | | | | | | | | | | | | | | | | | | | | 1 | 3 | 3¹⁄₂ |
| Yards (yd.) | | | | | | | | | | | | | | | | | | | | | | | | | 1 | 1¹⁄₁₂ |
| Millimeters (mm) | 0.40 | 0.79 | 1 | 1.59 | 3.18 | 6.35 | 9.53 | 10 | 12.7 | 15.9 | 19.1 | 22.2 | 25.4 | 50.8 | 76.2 | 101.6 | 127 | 152 | 178 | 203 | 229 | 254 | 279 | 305 | 914 | 1,000 |
| Centimeters (cm) | | | | | | | 0.95 | 1 | 1.27 | 1.59 | 1.91 | 2.22 | 2.54 | 5.08 | 7.62 | 10.16 | 12.7 | 15.2 | 17.8 | 20.3 | 22.9 | 25.4 | 27.9 | 30.5 | 91.4 | 100 |
| Meters (m) | | | | | | | | | | | | | | | | | | | | | | | | .30 | .91 | 1.00 |

# Converting Measurements

| TO CONVERT: | TO: | MULTIPLY BY: |
|---|---|---|
| Inches | Millimeters | 25.4 |
| Inches | Centimeters | 2.54 |
| Feet | Meters | 0.305 |
| Yards | Meters | 0.914 |
| Miles | Kilometers | 1.609 |
| Square inches | Square centimeters | 6.45 |
| Square feet | Square meters | 0.093 |
| Square yards | Square meters | 0.836 |
| Cubic inches | Cubic centimeters | 16.4 |
| Cubic feet | Cubic meters | 0.0283 |
| Cubic yards | Cubic meters | 0.765 |
| Pints (U.S.) | Liters | 0.473 (Imp. 0.568) |
| Quarts (U.S.) | Liters | 0.946 (Imp. 1.136) |
| Gallons (U.S.) | Liters | 3.785 (Imp. 4.546) |
| Ounces | Grams | 28.4 |
| Pounds | Kilograms | 0.454 |
| Tons | Metric tons | 0.907 |

| TO CONVERT: | TO: | MULTIPLY BY: |
|---|---|---|
| Millimeters | Inches | 0.039 |
| Centimeters | Inches | 0.394 |
| Meters | Feet | 3.28 |
| Meters | Yards | 1.09 |
| Kilometers | Miles | 0.621 |
| Square centimeters | Square inches | 0.155 |
| Square meters | Square feet | 10.8 |
| Square meters | Square yards | 1.2 |
| Cubic centimeters | Cubic inches | 0.061 |
| Cubic meters | Cubic feet | 35.3 |
| Cubic meters | Cubic yards | 1.31 |
| Liters | Pints (U.S.) | 2.114 (Imp. 1.76) |
| Liters | Quarts (U.S.) | 1.057 (Imp. 0.88) |
| Liters | Gallons (U.S.) | 0.264 (Imp. 0.22) |
| Grams | Ounces | 0.035 |
| Kilograms | Pounds | 2.2 |
| Metric tons | Tons | 1.1 |

# Converting Temperatures

Convert degrees Fahrenheit (F) to degrees Celsius (C) by following this simple formula: Subtract 32 from the Fahrenheit temperature reading. Then, mulitply that number by ⁵⁄₉. For example, 77°F - 32 = 45. 45 × ⁵⁄₉ = 25°C.

To convert degrees Celsius to degrees Fahrenheit, multiply the Celsius temperature reading by ⁹⁄₅. Then, add 32. For example, 25°C × ⁹⁄₅ = 45. 45 + 32 = 77°F.

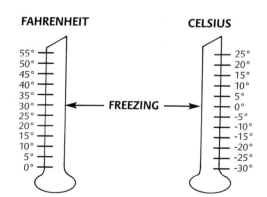

# Photo Credits

## Contributors

AIR-N-WATER: pp. 212, 224 (top)
800-734-0405
www.air-n-water.com

All American Wood: p. 210
© 2000 All American Wood
photo by James Kissenger
815-728-8888
www.allamericanwood.com

Andersen Windows, Inc: p. 134
800-426-4261
www.andersenwindows.com

CARDACO WINDOWS,
part of the JELD-WEN family:
sliding window p. 98
800-877-9482
www.jeld-wen.com

Daltile: p. 29
800-933-TILE
www.daltile.com

Hubbardton Forge: p. 166
802-468-5516
www.vtforge.com

Marvin Windows and Doors:
double-hung windows p. 98
888-537-8268
www.marvin.com

Mirage/Boa Franc Inc: p. 90
800-463-1303
www.boa-franc.com

Pella Storm Doors: p. 116
888-646-5354
www.pella.com

Silverline Windows:
pp. 122-123 (all)
800-234-4428
www.silverlinewindows.com

Wilsonart International:
pp. 82, 74
800-710-8846
www.wilsonart.com

Woodport Interior Doors Heritage
Veneered Products:
bifold doors p. 99
715-526-2146
www.woodport.com

## Photographers

Beateworks, Inc.
© Tim Street-Porter /
Beateworks.com: pp. 46, 202

Brand X Pictures
© Brand X Pictures: pp. 22, 32,
34, 36, 54, 72, 79, 96, 110, 176,
228, 261

Comstock Images
© www.comstock.com:
pp. 104, 138

Brad Daniels
© Brad Daniels for Barrington
Homes: fixed window p. 98

Fotosearch
© www.fotosearch.com:
p. 223

Getty Images
© Getty Images/PhotoDisc: pp. 38,
236, 259

The Interior Archive
© Tim Beddow/The Interior
Archive: p. 126

Karen Melvin
© Karen Melvin for the following
designers: Eric Odor: p. 80;
Mason Homes: p. 200

Brian Vanden Brink
© Todd Caverly/Brian Vanden
Brink: p. 196;
© Brian Vanden Brink: Back Cover
and for the following:
Centerbrook Architects: p. 4;
Sally Westin, Architect: p. 108;
Axel Builder: p. 238-239

# Index